1920: A Year of Global Turmoil

1920: A Year of Global Turmoil

David Charlwood

PEN & SWORD HISTORY

AN IMPRINT OF PEN & SWORD BOOKS LTD.
YORKSHIRE - PHILADELPHIA

First published in Great Britain in 2019 by
Pen and Sword History
An imprint of
Pen & Sword Books Ltd
Yorkshire - Philadelphia

First published in hardback in 2019, this edition published 2020.

Paperback ISBN: 9781526767172

Typeset in 11.5/14 Ehrhardt by Vman Infotech Pvt. Ltd.

Printed and bound by CPI Group (UK) Ltd, Croydon, CR0 4YY

Pen & Sword Books Ltd incorporates the Imprints of Pen & Sword Books Archaeology,
Atlas, Aviation, Battleground, Discovery, Family History, History, Maritime, Military,
Naval, Politics, Railways, Select, Transport, True Crime, Fiction, Frontline Books, Leo
Cooper, Praetorian Press, Seaforth Publishing, Wharncliffe and White Owl.

For a complete list of Pen & Sword titles please contact

PEN & SWORD BOOKS LIMITED
47 Church Street, Barnsley, South Yorkshire, S70 2AS, England
E-mail: enquiries@pen-and-sword.co.uk
Website: www.pen-and-sword.co.uk

or

PEN AND SWORD BOOKS
1950 Lawrence Rd, Havertown, PA 19083, USA
E-mail: Uspen-and-sword@casematepublishers.com
Website: www.penandswordbooks.com

Contents

PART FOUR

Preface

The year 1920 was both world-changing and uneventful. For most people, their pressing concerns were the same as ours today: food, shelter, warmth and love. Their world may seem smaller and slower-moving than our own – this was a time when crossing the Atlantic was undertaken by boat and took the better part of a working week, when news was only available via radio or newspaper and when most people rarely travelled beyond the borders of their own country – but, in reality, there is much in common.

The events of the past have echoes in the present. To speak of a British bombing campaign in Iraq, Russian soldiers annexing countries in Eastern Europe and an American president withdrawing the United States from international peace organisations in order to put 'America first' sounds more like news than history. But the aim of this book is not to draw comparisons, nor divine the future for our current age. It is simply to tell the story of the world one hundred years ago.

There are many books that deal with the social history of the 1920s, but this book takes a global view of events, focusing instead on the wider narrative and the political decisions that had the greatest impact in a single year. It is, therefore, only possible to tell the stories of a few individuals, those who held the reins of power, and to focus on international rather than domestic politics. The story of the year is told chronologically, weaving together the events as they unfolded in different countries. Many of the cast are familiar names – Churchill, Hitler, Roosevelt – but not as we know them: Winston Churchill has yet to be prime minister, Adolf Hitler is still forging the foundations of the Third Reich, while Franklin D. Roosevelt is working in a desk job for the US Navy. Their stage is a world emerging from the darkness of the first global conflict, as war-ravaged nations – winners and losers – try and find their feet again. In America, there are the beginnings of a new isolationism, and in Great Britain there is a desperate desire to secure an empire against the expansionism of Communist Russia. Nationalism is on the march and the rulers of distant lands are finding their subjects less inclined to acquiesce quietly to having little say in their own destinies. As the richest country in the world begins a decade of roaring prosperity, the writing is already on the wall. The storm clouds of war and the end of empires are gathering.

PART ONE

Chapter 1

'The birth of the new world'

On the morning of 16 January 1920, the newly elected Chairman of the League of Nations addressed its first Council meeting. Arrayed in front of him, beneath the ornate chandeliers of the clock room in the Quai d'Orsay in Paris, were representatives of governments from Asia to the Americas. Leon Bourgeois, the neatly-bearded former prime minister of France, began his remarks by acknowledging that the man who had tirelessly campaigned to bring the League into being – US President Woodrow Wilson – was regrettably absent. Bourgeois then went on to articulate the League's great ambition: 'January 16, 1920 will go down in history as the date of the birth of the new world. Decisions to be reached today will be in the name of all nations ... together for the first time ... to substitute right for might.'[1]

The main purpose of the League was to stop the world going to war again. Formed at the peace conference in Paris the previous year during the negotiation of the Treaty of Versailles, the League was intended to foster international cooperation and guarantee the political independence and territorial integrity of member states. The organisation comprised an Assembly, where all members were represented, and a Council, headed by five permanent members and four rotating members. The purpose of the Versailles treaty was to prevent Germany from ever starting another war, by enforcing disarmament and requiring Germany to pay reparations, while the League was supposed to provide a mechanism to protect all countries from aggression.

The creation of the League had generated a fair amount of optimism. Europe was only beginning to emerge from the deadliest conflict in its history and there was widespread support for a multinational body to prevent further wars. A popular organisation that sprang up in Britain in support of the League's ideals – the League of Nations Union – encouraged members into signing up by using a heady cocktail of unabashed optimism laced with religious ideology. A pamphlet distributed by the Union in 1920 proclaimed: 'Christian ideals find practical expression in the League of Nations ... Because where the doctrine of armed force has failed in abolishing war, the Christian doctrine of the universal brotherhood of man can succeed.'[2] Politicians also seemed to have grasped that, although it remained largely unclear what the League would actually do, its existence was probably a good thing. Lord Curzon, Britain's Foreign Secretary in 1920, described the League as 'the expression of the universal desire for a saner method of regulating the affairs of mankind,' while another British politician, Lord Cecil, stated, 'All, or almost all, of the House [of Lords] professed support of the League; very few knew anything about it.'[3]

An hour and twenty-five minutes after it had begun, the first meeting of the Council of the League of Nations was adjourned. The Council had discussed the single item on the agenda – the appointment of a commission to formalise the boundaries of the occupied Saar Basin industrial region in post-war Germany – and now it was time for lunch. A seemingly disappointed Leon Bourgeois ended proceedings, noting, 'Public opinion will perhaps be surprised that we have today made no greater stride and left no deeper mark upon the world.'[4]

The only prime minister present at the Council meeting was Eleftherios Venizelos of Greece; other nations sent ambassadors, foreign ministers, or, in the case of Italy, the Minister for Industry. The British prime minister, David Lloyd George, was actually in Paris at the time of the meeting. Rather than attending, he was spending the weekend of his fifty-seventh birthday with his mistress, Frances, as well as dining out and playing golf. Although absent from the first Council meeting, Lloyd George had supported Woodrow Wilson in his desire to found the League at the Paris peace conference in 1919. His motivation was less messianic than that of the American president, however, and Lloyd George had spent much of the conference watching with 'real joy' as Wilson annoyed France's hard-nosed premier, Georges Clemenceau, with his flights of fancy. Lloyd George later wrote: '[Wilson's] ... most extraordinary outburst was when he was developing some theme – I rather think it was connected with the League of Nations – which led him to explain the failure of Christianity to achieve its highest ideals ... Clemenceau slowly opened his dark eyes to their widest dimension and swept them around the Assembly to see how the Christians gathered around the table enjoyed this exposure of the futility of their Master'. When he returned home and was asked how it went, Lloyd George replied, 'I think as well as might be expected, seated as I was between Jesus Christ and Napoleon Bonaparte.'[5]

The British prime minister was well versed in religious metaphors. His father had died a year after he was born and his impoverished mother had taken her young son to live in Wales with her brother, who was a cobbler and a Baptist minister. Lloyd George was raised in an environment steeped in the Protestant work ethic and he excelled at school, partially teaching himself. He qualified as a solicitor before entering politics as Liberal MP for Caernarvon, a seat he held for fifty-five years. He had wit and charm, and a capacity to floor debating opponents. Behind a vibrant moustache and twinkling eyes, the stocky Welshman was determined, but prone to bouts of anxiety. His outlets were womanising and golf, which he played with sense of unencumbered enjoyment. He is said to have once remarked: 'Golf is the only game where the worst player gets the best of it. He obtains more out of it as regards both exercise and enjoyment, for the good player gets worried over the slightest mistake, whereas the poor player makes too many mistakes to worry about them.'

The day after the first Council meeting of the League of Nations, Lloyd George played a round at the Saint-Cloud golf course just outside Paris, and he and Frances – who was twenty-five years his junior and officially his personal secretary – joined a group at Ciro's restaurant for dinner. Among the select gathering was the Secretary of State for War and Air, Winston Churchill. Frances recorded in her diary that Churchill was 'raving on the subject of the Bolsheviks and ragging D. [Lloyd George] about the new world. "Don't you make any mistake", he said to D. "You're not going to get your new world. The old world is a good enough place for me, and there's still life in the old dog yet. It's going to sit up and wag its tail."'[6]

The 'old world' was at the time determinedly ignoring the earnest calls from politicians for the spread of goodwill among men. In January 1920, nearly eighteen months after the First World War had officially ended, conflict was in fact raging in Europe. Russia was entering its third year of civil war and the Bolshevik army was fighting to defend the new state across a front that stretched from the Baltic to the Caspian Sea. Far from standing idly by, Britain had supplied arms, equipment and military advisors in support of the anti-Bolshevik forces; the Royal Navy had exchanged fire with Russian ships in the Baltic and British pilots had launched bombing raids from the aircraft carrier HMS *Vindictive* and a forward air base established in Finland, while soldiers had also been deployed to the Caucasus. At the request of the British government, Woodrow Wilson had reluctantly agreed to send 5,000 American soldiers. They fought an eleven-month-long campaign – between 1918 and 1919 – in the Arctic wastes of Archangel, before being forced to withdraw as the winter weather and congressional opinion turned against the action.

The anti-Bolshevik confederation known as the 'White Army' achieved some early success, only for their gains to be reversed; a pattern that repeated itself until October 1919, when the White Army advanced to within two hundred miles of Moscow. Churchill jubilantly wrote in a memorandum to the Cabinet that the Bolsheviks would soon be finished.[7] He was wrong. The White Army was driven back and began a disorderly retreat in the depths of winter. The army's Polish-born commander, the devoutly Russian Orthodox and rabidly anti-Semitic General Anton Ivanovich Denikin, appealed to Britain for more aid. But the British government had already made up its mind: the military aid package he had received in the autumn of 1919, which took the value of British material assistance to the White Army to more than £35 million, was to be the last.[8] There was little appetite among any of the Cabinet members, other than the Minister for War, for foreign military entanglements. Churchill wrote to his private secretary on 1 January, 'It looks to me as if Denikin will come to an end before his supply of stores.'[9] This time Churchill was right. In the north, the General's starving, typhus-riddled shell of an army stumbled back across the Estonian border, while in southern Russia, the White Army was barely clinging on to a foothold near Rostov. Britain had backed the losing horse. Now the government had to figure out how to extricate itself from the mess. On 24 January, back in England, Lloyd George confided in his partner on the golf course, Lord Riddell: 'While we were in Paris, Winston was very excited about Russia. I had to handle him firmly. He was most insistent, and prepared to sacrifice both men and money. Now he is changing his views … He wanted to justify what he had done and also to withdraw. I would not agree to that.

I said, "You can withdraw if you like, but I will not be a party to any justification."[10]

What none of the leaders of the Western world were willing to acknowledge was that the League of Nations was founded on a fallacy: the peace that the organisation supposedly existed to maintain had never really begun.

Chapter 2

Troubles at home

The popularly held image of the First World War – known as the Great War in 1920, when it was presumed that no conflict could ever match its scale and devastation – is that of plucky 'Tommies' (British soldiers) in mud-filled trenches facing off against the Germans. Although the war was won and lost on the Western Front in the fields of France and Belgium, the conflict embroiled no fewer than nineteen nations and British soldiers' first shots in anger were actually fired at a German wireless station in Togoland, West Africa, on 12 August 1914.[1] When the war ended four years later, the map of the world had been redrawn.

The Allies' victory had expanded Great Britain's empire: Germany had lost her overseas territories and the surrender of the Ottoman Turks meant that British soldiers – although the majority of the men who carried arms for the Crown in the region were Indian – now guarded Jerusalem, Constantinople (Istanbul) and Baghdad. The result was that a further 1.8 million square miles had been added to the British Empire, along with more than 10 million additional subjects.[2] This expansion of British interests was, in part, intended to be retained under the sanction of the League of Nations through the thinly veiled colonial label of 'mandates', titles that would be given to the British control of Iraq and Palestine, while the former German colonies of Togoland, East Africa and Cameroon were simply absorbed into the Empire. The British Secretary of State for India, Edwin Montagu, who joined Lloyd George and Frances for dinner at Ciro's on 17 January, had casually remarked that it was difficult to find 'some convincing argument for not annexing all the territories in the world.'[3]

There was one convincing argument: post-war Britain simply could not afford it. In fighting the war, the British government had racked up a national debt of more than £7.4 billion, up from around £700 million before the outbreak of hostilities.[4] As well as raising domestic debt, Britain had received significant loans from the United States, most of which had immediately been spent to buy US war exports. As far as some critics were concerned, the debt had already been repaid, but requests for leniency went unheeded. President Wilson briefly toyed with the idea of asking the US Congress to consolidate the interest on all Allied debt obligations for a three-year period, but flatly refused to consider cancelling any debts.[5] In Britain it was hoped that the newly acquired territories would bring in money – particularly in the case of Iraq, where the British government was the dominant shareholder in the country's nascent oil industry – but in 1920 that hope would be violently dashed.

At the start of year, however, it was not Britain's far-flung territories that were causing problems; there was trouble much closer to home. On 20 January Constable Luke Finnegan was walking home from the police barracks in the town of Thurles in County Tipperary, Ireland. He was only a few paces from his front door when he was shot by several men armed with revolvers. He collapsed, seriously wounded, and called out to his wife, 'Mary, I am done. What will you and the little babies do?'[6] He died in hospital a few days later. In total, more than 100 members of the Royal Irish Constabulary (RIC) would be killed in the violence of 1920.

The Irish War of Independence had begun almost exactly a year before. In the December 1918 election the Irish Republican party, Sinn Fein, secured nearly seventy percent of the vote in Ireland. Before the First World War successive British governments had attempted to devolve power to Ireland through 'Home Rule', but efforts had been blocked by the upper chamber (the House of Lords) and the issue was overtaken by more pressing problems in England and by the outbreak of war. The newly empowered Sinn Fein demanded full independence. Home Rule was a non-starter, although there were British officials who still clung to the illusion that it might be workable.

The First World War had caused deep divisions in Ireland. More than 210,000 Irishmen served in the British armed forces, but those who signed up to fight were volunteers as there was no conscription. The disparity between Ireland and England – where, from May 1916 onwards, all able-bodied men between the ages of eighteen and forty-one could be called up – was deeply controversial. In 1918, with the army desperately short of manpower, Lloyd George's government voted in legislation to introduce conscription in Ireland.

Lloyd George had been deeply sceptical of the value of imposing conscription across the Irish Sea. In February 1917 he told his friend and golfing partner Lord Riddell: 'What would be the result? Scenes in the House of Commons, a possible rupture with America … If you passed the act you would only get 160,000 men. You could only get them at the point of a bayonet.'[7] The prime minister's premonition was correct. The response to the passing of the legislation in 1918 – which, to add insult to injury, had been attached to a bill on Home Rule – was a general strike across Ireland. Despite efforts to soften the policy, the British government was forced into a humiliating retreat and conscription was shelved. The attempt to compel Ireland's sons to fight in an 'English' war was not easily forgotten.

In January 1919 the seventy-three elected Sinn Fein members refused to take their seats in the Westminster parliament and instead formed a breakaway Irish government in Dublin. Their actions were completely in line with the Sinn Fein manifesto, which proclaimed the establishment of a republic by 'withdrawing the Irish representation from the British Parliament and by denying the right and opposing the will of the British government … to legislate for Ireland.' The manifesto also backed the 'use of any and every means available to render impotent the power of England to hold Ireland to subjugation by military force or otherwise.'[8] In swift fulfilment of the second pledge, Sinn Fein 'volunteers' – who would later become known as the Irish Republican Army (IRA) – began a campaign of violent resistance to British rule. In one sense, Ireland had voted for war.

Luke Finnegan's death marked a watershed moment in the conflict. The style of his killing was typical – the *Connacht Tribune* newspaper described it as 'one of those wicked murders which are unfortunately disgracing the country at present' – but there was nothing typical about the police response.[9] Some of Finnegan's colleagues from the RIC, along with soldiers from the Sherwood Foresters Regiment, which was garrisoned in the town, went on the rampage. Police and soldiers wrecked fourteen houses, targeting those known to be associated with Sinn Fein, and fired off live weapons, including grenades, in the streets.

Residents later referred to the violence as the 'Sack of Thurles'. A secret memo circulated to the British Cabinet a few weeks later highlighted the actions of police and soldiers to avenge Finnegan's death as a cause for concern: 'It is feared that the discipline of the Royal Irish Constabulary may break down, and that there will be a repetition of the indiscriminate firing at Thurles.'[10] The fears were well justified. From January 1920 onwards, increasingly indiscriminate reprisals by security forces, often with tacit approval from senior officers, became a familiar feature of the conflict.

The war in Ireland did not simply pitch Catholics against Protestants. Support for Irish nationalism had historically come from both sides of the religious divide and several important figures in the early movements for independence established in the nineteenth century were Protestants. However, the division between nationalists and unionists increasingly came to be viewed as religious, as well as regional. The most ardent opponents of independence were Protestants from the northern region of Ulster, which was the only part of Ireland to return unionist MPs to the Westminster Parliament in the 1918 election. While many Catholic Church leaders had expressed sympathy for the nationalist cause, the church hierarchy had publicly and repeatedly condemned the violence. A week after the Finnegan shooting and the sack of Thurles, a gathering of Catholic Bishops at Maynooth, the location of a historic Catholic seminary, signed a manifesto formally stating their position. The manifesto forthrightly condemned what it referred to as the British government's 'iron rule of oppression' and concluded that, 'The only way to terminate our historic troubles and establish friendly relations between England and Ireland is to allow undivided Ireland to choose her own form of government.'[11] After officially abstaining from supporting either cause, the Catholic Church had now firmly come out for Sinn Fein and independence. The men of God had been forced to choose a side.

Chapter 3

The world's best hope

The president was dying. Although any suggestion in the press that his 'illness' was affecting his work was vehemently denied by the White House, more telling was the month-long absence of his signature from legislation. It did not require much detective work to deduce that the leader of the 'Free World' was incapable of signing his name. In October 1919 Woodrow Wilson had suffered a stroke that left him half blind and paralysed down one side. He was completely incapacitated for four weeks. It was not his first stroke and it would not be his last. The *Washington Post* reported that the president had been diagnosed with 'nervous exhaustion'.

After recovering from a bout of influenza at the start of the year, by the end of January 1920 Wilson's condition was reportedly improving. A doctor from John Hopkins Hospital told journalists: 'The president walks sturdily now, without assistance and without fatigue. And he uses the still slightly impaired arm more and more every day ... [he] is able-minded and able-bodied and is giving splendid attention to the affairs of state.'[1] It was a lie. While Wilson's mobility may have been improving, his close advisors were questioning his faculties and his wife was shielding him from the serious concerns of doctors. He was certainly not showing anything more than a passing interest in most of his presidential duties. Wilson had decided to dedicate his broken body and ailing mind to the cause most dear to his heart: the League of Nations.

The absence of any US representative at the first League of Nations Council meeting in January 1920 was not due to the president's ill health; it was because politicians in Washington did not share the sentiment of their peers in London that the League's creation was 'probably a good thing'. Congress was not at all convinced that the country should participate in the president's world peace project. US legislators' primary concern centred around Article Ten of the League of Nations' Covenant, which stated that members of the League would undertake to 'respect and preserve as against external aggression the territorial integrity and existing political independence of all Members'. The fear was that joining the League would leave the US open to being drawn into another war not of its own making. Although there was no explicit statement in the Covenant that nations could be taken to war, those who objected in Washington insisted that any decision on the use force was the preserve of the US Congress. Wilson did not see it as a concern. He wrote to his ally, Democratic senator Gilbert Hitchcock, on 26 January: 'I have greatly appreciated your thoughtful kindness in keeping me informed concerning the conferences you and some of your colleagues have had with spokesmen of the Republican party ... I have never seen the slightest reason to doubt the good faith of our associates in the war, nor ever had the slightest reason to fear that any nation would seek to enlarge our obligations under the Covenant of the League of Nations or seek to commit us to lines of action which, under our Constitution, only the Congress of the United States can in the last analysis decide.'[2]

One of the most vocal opponents of the League was Republican senator Henry Cabot Lodge, who was leader of the Republicans in the Senate and chairman of the Senate's Foreign Relations Committee. Lodge's idea of foreign relations differed markedly from that of the president. Both he and Wilson were convinced that the United States should play a key role in the world, but for the Republican senator that key role was for the US to stand aloof. In a speech opposing the League in August 1919, Lodge declared: 'The United States is the world's best hope, but if you fetter her in the interests and quarrels of other nations, if you tangle her in the intrigues of Europe, you will destroy her power for good and endanger her very existence. Leave her to march freely through the centuries'.[3]

Wilson's Democrats had lost control of the Senate in the 1918 midterms and the upper house now represented the biggest roadblock to the president's international ambitions. Before his stroke, Wilson had attempted to drum up support for ratifying the Treaty of Paris and the Covenant of the League of Nations by undertaking a speaking campaign across America. The tour had had to be cut short because he was suffering violent headaches, a precursor to his near-terminal stroke. Wilson had been physically exhausted; in that regard the *Washington Post*'s diagnosis had been accurate. Although he gave multiple rousing speeches and was warmly received in several states, most notably in California, his real opposition in the Senate remained unconvinced. Bedridden for the early part of the year, Wilson was reliant on Hitchcock, not only to mobilise the Democratic vote in the Senate in favour of the League, but also to negotiate in person with the Republicans. The senator faced a formidable challenge, which was only made more difficult by the ongoing speculation over the president's health.

The country had changed markedly as a result of the First World War. The US was now the world's largest creditor and the wartime expansion of production had created an economic boom. With increased production came new employment opportunities, primarily located in major industrial cities in the Northeast, Midwest and West. For many African Americans, employment in these urban centres was a ticket to the American dream and a ticket out of the still-segregated South. A popular poem printed in the African-American newspaper, the *Chicago Defender*, in 1916 summed up the sentiment of those who set out on the Great Migration:

> From Florida's stormy banks I'll go, I'll bid the South goodbye;
>
> No longer will they treat me so, And knock me in the eye,
>
> Hasten on my dark brother, Duck the Jim Crow law.
>
> No Crackers North to slap your mother, or knock you on the jaw.
>
> No Cracker there to seduce your sister, nor to hang you to a limb.
>
> And you're not obliged to call 'em "Mister," nor skin 'em back
>   at him.[4]

Between 1916 and 1918 the black population of Chicago doubled. In industrial cities across America, returning demobilised soldiers discovered that the jobs they had left behind had been filled by African Americans who were willing to work for less. Racial tension simmered. As the post-war economy reacclimatised to the slower manufacturing pace of peacetime, some factories began to close. In the summer and autumn of 1919 the tension boiled over. There were at least twenty-five major riots in cities and towns across America.[5] The violence in Chicago lasted five days before the National Guard was deployed to restore order, by which time thirty-eight people had been killed. In October 1919 the *New York Times* reported that 'recurring race riots have made the public aware that the Negro problem has entered a new and dangerous phase'.

In Chicago it was housing, as much as jobs, that was the sticking point. The official commission into the Chicago riots, which did not report until three years later, recorded: 'Practically no new building had been done in the city during the war, and it was a physical impossibility for a doubled Negro population to live … Negroes spread out of what had been known as the 'Black Belt' into neighborhoods that had been exclusively white. This movement … developed friction.'[6] Clearly, not every white American city-dweller was racist, but the overwhelming experience for African Americans was that their arrival was not broadly welcomed. When Lucien B. Meriwether bought a house next to two white neighbours in Indianapolis in 1920, they built 12-ft fences on either side of his property.[7] It did not matter that Meriwether was a dentist and his family were thus decidedly middle class; they were black. The Chicago commission's report concluded: 'Mutual understanding and sympathy between the races will be followed by harmony and co-operation. But these can come completely only after the disappearance of prejudice.'[8] Far from being united by the First World War, the conflict had exposed America's deep divisions. Meanwhile, the president's attention was focused on forging peace overseas.

Chapter 4

Troubles abroad

Peace seemed a particularly hard commodity to come by in the freezing mountains of Waziristan. For three months the British Indian Army had been fighting to put down a tribal rebellion in what is now the north-west border region between Pakistan and Afghanistan. An army report, compiled by the General Staff in India, described Waziristan as follows: 'It is divided into Northern and Southern Waziristan, its shape resembling a rough parallelogram, 5,000 square miles in extent, practically the whole of which is a tangled mass of mountains and hills of every size, shape and bearing. At first sight the mountains appear to run irregularly in all directions, but a study of the map will show that there are well-defined ranges protecting the interior of the country and making penetration into it a matter of extreme difficulty'.

It was out of these mountains that raiders from the tribes of the Mahsud and Wazirs had swept as far south as the plains of the Punjab 'robbing and murdering peaceful villagers, especially Hindus'. When a British forward garrison was surrounded and cut off from resupply, it seemed that the nuisance raids were threatening to become a full-blown uprising, and in November 1919, a thirty-thousand-strong force was sent to teach the tribes a lesson.[1] The British were under no illusions of as to the difficulty of the task facing them. 'The Wazirs and Mahsuds, operating in their own country, can be classed among the finest fighters in the world, and at the present moment they include in their numbers upwards of 3,000 men who have served in our regular army or militia and who have intimate knowledge of our habits and tactics', noted the General Staff.

Britain had been embroiled in three wars in Afghanistan in the previous eighty years and generations of soldiers had become all too familiar with the fighting capabilities of the tribes in the region. The British force was under the overall command of Major General Skipton Hill Climo, a fifty-two-year-old career soldier who had spent almost his entire time in uniform stationed in India and the Middle East. In early January the advance of the lead column was delayed at Kotkai, as repeated attempts to force a narrow gorge failed. The British were wary of the exposed marching formation becoming trapped under fire. In January 1842, in the first Anglo-Afghan war, a retreating British force of over 4,000 men had been completely wiped out in the high passes. An Afghan poet recorded that the British army 'perished in the mountains, like a ship sunk without trace'.[2] Determined to avoid any repeat of past failures, the column's commander, General Andrew Skeen, ordered his men to march through the night until they had advanced beyond the pass. It was a tactic that would repeatedly be used by the British to outmanoeuvre their enemy. Conditions were atrocious for the men. They traversed mountains in temperatures which, according to one account, fell as low as twenty-five degrees below freezing: 'The Tank Zam [river] had to be crossed many times, and each time that our troops left the river their feet and legs were cased with ice'.[3] When General Climo inspected one of his regiments, the 5th Royal Gurkha Rifles, he was shocked to discover that most of them had not been granted any home leave since before the start of the Great War.[4] Many of the men under his command were weary of fighting. William Slim, a captain in the West India Regiment who would later famously command British troops in Burma in the Second World War, noted, 'On every village green in England monuments were rising which proclaimed that the war was over, yet here I had only to raise my eyes to see once more the piled sandbags, the rough stone parapet, and writhing strands of barbed wire.'[5]

On 19 January the Viceroy of India telegrammed London with an update on the campaign. Frederic John Napier Thesiger was, like nearly all of his contemporaries, a product of public school and Oxbridge. His career was one that was only possible during the years when the British Empire covered an impressive proportion of the world. He began as Governor of the Australian province of Queensland and eleven years later was appointed as Viceroy of India, in effective control of an area that included modern-day Pakistan, India and Bangladesh and was home to more than 200 million people. He reported to the Secretary of State for India, Edwin Montagu, who was nearly 5,000 miles away in London. Montagu came from a Jewish family, a heritage he only seemed to tolerate: his wife had to convert to Judaism before their marriage to allow him to keep his family inheritance and Montagu consistently opposed the Zionist ambition to create a Jewish homeland in Palestine. He was, according to some contemporaries, an ugly man; long-limbed with a big head and a coarse face. The daughter of Montagu's mentor, former Prime Minister Herbert Asquith, was aghast when her friend married him, writing, 'His physical repulsiveness to me is such that I w[oul]d lightly leap from the top story of Queen Anne's Mansions or the Eiffel Tower itself, to avoid the slightest contact.'[6] He was, however, said to be broad-minded and tolerant.

The Viceroy's communications to Montagu were generally short and to the point. Thesiger's message of 19 January read: 'Reports give conservative estimation of Mahsuds and Waziris killed on 14 January as 200 … Derajat Column advanced to new camp at Sara Rogha, about 1 mile south of Murgai Kach … As head of […] found in jar at Nai Kach, Climo has authorised Skeen to completely destroy village'.[7] The British were taking a methodical and utterly uncompromising approach to asserting their authority. General Climo wrote: 'I am of opinion that [the] days of lightening frontier campaigns, except against insignificant tribes, are over. Such campaigns must be more deliberate, will entail more troops for the defence of communications, will require more transport, and will be more expensive … but the results obtained will probably be better and more lasting.'[8]

In terrain where most of the military lessons learned during the Great War were largely useless, some of the war's new technology was at least proving a real asset. Another report sent to Montagu recorded: 'The work of the aeroplanes has been of great assistance … their moral effect on enemy is exemplified by an episode on 14 January. Two planes finding good targets finished their bombs and ammunition some time before their reliefs were due to arrive. The enemy were harassing our troops, and airmen knew the departure of our planes would be likely to be their opportunity to press attack. They therefore remained, and by continually diving low at the enemy succeeded in pinning them to their ground, thus preventing any offensive movement developing until the arrival of fresh planes'.[9] Aircraft were also used in attacks on villages, although it was admitted that the 'moral effect' of the raids was far greater than any material impact, as 'incendiary bombs created a considerable sensation among the tribesmen.' Having fought a pitched battle to cross the Tank Zam river, the British now found that their enemy had melted away.

While the daily number of Mahsuds and Waziris killed greatly exceeded the number of Climo's casualties, the enemy was refusing to stand and fight. The official account of the campaign produced the following year complained, 'It is exceedingly difficult to outflank the tribesman or to cut off his retreat, while if vigorously pursued and unable to get clear away, he will hide his rifle and appear as a peaceful villager ... when the troops begin to withdraw it is astonishing how large numbers of the enemy will appear in places which had seemed to be deserted'. Despite the slow progress, the Government of India notified Montagu on 13 January that the situation in Waziristan would hopefully be settled by the middle of February.[10]

There was also concern that the Russians were eyeing up Afghanistan. It was hardly a new development – the first Afghan war had in large part been a result of Britain's attempts to stop Russia gaining any foothold in the country – but it still exercised politicians concerned about the spread of Bolshevism. Ministers in India telegrammed Montagu warning that the Bolsheviks were willing to make 'considerable' concessions to secure the allegiance of the Amir, but that his main policy was to get 'as much as possible out of Bolsheviks and British simultaneously'.[11]

There was another factor: religion. After Bolshevism, the next greatest fear of the Indian Government was pan-Islamism, which they saw as having the potential to create a Muslim movement to oust the British across a westward arc from Kabul to Tehran and on to Baghdad. Both fears were combined into a single nightmare that there would be a Pan-Islamic uprising, aided and abetted by Bolshevik agents and money. Reports were filtering through to India that Bolshevik agents were arriving in Afghanistan, while simultaneously there was a disturbing suggestion that in the middle of January a Pan-Islamic and anti-Christian proclamation had been read out in a Kabul mosque.[12] Climo's campaign against the Mahsuds and Waziris was now more than a simple counter-insurgency; it needed to become a statement of British power and prestige of sufficient force to dissuade the Amir of Afghanistan from siding with the Bolsheviks, or fanning the flames of a pan-Islamist movement against the British. Montagu telegrammed the Viceroy in reply, asserting: '[the] view of His Majesty's Government is that while, as before stated, they desire friendly relations with Afghanistan, they are not prepared in order to gain this object, to take steps that would be misconstrued as weakness.'[13]

Chapter 5

Hopeless tangles

Gertrude Bell does not fit the typical image of an early twentieth-century British woman. She was an explorer, a scholar and a spy, and by 1920 she was one of the most influential British officials in the Middle East, at a time when politics was a male dominated arena. Rather awkwardly for some modern-day historians, Gertrude Bell campaigned vigorously against women being given the vote; she had never needed suffrage to sway the views of politicians.

After graduating from Oxford with a first in modern history in 1888, she had quickly made a name for herself travelling across the Middle East, writing three best-selling books and being awarded a medal by the Royal Geographical Society. A fluent speaker of Arabic and Persian, it was not long before her skills were noticed. She was first recruited to join a team of Middle East specialists in Cairo in November 1915, and in April 1917 was posted as Oriental Secretary to the British Government's Chief Political Officer in Baghdad. After her arrival, enamoured by her new surroundings and the prospects of what Britain could achieve in its newly acquired territory, she wrote to her father, 'There never was anything quite like this before, you must understand that – it's amazing. It's the making of a new world.'[1] Bell's letters home became her record of her time in Iraq as she had given up keeping her diary at the end of 1919. But within three years of her arrival, she had become less starry-eyed at the future prospects for the region.

At the end of the First World War, Britain had conquered Palestine and Iraq (Mesopotamia), but in the early part of the conflict that outcome was far from certain. British interest centred around defending the Suez Canal, which was the lifeline of the Empire's trade following the Ottoman entry into the war on the side of Germany and Austria-Hungary in November 1914. This brought 'the Arab question' into sharp relief. It was short but complicated: were Arab ambitions for autonomy a factor in the Middle East? In the heat of war, the debate was distilled to its most pressing elements: would the Arabs fight and, if so, for whom?

There was a significant difference of opinion on the matter, even among British officials. A special report to the War Office in 1915 stated: '[There is a] feeling in London that the Arab movement is unreal, shadowy, and vague; and that it cannot, on account of its incoherence, be of any value to us. [But] the reality and possible force of the movement is not doubted by any person of experience in the Near East.'[2] Those 'persons of experience' included Bell and an irascible former military cartographer working for the Cairo Arab Bureau called T.E. Lawrence. Crucially, this viewpoint also had the support of the then British High Commissioner in Egypt, Sir Arthur Henry McMahon. He exchanged a series of letters with the Hashemite Arab ruler Sharif Hussein of Mecca and, in *quid pro quo* for the Arabs joining with Britain against the Ottomans, McMahon agreed to the post-war creation of what was effectively an Arab state stretching from the Mediterranean into Iraq and Syria.[3] Following the agreement, T.E. Lawrence was dispatched into the desert to mould a group of Arab volunteers into a useful fighting force that later played a role in the British victory.

A year after McMahon had promised an Arab state to Hussein the British agreed a separate, this time secret, deal with the French – the Sykes-Picot agreement – giving them large chunks of what had been promised to Hussein. It was exactly the sort of quiet carving up of nations that Woodrow Wilson disapproved of. At the end of hostilities the historic *vilayets* (regions) of the Ottoman Empire had been divided between Britain and France. Violent resistance to French occupation began in Syria in 1919. On 1 February 1920 Bell wrote to her stepmother in England: 'The reason why I've been so busy is that people are beginning to come down the Aleppo road with news of Syria ... I, having now rather a satisfactory network of informants, hear of the arrival of most of them ... It's a distressing story which they bring. We share the blame, with France and America. for what is happening – I think there has seldom been such a series of hopeless tangles as the West has made about the East since the armistice. Meantime our administration in Mesopotamia is, contrary to all justice, reaping a profit.'[4]

While Bell may have seen it as an injustice – a rather progressive view at the time – reaping a profit was precisely what Britain intended to do in Iraq. Central to that purpose was the discovery of oil. The British government had first learned of the possibilities in Iraq from a German engineer in 1905, and as soon as soon as the Ottomans had been defeated and Iraq was in British hands, oil exploration began in earnest. A report by army surveyors in 1919 concluded that deposits in Iraq could rival the Persian oilfields, where the British-owned Anglo-Persian Oil Company (later to be renamed British Petroleum) had a few years previously completed the construction of the world's largest refinery.[5] However, at the start of 1920, no drilling had yet been undertaken, in part because there were ongoing debates with the French over logistics. Iraq may have had vast oil potential, but its only port was Basra at the top of the Persian Gulf and the hope was that the French could be persuaded to allow oil pipelines to run from Iraq, through Syria to the Mediterranean coast. A further benefit of these pipelines was that they would reduce the need for oil to be shipped through the Suez Canal.

In December 1919 the British Secretary for Overseas Trade agreed a provisional deal with the French. A month later it was in tatters. On 23 January 1920 Lloyd George declared that 'the profits arising from the exploitation of the oilfields of Mesopotamia should accrue for the benefit of the State rather than for the benefit of Joint Stock Companies'.[6] In short, the British government had paid to conquer Iraq and it was the British government that intended to benefit. Although it was a tantalising notion to entertain, full government control of Iraqi oil production was impracticable. As one minister quietly admitted: 'The proposal to develop the oilfields as government property may have attractions to some but the government does not possess the necessary organisation for so vast a business as the successful commercial exploitation of a large oilfield and the marketing of its products'.[7] At the start of February 1920 the entire enterprise was still up in the air.

The country to which Gertrude Bell had been sent was in fact still a province of the Ottoman Empire and not a country at all. Mesopotamia was the name given to the ancient region between the Euphrates and Tigris rivers, which stretched for over 500 miles from Mosul, near modern-day Turkey, to Basra on the Persian Gulf. Under Ottoman administration, the region had been divided into the three *vilayets* of Mosul, Baghdad and Basra. When British soldiers arrived in Baghdad in March 1917 they were warmly welcomed, but the fighting and the retreating Ottoman

Turks had left the city in a dire state. The war reporter Edmund Candler, who entered with British troops, reported in the *Manchester Guardian* a few days later:

> Crowds of Baghdadis came out to meet us: Persians, Krabe, Jew, Armenians, Chaldeans and Christians of diverse sects and races. They lined the streets, balconies and roofs, hurrahing and clapping their hands ... The people of the city have been robbed to supply the Turkish army for the last two years ... It appears that the enemy abandoned all hope of saving the city when we effected the crossing of the Tigris ... [after which] the Turkish government requisitioned private merchandise wholesale, and despatched it by train to Samara. Thirty or forty thousand pounds worth of stuff is believed to have been officially looted, including five thousand sacks of flour.[8]

The Baghdad the British inherited from the Ottomans was a city half in ruins and near starvation. A massive construction programme was initiated, adding a bridge over the Tigris, new streets and a power station. When the war ended, however, the British government began tightening its belt. Some investment projects were abandoned and a number of Arab employees were laid off, while the authorities continued to collect taxes in full, despite severe price inflation.[9] By 1920 the liberators were increasingly viewed as occupiers.

Chapter 6

A new faith

O fficially, the airmen of Number 47 Squadron no longer existed. In October 1919 the squadron had been disbanded and redesignated as an 'instructional mission' to the White Army in southern Russia. Their instruction included practical demonstrations of bombing and strafing runs against the advancing Bolshevik forces. They were part of a British contingent deployed in southern Russia totalling, in February 1920, 2,000 soldiers, sailors and airmen. Sadly, the British pilots' efforts to inspire the fledgling air force of the White Army were largely ineffective. While the air force did have planes – 138 obsolete RE8s – the Russian pilots were apparently disappointed that the British had not sent them more sophisticated aircraft: Number 47 Squadron was equipped with modern DH9 bombers and Sopwith Camel fighters. Worse still, the White Army's air force lacked dynamic leadership. Its chief, General Kravtshevich, was, it was officially noted, more interested in 'wine, women and song' than flying.[1]

The commander of the non-existent British squadron, Lieutenant Colonel Maund, had been recalled at the end of January and had left his men with warm words of encouragement: 'Although the fortunes of Russia are temporarily clouded I hope you will continue to show the same excellent qualities and high endeavour … necessary to restore the spirit of victory in our Russian allies.'[2] In line with this spirit of victory, a few weeks later the squadron received an order that 'All officers and ORs [ordinary ratings] must be in possession of a Rifle, Bayonet and 150 rounds of ammunition. These must in all cases be carried when travelling.'[3]

The British government's suspension of military aid was well known and there were rumours circulating that London was considering sending a trade delegation to Moscow. A British army colonel recorded in his diary on 13 February that he was ashamed to face his Russian colleagues, noting that the withdrawal of support was, 'a cowardly treachery. Winston [Churchill] is the only one who is playing honestly with [General] Denikin.'[4] Another British commander wrote to Churchill stating that, 'Without faith in us, the only people who have helped them materially, they are likely to be driven to despair. Nevertheless, Denikin and staunch elements are determined to fight on. They prefer to be driven into the sea.'[5]

The man in overall command of the White Army was, however, not helping his cause. Denikin was in the midst of a bitter dispute with rival commanders about their own ineptitude, with the result that the Bolshevik army had crossed the Don River and was making steady progress southward. Denikin finally gave in to reality and ordered the withdrawal of what was left of his army to the Crimea. The bulk would march on foot across the Kerch Strait, while the rest would be evacuated by boat from the Black Sea port of Novorossiysk. The Bolsheviks seemed to be advancing unchecked.

Churchill was not the only political figure concerned by the march of what he once called the 'foul baboonery' of Bolshevism. It was also of grave concern to a thirty-year-old German army corporal living in Munich. In September of the previous year, he had been sent by army intelligence to investigate and report on the activities of a small political group calling itself the German Workers' Party. Instead of supplying the army with intelligence, he had gone native. By February 1920 Adolf Hitler was a key member.

The German Workers' Party was the brainchild of Anton Drexler, a toolmaker and locksmith from Munich. The organisation was completely unremarkable: following the war there were many small groups of nationalist agitators and quasi-intellectuals casting around for someone to blame for Germany's defeat. Drexler's scapegoats of choice were the Jews and Freemasons, but he also had a strong antipathy toward Bolshevism, which he claimed was a 'Jewish swindle'. In his youth while in Berlin, Drexler had been forced to play the zither in a coffee house to survive, an experience he seemed to regard as a deep embarrassment. Despite his own industry, and that of the 'German workers' with whom he identified, the country's wealth seemed to be concentrated in the hands of a close-knit few; for Drexler, money really was the root of all evils. He wrote a short book, entitled *My Political Awakening*, which outlined his thoughts: 'The striving of international Free Masonry, whose leadership lies mostly in Jewish hands, is actually aimed at putting the world into a condition where 300 bankers are in a position to say "If we hold our pockets closed the gears of the world stop" ... all of productive mankind is supposed to be surrendered to the mercy or lack of mercy of a few hundred big bankers.'[6] Hitler later wrote that Drexler's book reflected his own development, and shortly after joining the German Workers' Party, Hitler began promoting the organisation by speaking in public. Many of his listeners were receptive; after all, it was less than eighteen months since the people had overthrown the monarchy.

At five in the morning on 10 November 1918 Friedrich Wilhelm Viktor Albert, Emperor of Germany and King of Prussia, shook hands with the members of his personal guard who were staying behind before the royal train pulled away from the station. A few hours later, as it crossed into neutral Holland, the relieved Wilhelm lit a cigarette.[7] Germany was now a republic. The following day, the new government agreed the Armistice and fighting ended on the Western Front. The king had left behind a country ravaged by war; roughly thirteen percent of the generation born between 1880 and 1899 had been killed in the space of four years. The Prussian elite were widely held responsible for the Great War and there was a strong reaction to Wilhelm's escape to Holland. A campaign started in the British press to extradite and then 'hang the Kaiser', a sentiment shared by many Germans. Even in 1920 the British were still pushing for extradition. Lloyd George wrote to the government of Holland on 14 February: 'It is indisputable that the permanent presence of the ex-Emperor ... a few kilometres from the German frontier ... constitutes, for the Powers who have made superhuman sacrifices to destroy this mortal danger, a menace ... the Powers cannot conceal the painful impression made upon them by the refusal of the Dutch Government to hand over the ex-Emperor.'[8] The reply was lengthy and full of caveats. The Dutch Foreign Minister stated: 'The Netherlands are not parties to the Treaty of Versailles ... their position with regard to the events of the war is different to that of the Powers ... it can only lay stress on the fact that it would be committing an act contrary to both law and justice and incompatible with national honour, were it to yield to the pressing demands of the Powers to violate such laws, thus abolishing the rights thereby granted to the fugitive within its territory.'[9]

The cause of the German revolution of 1918 was officially a mutiny among naval officers, but it had quickly spread to engulf most of the country. Even Germany's new government – headed by the leader of the historically accommodating Social Democratic Party – was still unpopular. The fear was that the seeds of revolution spread by Bolshevik Russia had taken root in Western Europe. The authorities acted decisively. Organisations purporting to stand up for workers' rights faced investigation – the very reason Hitler was sent to the meetings of the German Workers' Party in the first place – and worker uprisings were brutally suppressed by gangs of ex-servicemen organised into *Freikorps*, effectively government-run nationalist militia. Germany would not be allowed to turn to Bolshevism. In an environment of heightened nationalist sentiment, bitterness at the loss of the war, and the decimation of the economy, the German Workers' Party proposed a new future.

On 24 February 1920 Hitler addressed his largest crowd so far. The party had almost emptied its treasury to fund and publicise the event. Two thousand people crammed into a hall in Munich and listened to him outline twenty-five points he and Drexler had devised. They included the abolition of all unearned incomes, the revocation of Jews' German citizenship, and the creation of strong central state power. Hitler later wrote in *Mein Kampf* that when he announced each of the twenty-five points, 'One after the other was accepted with more and more joy, again and again unanimously ... I was confronted by the hall filled with people, united by a new conviction, a new faith, a new will'. His recollection may have been a little hazy: Hitler was heckled and his speech interrupted several times by left-wing agitators who comprised a good proportion of the crowd. A police informant described it as, 'Great tumult so that I often thought it would come to brawling at any minute'.[10] The meeting generated only modest attention in the local press, but gained the party new followers. However, the organisation they were encouraged to sign up to had changed its name. No longer was it the German Workers' Party. From February 1920 it was henceforth to be known as the *National-sozialistische Deutsche Arbeiterpartei*. The German mouthful was shortened to a pithy English abbreviation: the Nazi Party.

Chapter 7

'Native interests'

The very same day that Hitler was inspiring and antagonising a crowd in a Munich hall, Europe's leaders were concluding a twelve-day conference to finally settle a question that had been bothering them for nearly seventy years. The 'sick man of Europe' was dead at last and they had gathered to carve up the body.

Ottoman Turkey was first referred to as a 'sick man' by Tsar Nicholas I, in a meeting with the British Ambassador in 1853. The Tsar apparently said that Turkey was 'a sick man – a very sick man'; the sobriquet stuck.[1] The decline of the Ottoman Empire had been gradual. Successive sultans had acquired a habit of going to war in defence of the Empire's borders, only to find themselves defeated humiliatingly and forced to cede territory. The Ottomans had been supported by the British in the Crimean War, but twenty years later they were crushed by Russia and forced to hand over previously conquered Ottoman territories in the Balkans. In 1911 the Italians opportunistically snatched Libya and the following year more territory was lost after another uprising in the Balkans.[2]

Watching the slow death of the Ottoman Empire had become something of a spectator sport among European statesmen. They had even given the debates over the eventual outcome a name: the 'Eastern Question'. For years, European powers had been eyeing up the lands under Ottoman control, as much for strategic as well as economic reasons, and Ottoman Turkey's defeat in the First World War finally signalled the end. To the victor, the spoils. There were four nations around the table: Great Britain, France, Italy and Japan. Russia was not invited. Had King George V's cousin, Tsar Nicholas II, still been on the throne things might have been different – Russia had begun the First World War as an ally of Britain – but the rise of the Bolshevik menace meant Russia was now *persona non grata*. It was collectively decided by the nations seated around the table that the Allies could not countenance entering into diplomatic relations with the Soviets until the 'Bolshevist horrors' had come to an end and Lenin's government in Moscow decided it was 'ready to conform its methods and diplomatic conduct to that of all civilised governments.'[3]

Meetings began on 12 February with the intention that the decisions made would be developed into a formal document by a drafting committee. The result was to be a Treaty of Peace with Turkey, which would be signed at a later date. If the Ottoman representatives were in any doubt about their negotiating position, there were British-Indian soldiers marching around Constantinople to remind them. The French prime minister had originally not intended to stay in London longer than a week, but the British government not so politely informed Alexandre Millerand through official channels that if he went home, they might be forced to conclude separate arrangements with Turkey, an action Italy would almost certainly copy.[4] If the French walked away from the table, the British were determined to get their share regardless. Lloyd George himself had never liked Millerand. When he had defeated his predecessor, Georges Clemenceau, in the French elections the month before, the British prime minister had written to his wife, 'The defeat of Clemenceau upset all our plans. It is a monument of ingratitude [on the part of French voters]. From the point of view of policy I have not yet decided what it means, except that I shall dealing with very inferior men.'[5]

A group of generals were left to thrash out the military clauses of the treaty while the politicians dealt with the big questions, leaving the niggly details to be worked out by civil servants between the London meeting in February and the signing of the treaty itself. Although twelve days seems a remarkably short period of time in which to carve up a centuries-old empire, the Allies did have two significant factors on their side. The major decisions had already been made in the wartime deals cut with the French, and the presence of British troops in Palestine and Iraq, and French soldiers in Syria, meant that the Conference of London was, in many respects, meeting to confirm the reality that already existed on the ground. The treaty with Turkey would simply provide a respectable veneer for the Allies' acquisitions. There were a few more complicated issues, primarily centred around the claims of minority ethnic groups, and on 17 February it was agreed that there would be commissions on Armenia and Smyrna to assess the respective Armenian and Greek claims for sovereignty. The Armenian commission was already working on the 'assumptions' that Armenia would become an independent state and that included within its borders would be historically Armenian regions of eastern Turkey, which at the time of the conference were still officially under Turkish control.[6] It was an outcome that deeply offended the Turks; parts of their empire were being given to the minority groups they had repressed, or, in the case of the Armenians, attempted to eradicate from the pages of history.[7]

Like Germany, Ottoman Turkey was still intended to exist as a country, though it was determined that she should do so without her wider territories, and in a permanently weakened state. On 21 February the British Cabinet received a summary document of the principal decisions concluded in the negotiations. The borders of the Middle East had been redrawn. Regions which had been part of the Ottoman Empire for nearly 600 years had been splintered off and Turkey was now geographically bordered by Syria to the south, Armenia to the east and hemmed in by seas to its north and west. In addition, Turkey would agree to permit the Allies to maintain whatever military forces they wished on its territory, with the freedom to move them wherever they pleased.[8] The crucial statement in the draft was that 'Turkey renounces in favour of the Allied powers all her rights and titles over ... Kurdistan, Mesopotamia, Syria, Palestine, Arabia'.[9] With the exception of Kurdistan, the borders of which were still being debated, the Allies had already divided up the rest. Arabia was under the control of two Arab leaders, Ibn Saud and Sharif Hussein of Mecca, who was still smarting from the British government's refusal to honour the agreement he made with Sir Henry McMahon in 1915. The French would gain Syria under a 'mandate', while Mesopotamia and Palestine were to become mandates run by the British. The mandate concept was one invented by the League of Nations and set out in Article 22 of the Covenant. It stated:

> To those colonies and territories which as a consequence of the late war have ceased to be under the sovereignty of the States which formerly governed them and which are inhabited by peoples not yet able to stand by themselves under the strenuous conditions of the modern world, there should be applied the principle that the well-being and development of such peoples form a sacred trust of civilisation ... The best method of

giving practical effect to this principle is that the tutelage of such peoples should be entrusted to advanced nations who by reason of their resources, their experience or their geographical position can best undertake this responsibility.

In principle, France and Britain were benevolently taking on a sacred trust to tutelage the former Ottoman *vilayets* in Syria, Mesopotamia and Palestine until they could 'stand by themselves'. In February 1920 Britain and France were administering that sacred trust by trying to come to an arrangement to start extracting oil from Mesopotamia as soon as possible. In parallel with the discussions about military clauses and political areas of interest, Sir John Cadman, Director in charge of His Majesty's Petroleum Department, and his French opposite number, M. Philippe Bertholot, managed to agree the outlines of an oil deal on Iraq. The British would get free oil pipeline facilities in French-controlled Syria and in exchange France would get a twenty-five percent shareholding in any company permitted to develop the fields, or a twenty-five percent share of net oil output if the British government undertook the drilling itself. Under the same agreement, 'native interests' were granted the option of a twenty percent participation in oilfield developments.[10] They would be allowed to watch and learn.

In Palestine, the British also had native interests to content with, but the situation was further complicated by another wartime commitment made by the British government. In 1917 the then British Foreign Secretary, Arthur Balfour, had written to the influential Jewish banker Lord Rothschild, 'I have much pleasure in conveying to you on behalf of His Majesty's Government, the following declaration of sympathy with Jewish Zionist aspirations which has been submitted to, and approved by, the Cabinet.' The now historic letter went on to state, 'His Majesty's Government views with favour the establishment in Palestine of a national home for the Jewish people.' Much has been made of the fact that the British promised the Jews a 'national home' and not a state, and that the Balfour Declaration was also conditional on not prejudicing the rights of the existing non-Jewish communities in Palestine. But whatever Balfour thought he was promising at the time, the declaration set British policy fundamentally at odds with the wishes of the majority of the inhabitants of Palestine. It was another omen that Britain's mandates were to prove a costly endeavour.

By the end of February 1920 the organisation created to achieve world peace had achieved nothing of note, while the most powerful nation in the world was absent from its meetings; worse, the statesman who was the League's greatest advocate was gravely ill. The carve-up of the Ottoman Empire was proceeding as planned, but the British government faced the prospect of the White Army's defeat in Russia, violence in Ireland and rebellion in Waziristan. In Western Europe nations were still reeling from the war and there was growing discontent in Germany. Spring 1920 would bring even greater challenges.

PART TWO

Chapter 8

The man who would be king

Gertrude Bell was not impressed with the details of the proposed peace treaty with Turkey. She wrote a long letter to her friend Lord Robert Cecil – an ardent League supporter, who would later be president of the League of Nations Union – giving an exhaustive criticism of proposals that had arisen from the Conference of London. She viewed the continuance of the status quo in Iraq and Syria as a travesty: 'From first to last it's radically bad and there can't be any stability in existing arrangements.'[1] At the start of March 1920 the situation in Iraq was relatively stable; it was Syria that was giving the British and the French the greatest headache. The British had supported notions of Arab nationalism because it served their interests in the Great War, but now the genie was out of the bottle.

Feisal was the third son of Sharif Hussein of Mecca and it was Feisal's army that had fought with T.E. Lawrence against the Turks in the deserts of Arabia. Lawrence first met the prince in the Arabian village of Wadi Safra after being sent to the desert with the task of creating an Arab army to fight against the Turks.

> [A slave] led me to an inner court, on whose further side, framed between the uprights of a black doorway, stood a white figure waiting tensely for me. I felt at first glance that this was the man I had come to Arabia to seek – the leader who would bring the Arab revolt to full glory. Feisal looked very tall and pillar-like, very slender, in his long, white silk robes and his brown head-cloth bound with a brilliant scarlet and gold chord. His eyelids were dropped; and his black beard and colourless face were like a mask against the strange, still watchfulness of his body.[2]

Feisal possessed a magnetic charm, coupled with the ambition of a man fully aware that, as a Hashemite, he was descended from the lineage of the Prophet himself. Feisal assumed, because of his father's agreement with the British in the Hussein-McMahon correspondence, that after the Allied victory in the war, he would become ruler of a new Arab state. His ambitions were dashed in October 1918, following the triumphal entry of the Arab army into Damascus. Feisal, along with Lawrence who acted as interpreter, met with General Allenby in a room in the Victoria Hotel. Allenby, the Commander-in-Chief of British forces in the region, coolly informed Feisal of the terms of the Sykes-Picot agreement, under which Syria was to become a French protectorate; Feisal would only be permitted to lead an Arab administration that excluded Palestine and Lebanon. The prince was livid. Allenby turned to Lawrence and asked, 'But did you not tell him that the French were to have the Protectorate over Syria?' Lawrence replied, 'No Sir, I knew nothing about it.'[3]

Five months later, at the post-war treaty negotiations in Paris, Feisal and Lawrence led an Arab delegation lobbying for independent Arab rule in Syria and Iraq. Gertrude Bell travelled to Paris to support the cause. She stayed at the Hotel Majestic, a former palace on Avenue Kleber that lived it up to its name by providing its patrons with a view across the rooftop gables of Parisian apartments towards the Seine and the Eiffel Tower. While Feisal and Lawrence held formal meetings, Bell worked the back-channels: 'I'm lunching tomorrow with Mr Balfour who, I fancy, really doesn't care. Ultimately I hope to catch Ll.[oyd] George by the coat tails and if I can manage to do so, I believe I can enlist his sympathies … The Mesop.[otamia] settlement is so closely linked with the Syrian that we can't consider one without the other, and in the case of Syria it's the French attitude that counts.'[4] The French refused to be moved and there is no record that Bell managed a meeting with Lloyd George.

The British position towards Feisal had softened since the angry meeting in a Damascus hotel in 1918. Several British politicians – including Mark Sykes, who had negotiated the wartime agreement with the French – were increasingly of the view that the Sykes-Picot agreement should at least be modified.[5] Balfour noted, 'France, England and America have got themselves into a position over the Syrian problem so inextricably confused that no really neat and satisfactory issue is now possible for any of them'.[6] Lloyd George had some sympathy for the Arab cause. He wrote to Clemenceau, who was then French Prime Minster, 'His Majesty's Government cannot conceal the anxiety they have felt at the apparent determination of the French press to deal with the Emir Feisal and the Arab problem with a high hand. If this were indeed the policy of the French Government, the British Government are afraid that it would inevitably lead to serious and long-continued disturbances throughout the Arab territories.'[7] After much negotiation, the British agreed to pull their forces out of Syria. The pressing question was whether their place would be taken by French or Arab soldiers and who would officially have sovereignty. Feisal travelled to Paris to negotiate in person with Clemenceau.

The first proposal the French put on the table gave them complete control of Syria's economy and political apparatus. Feisal rejected it. His own position was a complicated one. Even within Syria, there were multiple Arab factions and while Feisal had become a figurehead for Arab nationalism, he faced criticism from some quarters for even negotiating with the French. The French came back with a revised proposal for a 'trusteeship' in Syria. They would provide military and civil administrators, but French troops would not be stationed in the interior and Feisal would be chief of the country, which would have a parliamentary government to determine its own laws and taxes. Feisal agreed to the terms in January 1920. Arab nationalists immediately began sporadic attacks against French forces.

Feisal left to return to Syria, having garnered some support in France. M. Philippe Bertholot, the French senior civil servant who was negotiating with the British over the Syria-Iraq oil pipeline, noted, 'The return of Emir Feisal, who is in agreement with us in the essential points, is going to help in the repression of that banditry ... [and] demonstrate the falseness of the accusations levelled against our policy of association with the natives and of respect for their liberties.'[8] Bertholot was sorely mistaken. On arrival, Feisal faced mass demonstrations in Damascus and accusations that he had collaborated with the French and given up his fight for Arab independence. Increasingly, he came under pressure to renounce any French claim over Syria. Within the French government, the agreement with Feisal also caused considerable division. To a significant minority it seemed that the Arabs were being handed far too generous a settlement in Syria, to the detriment of the French, when the British seemed to be getting their way in Iraq. France's new prime minister, Alexandre Millerand, was decidedly unenthusiastic about any agreement with the Arabs over Syria and when Feisal approached him to attempt to negotiate further concessions he flatly refused. Millerand was of the opinion that the Sykes-Picot agreement had granted France undisputed political control in Syria.[9]

In early March 1920 the General Syrian Congress convened in Damascus. The Congress had first met the year before and comprised Arab notables from Syria, Iraq, Palestine and Lebanon. They proclaimed the 'complete and unconditional independence of our country Syria,' and declared Feisal King of Syria and his older brother, Abdullah, ruler of a sovereign Iraq.[10] The French government quickly announced that it viewed the declaration as null and void, while the British Foreign Secretary indignantly asserted, 'Great Britain does not recognise that any committee in Damascus has the right to speak about Palestine and Iraq.' Syria, seemingly was another matter, but that was a French problem.[11] A week later, Bell wrote to her stepmother that she had heard 'the afternoon's news which was that Faisal [sic] had been crowned king of Syria and Abdullah king of Iraq. Well, we are in for it and I think we shall need every scrap of personal influence and every hour of friendly intercourse we've ever had here in order to keep this country from falling into chaos.'[12]

Chapter 9

The restoration of order

In March 1920 Adolf Hitler, while nurturing grand political ambitions, remained in the employ of the German Army. Having initially been used as an informant, he was also given the task of lecturing soldiers as part of their 'citizenship education'. He was taken under the wing of an army captain called Karl Mayr, who was head of the Army's Information Department, and who organised the education courses at which Hitler spoke. In January and February 1920 Hitler lectured soldiers on the Versailles Treaty and the significance of political parties, decrying both the treaty and Bolshevism in the name of German patriotism. Far from being contradictory, Hitler's two roles, one as part of the nationalist army propaganda machine and the other as a key member of the growing Nazi Party, were largely complimentary. His superior, Mayr, apparently shared his sense of outrage at the Versailles settlement and distaste for Bolshevism and Mayr himself had helped fund Nazi Party meetings. As well as encouraging Hitler, Mayr maintained contact with others in the German military and government who were deeply dissatisfied with the political situation.

One friend of Mayr's was the nationalist Wolfgang Kapp, a civil servant who had spent most of his career in government finance. Kapp had been born in New York after his father emigrated, but had returned to Germany with his family as a young boy. By March 1920 he was sixty-one years old. The best-known portrait of Kapp shows him staring down the lens, sagging chin hiding a once-square jaw, watery eyes peering through pince-nez. He does not look like the kind of man to lead a coup. General Walther von Lüttwitz, however, was precisely that kind of man: a decorated Great War general and a straight-backed and steely-eyed militant nationalist. Together, Kapp and Lüttwitz would attempt to bring down the German Republic.

Under Article 160 of the Treaty of Versailles, the German Army was effectively reduced to a skeleton security force: 'By a date which must not be later than March 31, 1920, the German Army must not comprise more than seven divisions of infantry and three divisions of cavalry ... After that date the total number of effectives in the Army of the States constituting Germany must not exceed one hundred thousand men, including officers.'[1] The German government had been steadily disbanding the German Army, but as the deadline loomed they instituted vicious cuts. The *Freikorps* units, now larger than the country's standing army, posed a dilemma. Although they had proved invaluable in putting down worker uprisings prior to 1920, they were now a threat. The German Defence Minister, Gustav Noske, therefore began issuing orders to some *Freikorps* units to disband. The six-thousand-strong *Marinebrigade Ehrhardt*, based near Berlin, was one of the *Freikorps* units slated for demobilisation. Its commander appealed to General Lüttwitz for support. It was the moment Lüttwitz and Kapp had been waiting for.

For more than a year, Kapp had been planning the overthrow of the government. He had contacted other disaffected nationalists and former military men and, in October 1919, founded the *National Vereinigung* (National Association), an umbrella organisation which aimed to unify German paramilitary forces, including the *Freikorps*. The Association encouraged anti-government sentiment within the *Freikorps*, establishing connections with different commanders, including Lüttwitz. It was agreed that, when the time came, the *Marinebrigade Ehrhardt* would enter Berlin to demand the removal of the government.[2]

On 10 March 1920 General Lüttwitz, after refusing to disband *Freikorps* units, consented to a meeting with the government. In the presence of Defence Minister Noske and the German president, Friedrich Ebert, Lüttwitz called for a reversal of the order to disband the *Freikorps* and presented a series of other demands, including Ebert's own resignation. Incensed, Noske ordered Lüttwitz to step down. He refused. Meanwhile, Kapp agreed the division of his future cabinet posts with his nationalist co-conspirators. At 7am on the morning of 13 March, Kapp and the other key leaders gathered at the Brandenburg Gate as, on the orders of Lüttwitz, the *Marinebrigade Ehrhardt* marched into Berlin. The president and government ministers fled to Stuttgart. Kapp declared himself Chancellor and made Lüttwitz Minister of Defence. Supporters of the coup handed out a proclamation in the streets of the German capital:

> Empire and nation are in grave danger. We are speedily approaching the total collapse of the state and legal system.

The people only vaguely sense the coming disaster. Prices soar without stopping. Misery is growing. Famine threatens … The ineffective government, lacking authority and tied to corruption, is not capable of mastering the danger … Militant Bolshevism threatens us with devastation and violation from the east … How will we avoid external and internal collapse? Only by re-establishing the authority of a strong state … restoration of order, and the sanctity of law. Duty and conscience are to reign again in German lands. German honour and honesty are to be restored.[3]

The London Globe newspaper, under the headline 'Drama of Berlin', reported that evening that the German government had ceased to exist and, according to the paper's military correspondent, the putsch was a plot to reinstate the monarchy.

While Kapp and Lüttwitz were both monarchists, there is little proof that they had any active intention of restoring the Kaiser to the throne. British Intelligence was completely fixated on a possible Bolshevist connection, apparently unaware of the coup plotters' vehement anti-Communist sentiment. The Home Office Directorate of Intelligence informed ministers, 'The military coup d'état which broke out on the 12th of March was evidently the result of a carefully prepared plot … It should be remembered that for some time there have been persistent rumours of an alliance between the German Monarchist Party and the Russian Bolsheviks … The danger of the present situation lies in the fact that the German Monarchists are ready to use any weapon which is calculated to assist their policy of a counter-revolution and the reconstruction of Russia under German domination.'[4] A union with the Bolsheviks was the last thing Kapp had in mind. After taking Berlin without firing a shot, the process of governing was already occupying all of his time. Crucially, other German army units had refused an order from Noske to put down the coup – the generals asserted that 'Reichswehr [German Army] troops never shoot on other Reichswehr troops' – but neither did they rally to Kapp's call to come out in support of the new government.[5]

From the outset, Kapp and Lüttwitz did not have the backing of the majority of the population. Civil servants simply refused to acknowledge the new administration. The ousted government, with the support of labour unions, called for a general strike across Germany. The country's entire economy ground to a halt. Mayr dispatched Adolf Hitler and a colleague to Berlin to update Kapp on the situation in Munich, which was also paralysed by the general strike. When Hitler landed at the airport, he discovered it had been occupied by picketing workers. Hitler only managed to extricate himself from the situation by passing himself off as an accountant.[6]

Kapp's government was now impotent: he had declared himself head of a state apparatus that refused to enact his wishes, while the country he claimed to run had no public services. Furthermore, his repeated pleas to other members of the General Staff to join Lüttwitz were ignored. The coup was beginning to unravel. On 17 March a delegation of high-ranking German Army officers called on Lüttwitz at the Chancellery to assert that the Kapp government did not have the backing of the majority of the German military. For the second time in a week Lüttwitz was asked to resign, this time from his position as Minister of Defence.[7] True to form, he refused. Later that day the *Freikorps* marched out of Berlin. Four days after he had stood at the Brandenburg Gate planning the first moves he would make once in power, Kapp was ignominiously forced to flee the city he had hoped would welcome him. Kapp fled to Sweden and Lüttwitz to Hungary. Two weeks later, Hitler was formally discharged from the German Army, one of the many who were culled from its ranks because of the Versailles Treaty restrictions.

Germany's first right-wing coup of the twentieth century was an embarrassing failure, but the ambitions of many nationalists remained undimmed. Mayr wrote to Kapp, now in exile in Sweden: 'The national workers' party must provide the basis for the strong assault-force we are hoping for ... Under this banner we've already won a good number of supporters. Since July of last year I've been looking ... to strengthen the movement ... I've set up very capable young people. A Herr Hitler, for example, has become a motive force, a popular speaker of the first rank. In the Munich branch we have over 2,000 members, compared with under 100 in summer 1919.'[8] Mayr's 'popular speaker' would later rise to a prominence his mentor could never have imagined.

Chapter 10

Nothing but force

The day that the *Marinebrigade Ehrhardt* marched between the columns of the Brandenburg Gate to establish the shortest-lived government in Germany's history, the members of the League of Nations Council gathered in Paris for their third session. They were supposed to have met in Rome, but urgent business led to the session being brought forward. It was entirely the fault of Lloyd George.

A few weeks before, the British prime minister had formerly written to the Council, stating that the Supreme Allied Council thought it would be 'highly desirable' for an investigation team to be sent to Russia to find out what exactly was taking place there. In the midst of rumours of widespread economic hardship following the Bolshevist takeover, the Allies were keen to discover what was actually going on. Lloyd George noted, 'This enquiry would be invested with even greater authority and with superior chances of success if it were made upon the initiative, and conducted under the supervision of the Council of the League of Nations.'[1]

Quick to oblige, the Council brought forward their planned meeting. After discussion, the Council decided that labour conditions in Russia were worthy of careful examination and it was desirable to extend the enquiry and to undertake a general survey. Following a period of deliberation, the Council arrived at the decision that two commissions should be sent to Russia: one dispatched by the League of Nations' main body and another from the International Labour Bureau, a body created by the League to consider labour conditions.[2]

In response to a request to investigate conditions in Russia, the League of Nations Council had decided to send not one, but two delegations on a visit. Members of the press immediately requested to be allowed to accompany them. Arthur Balfour, who was again the designated League attendee on behalf of Britain, put a dampener on the general enthusiasm by proposing that the first thing the Council should do was send a telegram to the Russian government to ask whether they would be allowed into the country. The Russian government replied a fortnight later: 'Your radio [telegram] of March 17th was handed to the Assistant Chairman of the Central Executive Committee, Lutovinof, who is now in Moscow. He sent it accordingly to the President of the Central Executive Committee, Kalinin, who is now travelling.'

At the same meeting, the Council also discussed an outbreak of typhus in Poland. M. Zaimoisky, the Polish Ambassador in Paris, was invited to address the members. He informed them that a fresh typhus outbreak was expected in the autumn of 1920 and, if left unchecked, would become an epidemic across the whole of Europe. The Council agreed that a permanent international body be established to assess the health of nations and proposed a resolution to collectively endorse a letter from Balfour to the International Red Cross urging them to urgent action. The resolution passed unanimously and at 5.20pm the members rose, with enough time to return to their hotels ahead of dinner in one of the French capital's famous restaurants.

In March 1920 the League of Nations Assembly had not yet met and the select members who comprised the Council had held three meetings – two in Paris and one in London – which had set up a series of commissions and inquiries to which the Council had appointed representatives from various member states. It had proposed the creation of a court of international justice, though no one had yet suggested how the select panel of judges would be chosen without offending the majority of the forty-four nations who were members of the League. In its three-month existence, the Council had demonstrated considerable ability to unanimously agree resolutions that assorted bodies, largely of its own creation, should take action on everything from minority rights to potential pandemics. Council members were well aware that US Senators were not alone in questioning the League's existence, but its power was limited. In a confidential memo to the British Cabinet after the Council meeting, Balfour reminded them:

> It must be remembered that the chief instruments at the disposal
> of the League are Public Discussion; Judicial Investigation;
> Arbitration; and in the last resort, but only in the last resort,

some form of compulsion. These are powerful weapons, but the places where they seem least applicable are those remote and half-barbarous regions, where nothing but force is understood, and where force is useless to preserve order unless it can be rapidly applied. It would seem that in those parts of the world where this description applies, the League of Nations can only play an effective part if there is a Mandatory through whom it can act.[3]

Publicly, Leon Bourgeois dismissed any criticisms. Two days after the meeting he told a Swiss newspaper, 'The Governments and peoples who want a difference settled or wish to make a complaint have already been coming to the Council, with the certainty that they are appealing to a powerful and moral authority which will be capable of having its decisions respected. All delegates are inspired with deep feelings of humanity and strict justice. Enormous progress has been made in the direction of world peace.' Privately however, even members of the League of Nations Council were admitting that the organisation lacked teeth. Balfour himself did not fear that the League would be neglected, but rather that 'the Governments and peoples of the world would throw upon the League a burden at least a heavy as that which it is able to bear.'[4] Already, the League was becoming an echo chamber for the world's ills, but the organisation's initial responses were ponderous.

Apart from anything else, achieving world peace was proving expensive. In addition to the funding required for the official bodies of the League – such as the Council – and their requisite administration, there were further costs accrued by other associated bodies like the International Labour Bureau. Up to 31 March 1920 expenditure totalled £130,500, equivalent to over £2.7 million in today's money.[5]

One of the 'half-barbarous regions' of which Balfour had spoken was eastern Turkey. Officially the region was part of the conquered Ottoman Empire, which the Allies were in the process of carving up. When the war ended, a wave of unrest swept the region and the government in Constantinople sent their most successful military officer to calm things down.

Mustafa Kemal Ataturk was the only Ottoman First World War general who had not been defeated in battle. Armed with extensive powers to command the obedience of the regional governors, he arrived in eastern Turkey in May 1919. On his arrival he went off script and announced to the crowds that greeted him that the Sultan was a prisoner of the Allies and that he had come to save Turkey. Ataturk ignored the instructions he received from Constantinople and was shortly afterwards dismissed by the Sultan, who issued orders for his arrest. Instead of arresting him, the local governors joined Ataturk, who had at his disposal the entire Turkish XV Army Corps, and helped set up a rival government in Anatolia. His congress rejected the agreement with the Allies and insisted that all the territory that had been under Turkish control at the end of hostilities should remain part of Turkey. Non-Turkish elements in the region were targeted by the nationalists, in particular Armenians. In January 1920 as many as 16,000 Armenians were massacred in the town of Marash. Although it was not openly admitted, eastern Turkey had effectively become a rogue state. This presented a problem for the Allies. The area under the control of Ataturk's administration, where Armenians were still being attacked, was supposed to be within the borders of the intended future state of Armenia.

As part of the former Ottoman Empire, the situation of Armenia was complicated; technically its future was to be decided through the peace treaty with Turkey. However, the Allies recognised that to simply announce the creation of a new state for Armenians would not solve the problem. They would need protection. The prospect of more British troops being deployed on foreign soil that was of little or no strategic value did not inspire action. The creation of Armenia itself was primarily a humanitarian endeavour and there seemed a natural solution: pass the problem to the League of Nations. On 12 March the Supreme Allied Council wrote to the League of Nations Council, proposing that the League should accept a position equivalent to that of a mandatory power to place the future state of Armenia under its protection. The message only reached the Council meeting at the end of its session, too late to make the agenda, although the Council briefly discussed it anyway. Balfour informed the British Cabinet: 'It is evident as yet, and probably for a long time to come, the League of Nations is not and cannot be adequately equipped to carry out duties which may well prove to be of the most onerous kind ... It is more than doubtful whether it should itself directly undertake large responsibilities of a mandatory character; especially in remote and half-civilised regions where civilised opinion, the chief weapon of the League, carries but little weight.[6]' He concluded, 'The League of Nations, with no force at its immediate disposal, would have no weapon except remonstrance; and remonstrance has been tried in Turkey for 100 years with singularly little effect.'

Chapter 11

The Frankenstein monster

There was no United States representative present at the League Council meeting on 13 March. The US Senate was still refusing to ratify the Treaty of Versailles and the League of Nations Covenant. While the Council members officially regretted the lack of US involvement, other politicians were more outspoken. A former British Foreign Secretary, Lord Grey, wrote a public letter, published in *The Times*, which stated: 'Without the United States it [the League] will have neither the overwhelming physical nor moral force behind it that it should have, or if it has the physical force it will not have the same degree of moral force, for it will be predominantly European and not a world organisation ... If the outcome of the long controversy in the Senate has been to offer cooperation in the League of Nations, it would be the greatest mistake to refuse.'[1] Wilson reacted strongly and issued a press release criticising what he claimed was an 'extraordinary attempt to influence the action of the president and the Senate,' adding that if Grey had been an ambassador he would have been ordered to leave the country.[2]

The machinations in the Senate had gone on for months. Henry Cabot Lodge had spearheaded the addition of a series of 'reservations' – effectively amendments – aimed to do away with any notion that the League could make demands on the United States without the say of Congress. Wilson resisted any suggestion of compromise. One proposal included a request to increase the number of US votes in the Assembly. This outraged the Canadians, who wrote a forthright note of complaint to the British Government stating that the proposed reservations were a 'direct challenge' to the status of the Dominions. They refused to countenance any grounds on which the United States could be given additional votes 'without changing the whole basis of representation and voting'.[3] They were joined in their protest by representatives from New Zealand and South Africa. The formal reply from the British Government was cautious; there were Cabinet members who hoped the US might still overcome the obstacles and become a League member. The government stressed that, in light of the fact that the fate of the entire treaty was still up in the air, any public fuss might consolidate American opinion in line with very thing the Canadians were opposing.[4]

Several senators secretly communicated with Wilson's Private Secretary in an attempt to create a compromise. Hitchcock, previously the president's go-between, was now of the opinion that agreeing to the reservations in some form was the best way forward. The general feeling was 'that the best interests of the [Democratic] party would be served if the president were to yield his opposition to the reservations.'[5] Wilson refused to be moved.

On 3 March Wilson was wheeled in his chair to the presidential limousine, driven along Pennsylvania Avenue and up to Capitol Hill, and then around the city for more than an hour. It was the first time in five months that he had left the White House. The Senate was in its second day of the final debate, which would continue for over two weeks. Existing reservations were heatedly discussed and new ones proposed. One Democrat called for a reservation in favour of the creation of an independent Armenia as a mandate for the League administered by the United States. A Republican Senator from Washington, one of the many 'irreconcilables' who were implacably opposed to the League in any form, told the Senate that such a proposal would require a billion dollars and showed how the League was 'this Frankenstein monster among the Governments of the world'.[6] Eventually, late in the evening on 19 March, the Senate held the final vote. The following day, Wilson's doctor recorded in his diary:

> The President slept all night through without awaking. The Senate yesterday rejected the Treaty of Versailles by a vote of 49 to 35. The result was announced to the President by Mrs Wilson this morning at nine o'clock. The President, after hearing this adverse news, showed every evidence of being very blue and depressed. He said to me: "I feel like going to bed and staying there." The weather was too inclement for him to venture out for a motor ride; it was cloudy and threatened to rain or snow. But for this I should have insisted on a ride in order to cheer him up.[7]

The report sent to London from the British Embassy in Washington was equally dejected: 'The Treaty is dead so far as the Senate is concerned, and it is difficult to see how it can possibly be brought to life again.'[8]

Among those in the Senate who voted against the League and ratification of the treaty was a Republican Senator from Ohio by the name of Warren Gamaliel Harding. He was no stranger to opposing the president. In August 1919 Wilson had invited members of the Senate Foreign Relations Committee to the East Room of the White House to discuss the treaty over lunch. Undeterred by his surroundings, the Ohio senator had clashed with the president, enquiring not only why Article Ten was necessary, but whether there was any point to the League at all. Wilson apparently responded that had America 'stood morally' with the Allies in 1914, Germany would never have started the war. Harding was unconvinced.[9]

A small-town newspaper owner who had made a modest fortune for himself, he had secured an unexpected but resounding election to the State Senate in 1899, in what had previously been a staunchly Democratic district. After navigating the Republican Party's decline in the early 1900s, he finally secured election to the US Senate in 1912. His easy manner and rugged good looks won him friends. While he was a cautious politician who took a laid-back approach – he missed two-thirds of Senate votes – his modest star was rising within the party. He only had one real weakness: women. Harding had multiple affairs, which became more complicated in 1919 when a twenty-year-old mistress became pregnant. In October of that year she gave birth to his first daughter, Elizabeth; Harding's marriage to his wife, Florence, was childless. His complicated personal life was counteracted by an uncomplicated public one: Harding's greatest trait was that he made few political enemies. In the summer of 1919 he was invited by a Republican cabal to consider running for the White House. Convinced that it might help secure his Senate seat, Harding declared his candidacy in December. He wrote to a friend a few weeks later, 'The only thing I really worry about is that I am sometimes very much afraid I am going to be nominated and elected. That's an awful thing to contemplate.'[10]

The current occupant of the White House was now in the twilight of his second term, largely scorned by Democrats and Republicans alike. Henry Cabot Lodge said of Wilson, 'His personal selfishness goes beyond what I have seen in any human being. It is so extreme that it is entirely unenlightened and stupid.'[11] On 25 March Wilson's Private Secretary requested that Wilson publicly announce that he would not run for a third term. The president claimed it would be presumptuous and still clung to an almost messianic perception of his own role in events, confiding in his doctor:

> No group of men has given me any assurance that it wanted me to be a candidate for renomination. In fact, everyone seems to be opposed to my running. And I think it would be entirely out of place for me to say now that I would not run ... The [Democratic] Convention may come to a deadlock as to candidates, and there may be practically a universal demand for the selection of someone to lead them out of the wilderness ... In such circumstances I would feel obliged to accept the nomination even if I thought it would cost me my life. I have given my vitality, and almost my life, for the League of Nations, and I would rather lead a fight for the League of Nations and lose both my reputation and my life than to shirk a duty.[12]

Chapter 12

Occupation

The high passes of Waziristan were still dusted with snow in early March. The region was not peaceful, but attacks against the British were becoming more sporadic and less organised. The regular dispatches sent to Montagu by the Viceroy struck a dull, monotonous note: 'Derajat column on 5th [March], three permanent picquets [outposts] established *en route* to Kaniguram without causalities ... On 7th nothing to report, except that parties revictualing picquets west of Kaniguram were sniped.'[1] The following day, General Skeen's men destroyed a tower from which some of the long-range shots had been fired.

Each of the permanent picquets held ten days' worth of food supplies and five days' water, as well as ammunition. Larger ones could be manned by as many as fifty riflemen, while smaller, temporary positions might be guarded by as few as seven soldiers, who, after constructing the picquet, would have to watch as their comrades in arms disappeared over the nearest ridge and out of sight. Sometimes men spent over a month enclosed behind the parapets. The British mission in Waziristan was strung out, with mile after mile of small defensive positions guarding supply lines and acting as early warning posts for the main force. The only communication between them was to send riders, who were often shot at as they travelled from one picquet to another. Waziristan provided a completely different combat experience, even for men who had spent most of the previous decade fighting. They had to learn new tactics, and quickly. Regular troops had to be taught how to mount attacks along the crests of converging hills rather than in ravines, and soldiers had to master the art of firing and reloading from behind the cover of rocks and boulders, as well as communicating with aircraft.[2] The supplied 'popham panels' used for vertical communication – white cloth panels with numbers on – proved completely useless in the snow and rocks of Waziristan and troops resorted to using simpler strips to mark their positions, although the markers occasionally fell into the hands of the enemy. It was assumed in official reports that the tactics used by the men fighting in Waziristan were exclusive to mountain combat, but in fact the men were learning methods of fighting that would become routine in the Second World War.

Despite all the problems posed by the weather, geography and the need for new tactics, the campaign appeared to have largely achieved its aim. Thesiger telegrammed Montagu on 20 March: 'Situation in North Waziristan is fairly satisfactory … Destruction of Makin and visit of Derajat Column to Kanigoram appear to have convinced Mahsud leaders that further resistance is futile … democratic constitution of tribes makes it unlikely that full compliance can be secured without prolonged occupation … We do not in any case anticipate much further serious resistance.' He closed the memo by stating, 'Viewed as a whole, situation on Frontier shows marked improvement. Severe punishment administered to Mahsuds is having salutary effects elsewhere.'[3]

The scorched earth policy of collective punishment adopted by the army appeared to be providing a deterrent against organised resistance. One of the main aims of the campaign was the disarmament of the tribes, particularly the recovery of British-made rifles that had previously been stolen, or held on to by deserters. The town of Makin was completely razed to the ground after residents failed to hand in the required number of 200. The official report by the General Staff impassively narrated the levelling of Makin as follows: 'The main column under Brigadier General Lucas gained its objective by 9.40am and the work of destruction continued until 12.30pm … the destructive work on this day included seventeen towers, one hundred and sixty houses and a large number of retaining walls in the fields.' The 'visit' of the Derajat Column to Kanigoram – mentioned by the Viceroy in his 20 March telegram – entailed the occupation of the city, which was only spared from the same fate as Makin by the Mahsud's payment of a fine and the delivery of 200 rifles. After months of fighting, the tribes were brutally being brought to heel. General Climo was pleased with his men: 'Immunity from serious attack on convoys is directly attributable to the skill and energy with which the pickets [sic] have been situated and constructed. The troops themselves are confident and contented, and have a feeling of elation that is fully justified by the difficulties they have overcome which cannot be realised fully without personal knowledge of the terrain.'[4] What is remarkable is that the men Climo praised were not British, even though they were part of the British army. With the exception of the airmen from the Royal Air Force and one mountain artillery battery, the entire rank and file of the Waziristan force were Indian. The General Staff admitted, 'This fact has, without doubt, considerably raised the prestige of the Indian Army on the Frontier and increased the esprit-de-corps of the troops engaged.' Despite this, the vast majority of the high-ranking officers were still drawn from the 'proper' British army.

Captain Amar Singh was one of only a handful of Indians who had achieved a commissioned rank in 1920. Singh was a Rajput – Indian aristocracy – from Jaipur. He was the third highest ranking officer in the 16th Cavalry Regiment. He was first given command of a squadron in March 1919, but when it was announced the regiment was to be deployed to Waziristan, Singh's superior questioned whether he should retain his command. Singh recorded in his diary, 'Yesterday [Col. Mears] told me that he did not think I knew enough work to command a squadron in the field and asked me whether I thought I could command it. I told him that it was no use his asking me as I would probably say that I could command the whole Waziristan Field Force.'[5] Once the regiment was deployed, Singh not only commanded his squadron but on several occasions, when Colonel Mears did not accompany the cavalry, was in de-facto charge of the entire regiment. The racist perception of Indian officers persisted, however, and Singh never secured promotion to Major, even though he spent another two years in uniform.

For all the men, conditions remained extremely difficult in spring 1920. The Derajat Column built a fortified camp just outside of Kaniguram, but heavy snowfall on 12 and 13 March disrupted supply convoys. Thunderstorms followed the snow and on 18 March two sentries were struck by lightning and severely injured. But the campaign seemed to be achieving its objective and shortly afterwards Thesiger proposed reducing the frequency of the weekly updates on the frontier situation from three to two; he appeared to be running out of things to report.

While the chastening of the Mahsuds was cheerily noted, the British Government in India was already grappling with the problem of what do when the campaign ended. Montagu, Secretary of State for India and therefore the senior minister in charge in London, was politely informed by the Indian Government that 'all officers, civil and military, are now agreed that permanent occupation of commanding position in central Waziristan is [the] solution which may ensure peace and security.'[6] Noting that the Mahsuds and Wazirs could not relied upon, even in 'good faith', it was suggested that if the British were to withdraw they would 'probably soon again be faced with necessity and inconvenience of another expensive expedition.' In the view of the Indian Government, if London did not want another war in Waziristan in the near future, the only option was a permanent occupation.

Chapter 13

The unhappy country

'It is painful to commence this report by stating the naked fact that in view of everybody whom I met in Ireland, the condition of that unhappy country has never been more deplorable in the memory of any Irishman now living than it is at the present moment.'[1] So began 'Some notes and observations on a recent visit to Ireland', compiled by the Honorary Secretary of the British Government's Irish Conciliation Group. While the violence in Waziristan gradually fizzled out, the violence in Ireland escalated. The summary by British Intelligence made for grim reading at the start of March. Young men suspected of becoming potential recruits to the RIC faced brutal intimidation, while the normal procedure of policing was in many areas impossible: 'A state of terror now exists in most localities which renders the task of attempting to procure evidence well nigh hopeless.' British Intelligence admitted that the IRA was now conducting 'guerrilla warfare' in the provinces and there was no way of knowing which police barracks would be targeted next.[2] It was not all bad news, however. On 4 March the Home Secretary passed on word that 'a correspondent reports that there will [shortly] be a lull in the militancy of certain Sinn Feiners on account of the manner in which certain of the Irish Bishops condemn crime, from a religious standpoint, in their Lenten Pastorals.'[3] In other words, some members of the IRA were giving up violence for Lent.

The RIC had been suffering a recruitment crisis for months. In autumn 1919 the British Cabinet had approved the expansion of the constabulary and adverts began appearing in the press for ex-servicemen who were willing to 'face a rough and dangerous task' for a pay of ten shillings per day, ten times the amount paid to a private in the British Army. Recruiting stations were established in Glasgow, Birmingham, Liverpool and London. The first of the new recruits arrived in Dublin in March 1920, having received three months training. As a result of a shortage of uniforms they were given combinations of British Army khaki and the dark-coloured RIC uniform: the Black and Tans were born. Contrary to popular myth, the temporary constables who made up the Black and Tans were not mostly former criminals and neither were they all English. Around a quarter of all the auxiliary forces recruited by the British government to serve in Ireland were from Ireland. The Black and Tans were distributed around the country to support isolated RIC barracks, which were frequently the targets of attacks by the IRA. In principle, they provided a force of trained and willing men who could bolster the flagging RIC and make up the numbers in areas where it was now impossible for the government to find recruits. However, the British Government's recruitment of auxiliary forces to fight the IRA in Ireland was a decision that was to backfire spectacularly.

The immediate blame for the situation in Ireland was conveniently laid at the door of the previous government. The Secretary of the Irish Conciliation Group drew a direct causal link to events which had taken place four years previously in the middle of the First World War, asserting: 'There is no doubt whatever that the visit of Mr. Asquith to Dublin following upon the rebellion on 1916, and his subsequent speech in the House of Commons on Irish policy, have done infinite harm ... and have been in no small measure responsible for the almost hopeless and helpless mess in which Ireland finds itself to-day.'[4]

On Easter Monday 1916 armed Irish Republicans took control of key buildings in Dublin and declared 'the right of the people of Ireland to the ownership of Ireland and to the unfettered control of Irish destinies'.[5] The insurrection, coming at the height of the war and with the known support of Germany – the British intercepted a shipment of German arms to the Republicans in April 1916 – was brutally crushed. After initially being taken by surprise, the British government deployed nearly 20,000 men and, rather than risk heavy losses in street fighting, flattened the centre of Dublin with heavy artillery. After five days of fighting in the shattered remains of buildings, the Republicans were forced to agree an unconditional surrender. The British government imposed martial law and over 3,000 people suspected of involvement in the 'Easter Rising' were arrested. The army held secret courts martial and began executing supposed ringleaders. As the death toll increased, so did public opposition to what appeared to be revenge killing by the British military. The deputy leader of the moderate Irish Parliamentary Party criticised the British policy in the House of Commons after the rising: 'With every fresh man killed it becomes no longer a question of malice or individual sentence; it has gone beyond that. This series of executions is doing more harm than any Englishman in this House can possibly fathom.'[6] In total, sixteen Republicans were executed by firing squad over a period of ten days. None was given a fair trial.

Three weeks after the start of the violence, Prime Minister Herbert Asquith visited Dublin. He toured the devastated centre of the city and travelled to Belfast and Cork. A few weeks later he made a statement in Parliament, proposing the swift introduction of the Government of Ireland Act – 'Home Rule' – which had been suspended at the outbreak of war. However, the proposed settlement was to exclude the six northern counties of Antrim, Armagh, Down, Fermanagh, Londonderry and Tyrone, as well the city of Belfast and the town of Londonderry. He concluded by saying, 'I believe we have now the golden opportunity, brought upon us by circumstances which we could not have foreseen – urged upon us by the exigencies of the War – to arrive at an arrangement already approved by the representatives of the two leading Irish parties, though in many of its features it is distasteful to both of them, and in some of its features, I know, distasteful to my colleagues, and, I will add, to myself – we have here an arrangement such as would never have been possible before.'[7] Far from being the perfect compromise 'distasteful' to all parties involved, the plan for Home Rule was a solution which would satisfy no one. Worse, by March 1920 the Westminster Parliament had still not passed the required legislation. London was now working to pass an Irish Home Rule Bill that was more than six years out of date with the realties on the ground, but Lloyd George's government could at least point the finger of blame at the Asquith administration.

The Home Rule Bill was now coming up for its second reading in the House. On 29 March 1920 the government's Chief Secretary for Ireland introduced the bill for debate. The government's position was simple: Northern Ireland would not be forced into a position of being dominated by the south and Ireland would never secede. In an uncompromising statement, the Chief Secretary assured the House that 'secession from the United Kingdom or from the Empire of Ireland, in whole or in part, can never be tolerated.'[8] In the absence of the Sinn Fein members, who refused to sit in Westminster, one Labour MP from Manchester articulated the absurdity of the debate:

> We are discussing this matter at a most inauspicious hour … when most abominable outrages are being committed in Ireland … when the vast majority of the people of that country look upon their present form of government as the most abominable form of government that has ever ruled in Ireland … We ought, therefore, not to deceive ourselves with the thought that any such measure imposed on Ireland and forced by this superior Parliament will allay that patriotic demand or settle this century-old claim. Two Parliaments are no substitute for the one Parliament which Ireland has so long claimed … This House can pass this Bill. The prime minister has a sufficient majority for any purpose, and is able to get anything through the lobbies of this building; but no one in the House, not even the Chief Secretary, would claim that anybody in Ireland who is anybody at all, with any influence or authority, or who is a representative person, can be found to accept this Bill, to welcome it, to say a good word for it, or to suggest that it would be a settlement of this thorny problem.[9]

Chapter 14

Withdrawal

The British had decided to help General Denikin evacuate his armies to the Crimea. There had been concern that Cossacks fighting for the Russian general might switch sides, join the Red Army and prevent the withdrawal – the famous Steppe cavalry were rather notorious for offering their fighting skills to the highest bidder – but in the end they remained loyal. It was a potentially fortunate development for Denikin. A British Lieutenant-Commander who toured the front to make a report on the situation had concluded 'if this course [withdrawal to Crimea] proved impossible it is to be feared that he [Denikin] might shoot himself.'[1] There was also a wider concern that went beyond the health of the British government's demanding ally: 'Without a leader the remains of the Volunteer Army would be at the mercy of the Red Army … they will admit of no peace, no truce, or understanding with them.'[2] Denikin had originally planned to march the majority of his army around to Crimea via the Kerch strait, but Red Army cavalry swiftly advanced to cut off his line of retreat. The entire White Army in southern Russia now fled south to Novorossiysk, a drab, industrial town on the north-east coast of the Black Sea, with a natural harbour surrounded by high, wooded hills.

In 1920 Novorossiysk was chiefly known for the manufacture and export of cement. It was the last toehold of the White Army on mainland Russia. The White Army's previous withdrawals had been lacking in organisation. In December 1919 the Russian personnel of a White Army air force squadron near Kiev fled overnight, leaving behind their planes, equipment and British instructors. At Taganrog, retreating soldiers had departed in the engine of the last train, leaving tanks and artillery stranded on their railway cars. The British were forced to destroy them, along with twenty aircraft, to stop them falling into the hands of the Red Army.[3] Higher ranking officers in the White Army had a disturbing habit of disappearing to the rear to take themselves and their families to safety, without informing their allies or even their own men. Novorossiysk, however, was to be different, because the British insisted on coordinating the withdrawal from the outset.

Their efforts were considerably hampered by the presence of an estimated half a million civilian refugees in the city. Some were related to soldiers of the White Army, others were simply civilians who feared for their safety with the imminent arrival of the Red Army. Typhus was rife. To aid the transfer of Denikin's ravaged army across to the Crimea, the Second Battalion of the Royal Scots Fusiliers was ordered to travel from Constantinople to Novorossiysk. The battalion spent three gut-churning days on board their transport ship outside the port as the sea was too rough for the vessel to dock. For two weeks after disembarkation, the soldiers of the Royal Scots manned a perimeter around the town before the remnants of Denikin's army began to arrive. Charles Francis, a twenty-six-year-old sergeant from a village in the Chiltern Hills later recounted:

> General Denikin's army came in after we had been there about the fortnight and a more pitiful sight I never saw. Men who had been prime of humanity were mere wrecks. Guns all dirty and in a bad state of repair, horses lame and dirty, but after them came thousands of women and children. Some of them had been driven from northern Russia, Petrograd, Moscow, Warsaw, Riga ... I was put on a job at the first gate with my battalion, with orders to allow only women and children through. Men only if they were old sick or wounded. I never had such an awful job in my life, just imagine thousands of refugees pushing and shouting in a language that I couldn't understand with just a handful of troops to keep them back. They were nearly all starving.[4]

The man in charge of the transportation was Lieutenant Colonel William Henry Bingham, a distinguished commander who had fought on the Gallipoli Peninsula and in France, where he had been mentioned in dispatches for his leadership during a gas attack at Loos in September 1915. Transport ships were officially allocated to military personnel, but Bingham still managed to organise the evacuation of some civilians, many of whom had their heads shaved to try to prevent the spread of typhus-carrying lice. By late March Bingham had successfully enabled 50,000 registered refugees – all related to White Army officers – to reach Constantinople or the Crimea. However, there were simply not enough ships and his office was besieged by civilians pleading to be taken to safety. Instead of defending the city, Denikin's men simply joined the refugees cramming the port. The Bolshevik advance was only slowed by gunfire from the British warships, which were covering the withdrawal from the sea, and by bombing attacks by the RAF.

Supplies continued to arrive at the port even as the White Army soldiers they were destined for hurriedly boarded boats to sail in the opposite direction. Charles Francis noted, 'generally speaking the only good thing was that all of us got new kit'; his men frequently appeared wearing new socks, boots or khaki. The port itself was a teeming mass of vessels arriving and departing under the cover of the Royal Navy's guns. Francis and his fellow soldiers were faced with desperate men, women and children, some of whom rushed the gates to the waterfront. Francis' platoon only held them off by fixing bayonets.

The stress of the evacuation was beginning to tell. Lieutenant Colonel Bingham attended a dinner with RAF officers in the final few days where it was remarked that he seemed troubled and deeply concerned at the number of women and children who would not be able to escape; he was also drinking heavily.[5] The following morning he was notified that no further civilians were to be evacuated and any places on remaining vessels should be reserved for military personnel only. On 18 March Bingham shot himself in his billets. He was forty-two years old.

As well as leaving behind tens of thousands of refugees, the British had no option but to discard large amounts of equipment and stores. Number 47 Squadron – officially an 'instructional mission' – was still flying sorties, but could not risk any aircraft falling into the hands of the Red Army. The squadron's Sopwith Camel fighters were lined up on the quayside and crushed by brand new tanks, which then destroyed new DH9 bombers still in their factory packing cases. Finally, the tanks were put in gear and sent over the side into the sea.[6]

On 26 March the Canadian squadron leader flew a final sortie, in which he strafed a Red Army cavalry troop and bombed an approaching armoured train. The same day, the Bolsheviks reached the outskirts of Novorossiysk. As the last of the British soldiers made their way towards the boats, they fought to hold off panicked refugees. Charles Francis recorded, 'We were the last platoon to leave, the CO [Commanding Officer] came up at the finish and told us to get back quickly keeping the people back as we went.' As night closed in, Francis' platoon boarded a destroyer. Behind them, Novorossiysk was overrun by the Red Army, while the forlorn figure of General Denikin watched on from a boat in the harbour. Five days later, on 31 March, the British Cabinet gathered at Downing Street at 6pm. In the absence of Winston Churchill, who was on holiday in France, the Cabinet decided to end all support for the White Army. Lord Curzon, the Foreign Secretary, drafted a telegram approved by the Cabinet, calling on Denikin to 'give up the struggle' and make peace with the Red Army.[7] He was offered asylum in Britain. Instead of surrendering, Denikin resigned and handed over command. The remnant of the White Army, around ten thousand men, was left stranded on the Crimea as the Royal Navy sailed away.

Chapter 15

The Holy City

For thousands of years, the setting sun has painted the ancient stones of Jerusalem gold; it is a city of long shadows and long memories. Although today it is the epicentre of the ongoing Israel-Palestine conflict, in 1920 Jerusalem had lived mostly in peace for over a hundred years.

The city and its surrounds were part of the former Ottoman Empire and had been acquired by the British during the First World War. After around a month of fighting near the city, the Ottoman Seventh Army retreated and Jerusalem surrendered on 9 December 1917. The British commander, General Allenby, famously refused to ride into the city, instead dismounting from his horse and walking through the Jaffa Gate as a mark of respect. The British were welcomed in Jerusalem by crowds throwing flowers. An interim report completed the following year by the British administration described Palestine as underpopulated due to 'lack of development', stating 'There are now in the whole of Palestine hardly 700,000 people, a population much less than that of the province of Galilee alone in the time of Christ ... Four-fifths of the whole population are Moslems [sic] ... Some 77,000 of the population are Christians, in large majority belonging to the Orthodox Church, and speaking Arabic ... The Jewish element of the population numbers 76,000. Almost all have entered Palestine during the last 40 years.'[1] In March 1920 the Jews in Palestine accounted for barely ten percent of the population – although over 5,000 more would emigrate to Palestine between September and December of that year – but their presence was to be the trigger for the first serious outbreak of violence.

The Jews who had emigrated to Palestine in the previous forty years had done so for a variety of reasons. There remained a strong religious attachment to the mostly arid strip of land on the eastern Mediterranean, enough for the notion of emigration to Palestine to have its own Hebrew word: *Aliyah*. It literally means to 'go up', an ancient Biblical image of Jewish pilgrims' ascension up to the temple at Jerusalem on holy days. In the traditional Rabbinical ordering of the *Tanakh* (Old Testament), the scriptures conclude with the account of the Persian King, Cyrus, allowing the return of the Jews to Jerusalem from exile around 538 BC. The king decrees: 'Whoever is among you of all his people, may the LORD his God be with him. Let him go up.' For centuries, the joyous endpoint of the Jewish scriptures had been the celebration of the first *Aliyah*, a poignant signpost of a promised future return, even as the Jewish people remained largely scattered around the world.

The first wave of the modern *Aliyah* was motivated as much by fear as by faith. In the 1880s a wave of pogroms against the Jews in Russia triggered a mass exodus. More followed in 1891 when, on the first day of Passover, the governor of Moscow rescinded the residency permits of the entire Jewish community in the city. It was not the first and it would not be the last time that Jews were expelled from a city on the European continent. The new arrivals in Palestine were not welcomed by the indigenous population and they also faced a hostile Ottoman bureaucracy.

Mosche Smilanky emigrated from Kiev to Palestine with his family in 1891 at the age of seventeen. He was from a farming family and was one of the early Jewish agricultural pioneers in Palestine. He began working on a settlement in Hadera, located on the coast between modern-day Haifa and Tel-Aviv. One day, as he wandered alone through the Roman ruins of Caesarea, he encountered a Bedouin tribesman on horseback. With a hatred that shocked the young man, the rider ordered the 'Jew' to leave. Smilanky replied, 'I am on my land, you go', to which the Arab responded by whipping him around the head.[2] Tension between the predominantly middle-class immigrants and the Arab population existed from the earliest days of the first *Aliyah*. However, the early settlers employed both Arab and Jewish workers on their land and many made efforts to forge relationships with the native inhabitants that would be deemed unnecessary by the majority of subsequent arrivals.

The Jews who arrived in the second and third wave of immigrants shared a very different outlook. Like their forebears they had fled anti-Semitic violence in Eastern Europe, which had surged following the Russian Revolution, but their *Aliyah* was a fulfilment of socialist ideals and prophecy. It was these men and women who become the founders of the Jewish state: the Zionists. The Zionist movement started in the late nineteenth century and called for return of the Jewish people to their historic homeland and for Jewish sovereignty over the 'promised' land. They revived the Hebrew language – which until the early twentieth century had barely been spoken in a thousand years – and vowed to create a Jewish state. The movement had powerful supporters, including the Rothschild family, and built strong lobbying movements in the United States and Britain, which in part led to the 1917 Balfour Declaration, in which the British government declared its support for the establishment in Palestine of a 'national home for the Jewish people'. General Allenby's capture of Palestine from the Ottoman Turks in 1917 meant that the region was now governed by a nation officially sympathetic to the Zionist ideal. Despite the apparently favourable conditions, there was no significant mass migration to Palestine. The popular view that the Balfour declaration and Britain's acquisition of Palestine as a mandate led to an immediate and dramatic influx of Jewish refugees was simply not the case in the early part of the twentieth century; in 1919 there were in fact 20,000 fewer Jews in Palestine than there had been in 1914. What mattered, however, was the perception. As far as the Arabs were concerned, they had lost control of their own destiny. At the height of the war, the British had promised a homeland to the Arabs and their reneging on that promise, and instead promoting a homeland for the Jews, was the single most significant cause of the unrest in the region in 1920.

Easter Sunday 1920 dawned pleasantly cool: good weather for a day of religious processions. By mid-morning as many as 70,000 Arabs had gathered in Jerusalem to celebrate the *Nebi Musa* festival. It was no coincidence that *Nebi Musa* usually took place over Passover and Easter Sunday. The festival commemorates the Prophet Moses – *Musa* in Arabic – but had only become popular in Palestine under late Ottoman rule and was basically created to give the Muslim Arabs their own opportunity to congregate in Jerusalem so that the city was not entirely overrun by Jewish and Christian pilgrims. Previous years' processions had been peaceful, but in 1920 there would be an outbreak of rioting that would lead to multiple deaths and leave more than 200 injured. The British administration had been warned by Zionist leaders that a riot was in the offing, but had completely ignored the signs, including a series of Arab demonstrations over the winter in which thousands of Arabs had called for independence. Four days before the riots, the British Chief Political Officer cabled the Foreign Office, 'I do not anticipate any major trouble in Palestine.'[3] When a major inquiry was subsequently launched into the disturbances, the British would lay much of the blame for inciting the violence at the feet of one man: Haj Amin al-Husseini.

Amin al-Husseini was a former artillery officer in the Ottoman Army who was convalescing in Jerusalem after an illness when the city fell to General Allenby in 1917. The young former officer embraced his new predicament and became a recruiter for T.E. Lawrence's Arab army on behalf of the British, encouraging potential recruits that they should join up to liberate their country from the Turks. After the war he founded the Jerusalem branch of the Arab Club – the *Al-Nadi al-arabi* – which advocated that Palestine be incorporated in an independent Greater Syria. Viewed straight on, Amin al-Husseini had overly prominent ears, which he would draw attention to throughout his life by wearing a white Ottoman-style hat and trimming his beard. There was nothing comical about his character, however. He was an opportunist who possessed a violent hatred of Jews, and would have no qualms about making friendships with anyone who he felt could advance the Arab cause, including the future leader of the Third Reich.

Amin al-Husseini was one of those to address the crowd on the morning of Easter Sunday. Shortly afterwards, chanting reverberated off the ancient walls: 'Independence, independence. Palestine is our land, the Jews are our dogs', a phrase that rhymes in Arabic. Then a mob began to ransack the Jewish quarter of the Old City.

Chapter 16

Choosing a candidate

The Democratic Party was in a quandary. The party's sitting president was manifestly incapable of running for another term, a fact recognised by almost everyone except the president himself. The Democrats needed another candidate: someone who could take the fight to the Republicans.

There was one obvious choice. William Gibbs McAdoo was able, experienced and a born leader. McAdoo had served in Wilson's Cabinet, presided over the establishment of the Federal Reserve, run America's railroads with distinction throughout the First World War and then married the president's youngest daughter. He was the perfect candidate for the White House and he would never make the ticket.

While high office would forever elude the urbane McAdoo, it would come naturally to another Democratic hopeful. Franklin Delano Roosevelt simply looked like a president: '[he] has a bearing … His face is long, firmly shaped and set with marks of confidence … Intensely blue eyes rest in light shadow. A firm, thin mouth breaks quickly to laugh, openly and freely. His voice is pitched well, [and] goes forward without tripping', remarked one newspaperman a few years later.[1] In April 1920 FDR was Assistant Secretary to the Navy, prior to which he had been a state senator. For all his presence and poise – he stood around 6ft 2in tall – he was only in his late thirties and did not have enough experience to be the first name on the ticket. His family name, however, carried weight, as he was the fifth cousin of the twenty-sixth president, Theodore, 'Teddy', Roosevelt.

McAdoo was not the only member of Wilson's Cabinet who had put their name forward for the presidency. Alexander Mitchell Palmer, who abbreviated his first name to a simple initial, was Wilson's Attorney General. As a Quaker and a pacifist, he had declined an earlier offer of Wilson's to become Secretary of State for War, but had had no reservations about seizing German-owned property during the war. Appointed as

Alien Property Custodian, he confiscated over $700 million worth of German real estate and sold it mostly to his associates.[2] As Attorney General he made a name for himself aggressively pursuing radical left-wing groups at the height of the 'Red Scare' in 1919. That autumn he rounded up thousands of suspected Bolshevists on often circumstantial evidence, culminating in the forced deportation to Russia of 249 men and women aboard the USS *Buford* on 21 December. American public opinion soon turned against his aggressive methods and even members of Wilson's administration moved to block many of his deportation orders. He was an astute political animal and adept at getting on side with party Democrats, but in the Michigan primary, on 5 April, McAdoo took twenty one percent of the vote compared to Mitchell Palmer's twelve per cent.

Both McAdoo and A. Mitchell Palmer were firmly establishment candidates, despite Mitchell Palmer being a divisive figure amongst the American public. The Democrats' Washington outsider was the governor of Ohio, James 'Jimmy' Cox. Like Republican candidate Warren G. Harding, Cox was a newspaperman who had found his way into politics. Like Harding, he had courted scandal; he was one of the few divorcees to succeed in US politics in 1920. One of his key attractions was that, as a state governor, he had been able to keep his distance as the debate raged over the League of Nations. He was fairly sanguine about his chances and aware that he only had one trump card: that he was a Democratic governor of the swing state of Ohio. 'My friends are urging me to open up a vigorous campaign. But I prefer to wait,' he said. 'If, when the [Democratic] convention opens, they finally turn to Ohio, oh all right. We either have an ace in the hole, or we haven't.'[3] He also had one other attraction: he was an opponent of prohibition.

At midnight on 16 January 1920 the sale, manufacture and importation of alcohol became illegal in the US. The era of prohibition had begun. Crucially, drinking alcohol was not illegal, a glorious loophole that, in time, would result in the repeal of the legislation. The Volstead Act, which introduced prohibition, would go on to become one of the most ridiculed laws in history. Outside of the US there was general bemusement at the legislation. Winston Churchill – a man known to occasionally enjoy a drink with his breakfast – would later famously call it 'an affront to the whole history of mankind', while Lord Curzon described prohibition as 'Puritanism gone mad'. Proponents saw it as a bringing sobriety to a

country awash with the vices of drink, although a sturdy whisky ration
of four ounces a day had fired the bellies of Washington's revolutionary
army. The founding father once remarked, 'The benefits arising from
moderate use of strong liquor have been experienced in all Armies, and
are not to be disputed.'[4]

The presidential hopefuls of 1920 would all be forced to declare their
stance on prohibition. It was, after all, the pressing moral issue of the day.
Republican Warren G. Harding, as a hardened newspaperman, declared
'I am not a prohibitionist ... and never have pretended to be ... I am unable
to see it as a great moral question.'[5] McAdoo was firmly for prohibition,
but Mitchell Palmer hedged his bets. James Cox began the year as a
vocal opponent, but the travails of the campaign trail were to make him
change his mind. Franklin Roosevelt, on other hand, was officially a 'dry',
but his public conversion appears to have perhaps been for the benefit of
his wife, or his senate seat. Before prohibition began, Roosevelt hid four
cases of whisky at his home, although alcohol was banned in the house by
his wife, and told friends that his address was 'for the time being at least
on the "wet" list!'

There were now just over two months until the Democratic Convention in San Francisco, when the party would vote to decide the party
ticket. Despite the lack of support from anyone within his own party,
Wilson still had supporters among the general public who hoped he
would go for a third term. A friend of the president's doctor wrote to
him in April: 'The health of the President is, I trust, not so severe as to be
classed a breakdown ... We need Mr Wilson's leadership continued, and it
is the hope and desire of all right thinking people, who have a democratic
conscience and hearts to appreciate great service, that Mr Wilson may not
be unwilling to give a grateful people a chance to show their appreciation.
Is it asking too much to hope for a word of encouragement from you,
in strict confidence? I feel hopeful that the President has regained his
health.'[6] Sadly, Wilson's health was largely unchanged and he was still
depressed by the Senate's decision not to ratify the League of Nations
charter. One day when his doctor greeted him, 'Good morning; it is a
beautiful spring day and warm', the president replied, 'I don't know
whether it is warm or cold. I feel so weak and useless.'[7]

Wilson did muster enough strength to chair cabinet for the first time
since his 'illness' on 14 April, but the members of his inner circle jostling

for position on the campaign trail were already assuming he would not run. When Mitchell Palmer gave a speech in Savanah, Georgia on 10 April, ahead of the Democratic primary, he declared his firm solidarity with the president: 'I am one of those who believe in all honesty and candor that history will never write a brighter page of political life in this Republic than has been written by the Democratic party under the leadership of Woodrow Wilson ... I want America to continue to be led by the great Democratic party under the management of men who believe in the same high ideals that have moved Woodrow Wilson in all things.'[8] They were kind and affirming words, but they more closely resembled a eulogy than a stump speech for the president.

Chapter 17

Nebi Musa

The initial violence in Jerusalem was typical, but still frightening. One eye witness recounted, 'The people began to run about and stones were thrown at the Jews. The shops were closed and there were screams. Afterwards, I saw one Hebronite [an Arab from Hebron] approach a Jewish shoeshine boy, who hid behind a sack in the corner next to Jaffa Gate, and take his box and beat him over the head. He screamed and began to run, his head bleeding ... The riot reached its zenith. All shouted, "Muhammed's religion was born with the sword."'[1] As the violence escalated, police rushed to inform the governor.

Ronald Storrs was the British civil servant who had been appointed governor of Jerusalem in 1917. In the absence of any civil administration, he was temporarily given the rank of a Lieutenant Colonel, which led the thirty-nine-year-old to jovially describe himself as 'the first military governor of Jerusalem since Pontius Pilate'. He was a brilliant linguist and spoke Arabic, Hebrew and Italian, as well as the diplomatic staples of French and German, plus Greek and Latin from his days as an undergraduate classicist. T.E. Lawrence once described Storrs as 'the most brilliant Englishman in the Near East', although he also thought he was diverted by a love of music and letters. Above all, Storrs was a quintessential Englishman, replete with receding hairline and compensating combed moustache, as much at home discussing the merits of Debussy as democracy. His attempts to be consistently even handed as governor successfully earned him the ire of both sides. When the riot broke out on Easter Sunday 1920, he was in church. Storrs was not unaware of the potential for public disorder. In his memoirs, he stated, 'Eastertide, the culmination of the Christian year, is almost throughout the world the season when, if only for three days, the death of strife becomes the victory of peace. Easter in the Holy Land, and most of all in the Holy City, had meant for generations of the sharpening of daggers and the trebling of garrisons.' The collision of Passover, Easter and Nebi Musa, he wrote, 'summon into Jerusalem, together with the genuinely pious, hordes of the politically and criminally turbulent, in the very crisis of the riotous Eastern Spring.'[2] He only had 188 policemen and eight officers at his disposal and therefore he was almost entirely reliant on the army to maintain order.

In what had become an increasingly explosive atmosphere in recent months, Jewish groups had begun to train and arm themselves. The most notable self-defence force was led by a Russian Jew and former British Army Officer, Ze'ev Jabotinsky. When violence began on Easter Sunday, he straight away requested permission from Storrs to deploy his self-defence group. Storrs refused and instead made limited arrests and ordered a night curfew. The following day the violence intensified. Jewish homes were ransacked and Jews walking the streets were targeted: two were stabbed. The British evacuated all the forces of law and order from the Old City and sealed it off, forbidding anyone from going in or out.

Once disorder began in the Old City it was remarkably difficult to restrain without resorting to overwhelming force. It was a nightmare to police and its ancient narrow, cobbled and stepped streets were impassable for armoured cars and problematic for mounted soldiers too. Storrs later wrote, 'I have often wondered if those who [afterwards] criticised us in Europe could have the faintest conception of the steep, narrow and winding alleys within the Old City ... the deadly dark corners beyond which a whole family can be murdered out of sight or sound of a police post not a hundred yards away.'[3]

On Tuesday 6 April, two days after the disturbances had first started, one particular incident brought home the seriousness of the violence. Arab rioters broke into several Jewish houses contained within a courtyard close to the Temple Mount, which had effectively been under siege since the violence had begun. Frightened families congregated in an upper room listening to the sounds of furniture being smashed down below. The rioters climbed the stairs and attacked the Jews, including children, with iron bars. Some of the attackers then took turns raping one fifteen-year-old girl and a young married woman. Days of attacks encouraged some Jews to fight back. Jabotinsky had managed to smuggle some weapons into the Jewish quarter and a few militarist Zionists helped residents to defend themselves by throwing rocks and pouring boiling water down on attackers from the flat-roofed buildings.

Finally, the British imposed martial law and the violence subsided. The riots had lasted from Sunday 4 to Wednesday 7 April. On 8 April, *The Times* newspaper reported: 'It must be admitted that trouble has been brewing for some time. Travellers say that the acuteness of Arab feeling against the Jews is probably not realised in England.' In all, five Jews and four Arabs died in the *Nebi Musa* riots, while 216 Jews were injured.

Murder, rape and pillage were nothing new in Jerusalem, but they were not supposed to occur on the British watch. An apologetic Storrs visited one Zionist Jewish leader. He gave his official condolences: 'I have come to express to his honour my regrets for the tragedy that has befallen us.' 'What tragedy?' the Jewish statesman replied. 'I mean the unfortunate events that have occurred here in recent days', Storrs said. 'His excellency means the pogrom', was the bitter response.[4] Storrs vehemently denied that it was anything other than a riot, but the Jewish perception was that an Arab mob had been allowed to run amok in the city and murder Jews. In response the British had only belatedly acted and, at the same time, had tried to prevent the Jews from defending themselves by detaining many of those who had tried to get arms into the Old City.

A wave of arrests followed the end of the violence and more than 200 people were tried in military courts. The British authorities handed down severe sentences. Two Arabs who had raped the Jewish women in the upper room were jailed for fifteen years, while seven Arabs and nineteen Jews were charged with possession of firearms. Among them was Jabotinsky. His actions, instead of being viewed as self-defence, were claimed to be an incitement to riot and led to him being sentenced to fifteen years. Haj Amin al-Husseini received ten years for incitement to riot, but he was tried in absentia, having already fled the country. The seemingly disproportionate sentencing, which saw Jabotinsky jailed for longer than Haj Amin al-Husseini, caused uproar, even in the British press. Almost as soon as the sentences were made public, the commander of the British forces in Palestine admitted that the prison terms given to the various Jews were 'much too severe … and I shall have to greatly reduce them.'[5]

As the military court got underway, the inquest began in the House of Commons. Gertrude Bell's friend, Lord Robert Cecil, was among those who called on the Prime Minster to explain the recent disturbances in Palestine. The government was also asked to explain why prior warnings of the violence had not been heeded and why the Jews had been expressly forbidden from forming a self-defence organisation. Answering questions on 29 April, Winston Churchill informed the House: 'I am not in a position to state what actual damage occurred in the city, but there were, undoubtedly, certain cases of arson. As the House will realise, these events took place among Eastern people, and feeling appears to have run high … The chief offenders have been tried before a military Court, and heavy sentences imposed.'

The *Nebi Musa* riots brutally demonstrated to the British that the mandate they were about to acquire was going to prove far more problematic to administer than most had imagined.

Chapter 18

Territories, not colonies

When the League of Nations Council gathered for their fourth session of the year in early April, the League had still not yet officially agreed the proposed mandates over the regions of the former Ottoman and German empires captured by the Allies. There were many who just wanted the League to get on with it.

Palestine was not the only place conquered during the war. The British had fought a brutal and little-known campaign across East Africa and, just as with the Middle East, the entire region was to be divided up among the victors. The problem was that the civil servants who found themselves in de-facto control literally had no mandate. Alfred Milner, the British government's Secretary of State for the Colonies, was constantly being pressured on the issue by government officials from far-flung territories. In one report he lamented, 'My life is rendered a burden to me by telegrams from the Dominions ... clamouring for the issue of Mandates for the Pacific Islands, German South West Africa, etc. etc. I fully realize the awkward position in which [the Dominions] are all placed ... For my own part I am in quite the same kind of difficulty over East Africa. Almost every day some problem arises which requires for its solution that we should know whether we have or have not the authority of a Mandatory Power over that country.'[1]

In East Africa one problem had finally been solved simply by executive decision. Fed up with waiting for the League of Nations to ratify the new mandate, it was unilaterally decided that Britain's newly acquired possession was to be called the Tanganyika Territory. It was a new category of British possession – all the others were either colonies or protectorates – but it was better than no name at all. Everything else, however, was still up in the air. No one had made any new maps of the territory, there was debate about whether it was appropriate to fly the Union Jack from government buildings, and no vessels could be registered in Dar es Salaam, one of major ports on the East African coast. The Foreign Office had dispatched a telegram in July 1919, helpfully informing all officials that the laws of any states that had been conquered were no longer in force, but the Foreign Office's legal advisor immediately decided that this was not applicable in German East Africa: '[the] German territories "mandated" to some other state are presumably neither "conquered" nor "ceded" in the strict sense. This seems to form a new class of acquired territory ... [and] I should think that the German law remains until altered by the Mandatory Power.'[2] By a quirk of international law, in April 1920 British civil servants and soldiers were still enforcing German-devised law in territories they had liberated from the Germans years previously.

The 2nd Battalion of the Kings African Rifles, based at Tabora, was inspected on the final day of March. As with the Indian Army, the Kings African Rifles was comprised of soldiers recruited from the region, although they were commanded by British officers. The Battalion generally passed muster – the men were reported to look 'cheery and contented' – but other than honing their shooting and bayoneting skills, they had nothing to do. Boredom led to an increase in petty offences. The Inspector General recorded, 'The majority of the offences are committed by Atonga, who form only a small proportion of the battalion. Though excellent on service, the Atonga are always apt to give more trouble ... in peace time.'[3] It was suggested that the entire battalion should be given Thursdays off. There were other side effects of inactivity, including a 'somewhat high' number of admissions to hospital on account of venereal disease. While British soldiers in East Africa occupied themselves with local liaisons, exasperated civil servants muddled through as best they could.

The League of Nations Council was preoccupied by other administrative issues related to mandates, namely the problem of protecting the proposed state of Armenia. Everyone agreed that it was a good idea, the Council noting the creation of Armenia was 'an object which will receive, and which will deserve to receive, the sympathy and support of enlightened opinion throughout the civilised world.' The problem was that no one wanted to be the mandatory power in charge. Britain, on behalf of the Supreme Allied Council, had volunteered that the task should be undertaken by the League of Nations, although the request had arrived late to the Council's March meeting. Having now had time to properly discuss the issue at their fourth session, the Council agreed that the acceptance of a mandate for Armenia by the League of Nations was 'on all hands admitted to be desirable', but presented a few practical difficulties. The Council's official minutes concluded that the decision of any nation to accept the mandate depended on solving the military problems – the measures needed to protect the frontiers of the new state – and also on finance. Nation building, as it transpired, was expensive. The difficulties were not deemed to be insurmountable, particularly if the eventual mandatory power could be relieved of the associated financial burden. In the absence of the approval of the full Assembly, which would not gather until the autumn, there was only one place to which the League of Nations Council could turn to source the needed military capability and funds: the Allies. After being handed the problem of Armenia by the Allies in March, the League of Nations Council simply handed it back to the Supreme Allied Council a month later.

Time was running out, however, as the borders of the new state of Armenia were set to be finalised at another conference of the Supreme Allied Council later in April, which would conclude the peace treaty with Turkey. The Allies were in danger of creating a nation that could not defend itself. Edwin Montagu waded into the argument at the eleventh hour, circulating an extended letter to his Cabinet colleagues, condemning nearly every aspect of the proposed treaty with Turkey. Regarding Armenia he wrote, 'I should be failing in my duty both to India and to Cabinet, if I refrained from pointing out in the time that is left the disastrous consequences which must result ... Whatever the frontiers [of Armenia] accepted, there must remain Christians under Moslem and Moslems under Christian rule. The settlement, therefore, should be such as to give neither cause for bitterness against the other. It is now certain that no Power will accept a mandate for Armenia; it is therefore essential that the new republic be on friendly relations with her western neighbour [Turkey].'[4] It was deeply wishful thinking to suggest that Armenia could be on friendly terms with Turkey, given the fact that most of eastern Turkey – which was supposed to be included in the future Armenia – was under the control of Ataturk's nationalists, who were adamantly against any post-war settlement that would see Turkey lose what was left of the former Ottoman Empire. Montagu was not the only political figure to express his opinion on the matter: President Wilson helpfully wrote a note to the British Ambassador affirming the 'genuine interest' of the United States' government in what he described as 'the plan for Armenia'. He was still fixated with the ideal of a new world in which the meek would inherit the earth and there would be peace among men. In his letter, Wilson helpfully suggested, as if the idea had never crossed anyone else's mind, that 'Armenia's boundaries therefore should be fixed in such a way as to recognise all the legitimate claims of the Armenians.'[5]

Chapter 19

Old enemies

Under the Treaty of Versailles, the Rhine river marked the limits of German power. German troops were not permitted to cross onto the river's western bank and the entire Rhineland became a demilitarised zone, a buffer between France and Germany. This presented a particular problem for the German government in early April 1920. Following Wolfgang Kapp's attempted coup in March, what had begun as a general strike in protest at the coup among industrial workers in the Rhineland had developed into a full-blown Communist uprising. Upwards of 50,000 armed workers calling themselves a 'Red Army' took control of the entire Ruhr valley. The German government requested permission to enter the neutral zone to put down the revolt. Britain and the other Allies were in favour, but the French refused. After holding out for several days, the German government felt it had no choice and *Reichswehr* soldiers crossed the Rhine.

The moment of discord was unfortunate timing for the Allies. The concluding negotiations over the Treaty of Peace with Turkey were scheduled to take place at San Remo in Italy a fortnight later and there were significant aspects that still needed to be agreed, not least the oil negotiations in Iraq. The French prime minister, Alexandre Millerand, responded uncompromisingly to the German action, which he viewed as a clear violation of the terms of Versailles. On 6 April French troops marched into the neutral zone and occupied Frankfurt, Hanau and Darmstadt. On 8 April in London, at the midday Cabinet meeting at 10 Downing Street, the problems in the Ruhr neutral zone were the first item on the agenda. The whole Cabinet agreed it was desirable 'to dispel the cloud hanging over the Ruhr valley before meeting at San Remo.'[1] Lloyd George was annoyed by the French provocation following what he saw as perfectly reasonable steps on the part of Germany to counter a Bolshevist uprising. He wrote to his wife the following day, 'In the throes of the Franco-German crisis … The French have played the fool & we must act firmly with them if we are to keep out of great trouble.'[2]

The French, meanwhile, were increasingly bitter at what they perceived as British inaction in response to Germany's flouting of the agreements made at Versailles. Around the time Lloyd George was writing to his wife, the British Ambassador in Paris received an angry note from the French government: 'What proof has the German Government given of good faith in executing Treaty of Versailles? It would be too long to recite all the violations of Treaty during last few weeks … Do not [the] British government measure [the] danger of these successive and systematic violations? When will they call a halt to Germany?'[3] The French claimed the German entry into the Ruhr was the latest in a string of slights against them and the treaty, and that they had given the Germans, and their allies, ample warning of their intended action. In fact, the French had dispatched a telegram to the British Foreign Office announcing their intention to invade the neutral zone, apparently timed deliberately to arrive on Easter Sunday. Millerand had then ordered his men to take Frankfurt before receiving a reply. The British response to the French accusation of inaction in the face of German violations, sent via the British Ambassador in Paris, was scathing: 'His Majesty's Government fear that they cannot accept this narration as being a complete or accurate statement of the facts … the German government should be permitted to restore order in a disturbed area in their own country with the only means which were available to them.'[4] The Franco-British friendship showed every sign of turning sour.

While French officials may have deliberately misled their allies regarding the Rhineland, it was correct that Germany was barely paying lip service to some of its Versailles Treaty commitments. The previous month the famous French Great War General, Marshall Ferdinand Foch, had compiled a dossier of Germany's failure to hand over arms. The Germans claimed to have destroyed some stockpiles of military material, but Foch noted that the Allies had not been able to supervise these.[5] The German army was still larger than 200,000 men on 10 April, the deadline by which it was supposed have been half that size. In some areas, the level of Germany's non-compliance was almost laughable. On 7 April the Cabinet received a statement showing the 'Amount of Aeronautical War Material handed over or Destroyed by the Germans in Accordance with the Treaty of Versailles'. It consisted of single sheet of paper with a list of material – aeroplanes, seaplanes, airships, balloons, sheds, hangers, bombs – next to which were two columns, one marked 'handed over' and the other 'destroyed'. In both was neatly typed in capitals the word 'NIL'. French anger was not unfounded, and they had firm British support in their quest for demilitarisation in the person of Winston Churchill. He travelled to Paris on 13 April for a conference with Marshall Foch. When he was informed that, in total, the Germans had surrendered only 500,000 rifles, Churchill agreed the number was 'absurd'.[6]

The German failure to comply was not simply based on disdain for the terms of the Versailles Treaty. For centuries, militarism had been held in high esteem and the gutting of the country's military apparatus had a psychological and cultural impact on its people. On 12 April the German Chancellor confided in a British army colonel based in Berlin that the German people 'have nothing to look up to – to respect. Before the War there was nothing in Germany that really counted as a moral or physical force but the army. That one idol has failed them and there is nothing to replace that on its pedestal.'[7] The British colonel promptly wrote up the conversation and sent it to the Minister for War. Barely three days after the event, the German Chancellor's wistful and possibly schnapps-induced comment sat on Winston Churchill's desk. Germany was still reverberating with the aftershocks of the attempted coup a few months before. Along with the report of the Chancellor's words, the British colonel noted, 'The *Kapp-Putsch* might be described as a still-born child which nearly caused the death of the mother and which has left her in a state in which it is difficult to foretell whether the result is to be recuperation or insanity.'

The German government attempted to negotiate to keep the *Reichswehr* at a strength of 200,000 men, but the request was denied. The joint reply from the Supreme Allied Council was a firm rejection. They refused to examine any such proposal while Germany failed to keep to its obligations to disarm 'upon which depends the peace of the whole world'. It was a rather exaggerated statement from the Allies – the world seemed to be managing very successfully to carry on wars without the assistance of Germany – but the Allies were correct to point out that Germany was failing in several areas: 'Germany is not living up to her engagements either in the destruction of the material of war, or in the reduction of her effectiveness ... or with regard to reparations.'[8]

Reparations were, however, a point of contention between the Allies themselves. The French were strongly in favour of crippling Germany, but not all their allies agreed with them. While Britain had lost a generation of young men and the population had endured rationing and German bombing raids, England's green and pleasant land had been largely untrammelled by the war. The guns of the Western Front had been heard in Kent, but the shells had all landed in France. The country had been ravaged; whole towns and regions had been overwhelmed by a putrid sea of mud. The flowers of the French countryside, as well as the flower of French youth, had been trampled by the most devastating war in history. Half a million homes in 1,600 different towns and villages had been destroyed and 6,000 square miles of French territory had been rendered wasteland. Naturally, the French wanted the Germans to pay.

The British government, and particularly Lloyd George, did not share the French desire for material revenge. On 22 April he wrote to his wife from San Remo: 'Things are difficult here. The French mean to be troublesome I fear. They are anxious Allies. For the moment their papers & politicians are in full cry against me because I refuse to support their mad schemes for the destruction & dismemberment of Germany.'[9] The British prime minister's private view was that 'They must disarm and they must pay. But subject to that we are in favour of rehabilitating Germany.'[10] Lloyd George did have support from across the Atlantic. A similar stance was taken by representatives of the United States. This was an important factor, as the Allies needed US money. In April the British Foreign Secretary Lord Curzon noted that Washington was 'determined not to do anything which will help the European allies to extract more reparation from Germany', adding, 'On this rock all suggestions for American help in European reconstruction have shattered and will continue to shatter.'[11] At the very moment the Allies needed to draw closer together to define their plans for reshaping the post-war world, the Franco-German crisis was creating a widening gulf between them.

Chapter 20

San Remo

The town of San Remo lies on the sun-blushed Mediterranean coast in north-west Italy. Between 19 and 26 April 1920 the sleepy setting on the Italian Riviera was the location for the final discussions over the peace treaty with Turkey, which would redraw the map of the entire Middle East. The conference at San Remo would later lead to the creation of the countries of Armenia, Iraq, Syria, Lebanon and Palestine. Three prime ministers were in attendance: Lloyd George on behalf of Britain, Alexandre Millerand for France, and Francesco Nitti for Italy. In principle, San Remo was the formal rubber-stamp of the decisions made in February at the Conference of London, but, in reality, significant aspects remained undecided. The British Foreign Secretary, Lord Curzon, and the head of the French Foreign Service, M. Bertholot, also accompanied their respective prime ministers, although there seems to have been little love lost between them.

The British delegation travelled together by boat to Marseilles, enduring a rough crossing through the Bay of Biscay, before taking the train to San Remo. They stayed at the Hotel Royal, from where Maurice Hankey, the senior civil servant who was Secretary to the Cabinet, dispatched telegrams notifying London of each decision that had been arrived at. What he neglected to mention was that the British and French prime ministers could barely stand to be in the same room; the French were, as Lloyd George wrote to his wife, 'troublesome'. It was not an auspicious start to a conference that was supposed to be the grand climax of months of negotiation and diligent work by British, French and Italian civil servants.

On the first day, discussion was taken up by Armenia. Most of the country's borders had been agreed, but if they were confirmed they would leave Armenia without a port. The proposed solution was to give Armenia access to the Black Sea port of Batum, but as it was not part of the former Ottoman Empire, access would have to be negotiated with Georgia and

Azerbaijan. Ensuring the security of the future state was still the biggest sticking point, especially given the situation with Ataturk's nationalists who were occupying the regions that had, historically, had a significant Armenian population and were planned to be included in the new nation. The current position was that none of the Allies were willing to provide troops and the League of Nations had thrown the problem back at the Allies at their Council meeting earlier that month.

Over Syria and Iraq there was general agreement, and all parties accepted the decision that they were to be recognised as independent states but would receive 'assistance' as mandates under the League of Nations until they were able to 'stand alone'. Gertrude Bell's worst nightmare was coming to pass: white European politicians were deciding the fate of her beloved countries behind closed doors. Not all of the residents of the regions being redrawn accepted the decision without complaint. Sharif Hussein of Mecca – now King Hussein of the Hejaz – was the source of most of the complaints from the Arab side. After all, it was his two sons, Abdullah and Feisal, who had just declared themselves the rulers of 'independent' countries in Iraq and Syria. Hussein was more measured than his sons, but on 7 April he wrote to General Allenby stating that his relations were with Great Britain and not with the Peace Conference. In sum, if his sons were to be denuded of their kingdoms, the only power he respected to have any opinion on the matter was Britain. The Allied Council (and San Remo) could go hang. Hussein also took the opportunity to re-open the old wound of Britain's failure to deliver on the promises made to him during the war, noting that when he had been induced to revolt he had done so after accepting independence for the Arabs, trusting in Britain's honour and 'relying on her reputation for keeping her word'.[1] What the bitter Arab ruler failed to recognise was that the promises made to him were words spoken in the heat of war, when the British government feared that the imminent collapse of the campaign at Gallipoli would lead the Arabs to side with the Turks. In victory, the British were less accommodating.

There was still no oil agreement with the French over Iraq, a situation that was deeply unsettling for the minister in charge of the British government's petroleum department. Ahead of San Remo he warned the Cabinet, 'If the proposed settlement falls through now, after the principle has been regarded as settled and after many months of discussion on intricate matters of detail, further negotiations on other lines will be impossible ... this would be a most disastrous occurrence ... when our dependence on foreign controlled fields is such a source of danger.'[2] For all its urging, the petroleum department still sounded a note of caution: 'As regards the oil wealth of Mesopotamia, it should be remembered that this is still entirely unproved.' The British and French were effectively fighting over buried treasure for which they did not yet even have a map.

They had, however, agreed enough to put pen to paper. On 24 April Lloyd George and Millerand signed a memorandum of agreement on oil. In an era of impressively verbose treaties, it was only two pages long. The Mesopotamia section began, 'The British Government undertakes to grant to the French Government or its nominee 25 percent of the net output of crude oil at current market rates which His Majesty's Government may secure from the Mesopotamian oilfields.'[3] The French also agreed to the construction of two separate pipelines and railways, which would enable oil to be transported from wells in Mesopotamia and Persia through the areas under French control to ports on the eastern Mediterranean. The British finally had their pipeline, but it was still undecided whether it would be the government or private enterprise that would meet the cost of sinking the wells and, hopefully, reap the rewards.

Discussions about the mandate for Palestine came to a head on the same day. The mandate was accepted, but to placate the Zionist lobby the British proposed the inclusion of the Balfour Declaration, verbatim, in the treaty. Bertholot commented he 'had no desire at all to embarrass the British Government,' but felt he should state, 'so far as his recollection went, there had never been any official acceptance of Mr Balfour's declaration by the Allies of the British Government.' Curzon witheringly replied that he thought Bertholot was 'possibly not fully acquainted with the history of the question.' The Italian prime minister headed off a major disagreement by saying it was 'useless to go into past history,' and that it appeared to him 'the Powers were generally in agreement [on including the declaration]'. Palestine, then, was at least officially resolved. In reality, the *Nebi Musa* riots had shocked the British and there was, briefly, a renewed vigour for a pro-Jewish settlement. Chaim Weizmann, the founding father of Zionism, had travelled to San Remo to press his case, but Lloyd George was already on his side. The prime minister's parting private words to the tireless Jewish campaigner were, 'You have got your start. It all depends on you.'[4]

The conference was a significant amount of work. Curzon stayed up writing dispatches until three in the morning and, while he seemed to revel in it, one of the members of the British delegation remarked that he 'nearly killed his secretaries by robbing them of their sleep.' Dividing up the spoils of war was an arduous business.

After batting the issue back and forth, the Allies hit upon a solution to the Armenian problem. On the morning of 24 April, ahead of the formal meeting, Millerand and Lloyd George discussed Armenia. As Lloyd George did not speak French, he used an interpreter, a policy he preferred because 'the breaks give more time for thought.' The British prime minister proposed an alternative option, which Millerand describes in the minutes of day's proceedings as 'doubtful', but which, in the absence of any other ideas, was adopted. In wilful defiance of the fact that the United States was not a member of the League of Nations, the Allies decided to take advantage of President's Wilson's weakness for solving the world's ills: they would invite America to take on a mandate for Armenia and suggest President Wilson as the arbiter of the boundaries of the new state. At San Remo the Allies agreed revised wording for the treaty with Turkey, which now stated that the parties would refer the arbitration of the future boundaries between Turkey and Armenia to the president of the United States.[5] After deciding on the wording, the Allies immediately dispatched a telegram to President Wilson. They used the rebuff of the League of Nations earlier in April to their advantage: 'The Supreme Council, in consideration of their reply [to the League of Nations], were at once reminded of the conviction long entertained by them that the only great Power which is qualified alike by its sympathies and its material resources to undertake this task on behalf of humanity is America … Nor could the Supreme Council forget that the inclusion of a liberated Armenia among the objects for which the Allies and Associated Powers fought and won the war, nowhere received more eloquent expression than in the speeches of President Wilson.'[6] The message was blatant lies and sycophancy: the Allies had not fought to liberate Armenia in the Great War, they had fought to liberate France and capture Constantinople. A liberated Armenia was by-product that was initially warmly welcomed, but which had become a headache.

Chapter 21

A nation reborn

Poland was another nation that was re-created by the war. From the late eighteenth century until the end of the Great War, Poland had not existed, save for a tiny nominal kingdom which was, in truth, a vassal state of the Russian Tsar. With no natural geographical defensive lines, the country had been repeatedly invaded and eventually divided up between Russia, Prussia and Austria. Poles had fought on all sides in the Great War, under flags that were not their own, many still harbouring hopes that, somehow, they were fighting for independence. When the war ended, Polish nationalists hastily formed an army and declared a government, but they faced the reality that their country was occupied by large numbers of German soldiers – technically defeated but with nowhere else to go – and by Russian soldiers who also refused to move.

In spring 1919 the Poles forced the Russians out and the Germans gradually withdrew their forces, leaving Poland largely in Polish control. However, they still had to fight the Czechs to secure the country's southern border, and acquired a new problem in late 1919 when the Bolshevik army occupied Ukraine. The Ukrainian army took refuge in Poland and Ukrainian and Polish interests became suddenly aligned. The reborn nation was also receiving assistance from France and Britain, both of whom sent military missions. The French was the more active of the two and included 1,500 officers who provided training to the Poles, among them a young major by the name of Charles de Gaulle. He admitted in a letter home that the Polish army was in a state, writing, 'Literally everything needs to be rebuilt.'[1]

In January 1920 Lenin, the Russian revolutionary leader who had become head of the Soviet government, committed the Red Army to attacking Poland, but the planned offensive was delayed because of a lack of men; all available forces were fighting the White Army in southern

Russia. The fears of Winston Churchill and others that Bolshevists had designs on conquering Europe were not without basis. Lenin saw Poland as the gateway to Germany – which was still racked by left-wing agitation and, therefore, seemingly ripe for revolution – and the next step in Bolshevism's sweep into Western Europe. He decreed, 'By attacking Poland we are attacking the Allies … by destroying the Polish army we are destroying the Versailles peace, upon which rests the whole present system of international relations.'[2] The world, in the eyes of Lenin, was at a tipping point: the Treaty of Versailles, the League of Nations and the peace treaty with Turkey were only papering over the cracks in the foundations of capitalist imperialism. All that was needed to bring the edifice crashing to the ground was a single big push. But before the Russians could put their plan into action, the Poles seized the moment to attack first. Polish ambitions were not confined to delaying the Russian threat.

Beginning in late April, nine Polish and one Ukrainian division launched an assault through Ukraine. Pinned at their front by a superior force and harried by encircling cavalry, the two Red Army groups panicked and fled en masse. The Polish cavalry, which had so neatly encircled them, were simply unable to stop the tide of men, most of whom had discarded their weapons as they streamed back towards Russia.

On 6 May Polish forces marched unopposed into Kiev. It was an utterly unexpected victory. In less than two weeks, they had routed two Soviet army groups, captured 30,000 prisoners and advanced over one hundred miles. But the attack had not inflicted a crushing blow on the Russian army. The Poles had acquired a newly expanded area of territory in the Ukraine that they did not have the manpower to defend, and because they had attacked first, in the eyes of the world they were the aggressors. Three days after Polish columns marched triumphantly through the streets of Kiev, Lloyd George mused, 'Unless the Poles are careful they will revive and intensify the spirit of Russian nationality … The Poles are inclined to be arrogant and they will have to take care that they don't get their heads punched.'[3]

The Russian commander tasked with doing the punching, Mikhail Tukhachevsky, was a man of two halves: he was both an ardent Bolshevist and a son of Russian nobility, a contradiction that meant his meteoric rise through the ranks was deeply controversial. Tukhachevsky had fought in the Great War as a lieutenant of an elite infantry regiment. He had been decorated for bravery six times and then escaped from the Germans' highest security prisoner-of-war camp, where he had shocked his fellow prisoners by engaging in in-depth discussions about literature, while at the same time declaring all books should be burnt. He reached Moscow, offered his skills to Leon Trotsky and found himself in charge of soldiers of the rag-tag revolutionary army in Siberia. His instant success led to his reposting to southern Russia, where his men were responsible for hounding Denikin's army into the sea. In May he was sent west to stop the Polish advance. When he was put in charge of coordinating the Russian counter-offensive he was just twenty-seven years old. Modesty was not one of his qualities: his promotion was simply the fulfilment of the aim he had once stated, to be either a corpse or a general by the age of thirty.

The Polish army arranged against him was made up of men wearing the French, German, Russian and Austrian uniforms they had worn during the war. It is quite probable that some of them had been shooting at each other a few short weeks before they were united into the ranks of the new Polish army. They had also kept their rifles. Soldiers fought side by side using German Mausers, British Lee-Enfields and other weapons they had managed to acquire, meaning that organising the supply of ammunition was a complete impossibility. The Polish army had an armoured regiment equipped with French Renault FT tanks, but they were unreliable and spent most of the war being repaired. The army's proudest units were its cavalry, drawn, as with the foot soldiers, from the ranks of multiple armies that had fought each other in the Great War. The result was a collection of regiments that one observer described as 'like so many children born of the same mother, but conceived by different fathers.' The riders still carried lances and sabres and would not have looked out of place galloping into battle in the time of Napoleon.

The Russian counter-offensive was launched on 14 May, after Tukha-chevsky had waited until he had achieved numerical superiority. A total of 115,000 Russians faced 95,000 Poles, who were thinly strung out across a defensive line, with a concentration in the city of Kiev. Tukhachevsky's army was largely comprised of conscripted peasants who were badly trained and even more badly equipped; Russian-made rifles were of an archaic Imperial-era design that was notoriously inaccurate. Any Red Army victory would rely on weight of numbers and the quality of its legendary cavalry. Tukhachevsky had at his disposal the first cavalry army – the *Piervaia Konnaia Armia*, which was effectively a self-contained fighting force of four divisions of 18,000 mounted men – a brigade of infantry and over fifty artillery pieces. It represented a fusion of cavalry tradition and modern weaponry and made excellent use of horse-drawn Maxim machine guns mounted on open buggies. In battle, the mounted machine guns were used in the style of Mongol horse archers: galloping towards the enemy before slowing to open fire, and then galloping away again without allowing the enemy to get close enough to engage. Tukhachevsky planned to hold the Poles with a frontal attack and then drive them north-west into the Pripet Marshes, where they would be immobile and easily destroyed.

The Poles were initially caught by surprise in Kiev and forced back, but soon rallied in what, to a casual observer, must have seemed like a war from another age. On the evening of 29 May, near the town of Volodarka, south of Kiev on the Ros River, the setting sun cast its rays over a scene reminiscent of past centuries: a style of war that most people thought had been left in the mud of Flanders. A Polish lancer recorded: 'As we came over the ridge, we caught sight of a huge wave of … [Russian] cavalry descending from the opposite ridge into the dip, also at a trot.' The mounted ranks halted and one Cossack rode forth demanding a challenger. A Polish captain responded, drawing his sword and slashing the Cossack from his neck to his waist. The Cossacks charged, the Polish lancer remembering, 'We moved off at a gallop, arched low in the saddle, lances at the horse's ear, sabres raised high for the cut.'[4] The skirmish ended in a Russian withdrawal, while across Ukraine the Polish front creaked and then held. Although most of the world was largely ignorant of the events unfolding near Kiev, once again war was raging in Europe.

Chapter 22

'Indian measures'

On 10 May 1920 the British prime minister wrote to his Minister for War: 'My Dear Winston, I am very anxious about Ireland, and I want you to help. We cannot leave things as they are. [Eamon] de Valera [the official leader of the breakaway Irish Parliament who spent 1920 in exile in the US] has particularly challenged the British Empire and, unless he is put down, the Empire will look silly. I know how difficult it is to spare men and material, but this seems to me to be the urgent problem for us.'[1]

In the month before, 300 police barracks had been burnt or destroyed around Ireland. On the night of 8 May there were attacks on barracks in Newtownhamilton and in County Cork. At Newtownhamilton, police succeeded in driving off the attack, but in County Cork the barracks was set on fire and had to be evacuated. Outside the northern province of Ulster, the police waited, holed-up in their barracks, for the inevitable assaults. This led, increasingly, to the evacuation of police stations. The Royal Irish Constabulary, a police force staffed almost exclusively by Irishmen, was being viciously targeted by the IRA because its members were viewed as the principal agents of the British government in Ireland.

The introduction of the Black and Tans in March 1920 has been harshly criticised by historians for decades. However, the British government was faced with little choice. The RIC was, by May 1920, utterly unable to maintain order in the country, except in Ulster where the majority of the population was on the side of the British government. The Home Office noted, 'A cowardly campaign against the families of members of the force is now in progress. Persons who venture to let them houses or lodgings are intimidated and the women and children are compelled to move from place to place. Nothing is left undone, even to attempts on their lives, to deter recruits from joining the force.'[2] Even local government aided and abetted the banishment of police: 'After next month [June], it is expected that Sinn Fein will command a majority on most of the County and Rural District Councils outside Ulster, and it is then intended to refuse to levy any rates to pay compensation awarded for the murder or injury of police.' In one week in the middle of May there were eleven murders in Ireland and seven of the victims were members of the RIC. It was openly admitted in government that large tracts of Ireland were 'practically in a state of anarchy' and it was not known how long the RIC could cling on 'without greatly increased military assistance'. A total of 250 RIC constables had resigned in April alone. In some ways it is remarkable that the hawks in the Cabinet – Curzon and Churchill foremost among them – could not persuade the government to agree to the wholesale deployment of the British Army; the approach that was adopted in Northern Ireland during 'The Troubles' nearly fifty years later.

Great Britain's Foreign Secretary, George Curzon, regarded Ireland as nothing more than another unruly province of the Empire, and saw no distinction between it and India, where he had been Viceroy from 1899 to 1905. Curzon was a man who had grasped his own destiny with both hands. A product of Eton, Oxford and the ministrations of a sadistic childhood nanny, he went from becoming a member of Parliament to being appointed Viceroy of India at the age of thirty-nine. His time as Viceroy was the highlight of his life. Curzon once confided in a colleague, 'When in India I did things that will stand for hundreds of years – things that will be a monument to my rule.'[3] In his youth, he had a haughty face, with a strong jaw and piercing gaze, but age left him balding, with a beak-like nose. He possessed a manner and an intellect that alienated many of those he met. The wife of the war-time prime minister, Herbert Asquith, once recorded in her diary, 'Curzon is detested [in Parliament], and no doubt he will never get past this. He is not a gentleman and is not generous or grateful.' Curzon even managed to rile the staff at the Foreign Office over simple matters. When presented with a new mural to decorate the interior of the main building in Whitehall in May 1920, he was deeply unimpressed. The government's official Commissioner of Works, who had the problematic duty of marrying artists' inspiration and civil service décor, remarked that the Foreign Secretary 'does not profess to be an art expert, but this does not prevent him launching into a long and destructive criticism regarding the works of art in question and his reasons for disliking them.'[4] However, despite Curzon's many and obvious flaws, fifteen years after he had resigned as Viceroy as a result of a bitter political dispute, his knowledge of Central Asia was unrivalled in Cabinet.

Curzon's proposed solution to the problems in Ireland was to impose 'Indian measures' to deal with what he rightly described during a Cabinet meeting in May as the 'state of war' in Ireland. By 'India', Curzon was referring to the north-western frontier of what is now Pakistan. His suggestion was simple: treat Ireland like Waziristan, where the British Indian Army's retributions had been in adherence to a policy of 'collective tribal responsibility'; punishing populations that housed, clothed and hid the Waziri and Mahsud fighters with fines. Failure to pay was answered with the wholesale wiping out of towns and villages. The Dejerat column's advance across Waziristan in 1920 left behind charred homes and torn-down buildings, leading eventually to the majority of the population being cowed into submission. By comparison, the destruction of property in sporadic unofficial reprisals, and the imprisonment and brutal treatment of IRA suspects experienced in Ireland up to the late spring of 1920 demonstrated a level of restraint that would not have been granted to any of Britain's other dominions at the time.

Winston Churchill strongly advocated an expansion of the use of auxiliary forces to supplement the dwindling ranks of the RIC and pulled together a proposal in short order to recruit, 'men between the ages of 25 and 35 who have served in the war', who would receive four shillings on signing up and then, for privates, five shillings a day.[5] This was half of what the Black and Tans earned, but the new auxiliaries were not intended to be attached to the RIC. The Cabinet accepted the proposal at an afternoon meeting on 21 May, on the basis that the auxiliaries were to be raised and paid for by the War Office. The British Government had agreed to recruit mercenaries to fight in Ireland.

As well as men, transport was in extremely short supply. The tactical transport available to the small contingent of soldiers in Ireland consisted only of 175 lorries. The assessment by the authorities in Ireland was that they needed over 350, simply to be able to respond. The desire was to create a mobile force that could react more quickly to attacks. While in principle this was a sensible notion, in reality there were very few sustained assaults by the IRA and, even if larger scale attacks could be stopped, there was nothing a mobile force could do to prevent the IRA assassinating RIC members on the streets.

Wider army deployment was discussed in the morning Cabinet meeting on 11 May, but the British Army was already stretched almost to its limits. It was suggested that eight battalions be placed in readiness to go to Ireland, but even the War Office objected to the number 'in view of the smallness of the force which would left [in Britain] after their withdrawal … either for purposes of maintaining order or as the central reserve of the Empire.'[6] The British government – in their singular mission to put down what was regarded by many simply as another uprising – was running out of options. The most common narrative in London was that the Irish, having been offered Home Rule, were bringing the violence on themselves by voting for Sinn Fein and allowing the IRA to run amok on the streets. IRA members may have felt that they were fighting for independence, but the British government's Chief Secretary for Ireland described their actions as a 'campaign of murder and arson' that he intended to 'stamp out'. He was confident that improving the transport capabilities of the forces already in Ireland, and bolstering their numbers with the new auxiliaries, would make a marked difference.

On 31 May there were the first early signs of the future direction of British policy. For the first time, martial law was openly discussed and official Cabinet conclusions noted support for 'some plan whereby Irishmen were made to feel the effect of the campaign of murder and arson along economic channels', with suggestions including shutting down the railways, postal service or stopping sales of local goods.[7] Although there would be more months of violence before the government fully came round to the idea, the entire Irish population was now going to face the consequences of the majority's support for Sinn Fein. Curzon was about to get his way.

Chapter 23

Taking the initiative

On 14 May the League of Nations Council held their long-planned meeting in Rome. The previous day, the League of Nations had finally received a reply from the Russian government regarding the proposed trip to investigate labour conditions. The letter began, 'The Central Committee of the Soviets of the workers, peasants and Red Army deputies and of the Cossacks, welcomes any sign which would show that the Governments, which up to the present have made war on Soviet Russia ... now realise the uselessness of their attempts to strangle the great Russian people.'

Rather than a reflection of world concern for what was going on in Russia, the Russian government publicly suggested the proposed visit from the League was an invitation to the Soviets to come back in from the cold: 'The decision of the League of Nations to send a delegation to Russia ... [is] a sign that some of the Powers belonging to the League of Nations are trying to renounce the policy of strife against the Russian people.' It was nothing of the sort, but it suited Russian interests to point out the inconsistency between the aims of the League and actions of the great powers who were members. The League of Nations Council was about to receive its first dressing down. The Soviet Central Committee pointed out, 'at the same time, the League of Nations has imposed war on the Russian people'. Poland, it was noted, had 'tried to seize territories belonging to Russia ... and in this criminal policy, the Polish Government has not met with any opposition from the League of Nations, but has even received active support from certain Powers, members of the League, which have invariably supported all revolutions ... against Soviet power.'

The actions of the Allies, and specifically Great Britain, to try and hold back the spread of Bolshevism were coming back to haunt the League. Although it was not articulated, the British were treating the League not as the international arbiter of disputes or a force for peace, but as a vehicle to deal with their own problems – among which was Armenia – while working on the assumption that the League was not affected by British actions anywhere else around the globe. The League dashed off a reply, stating that its delegates represented 'no particular state' and that the League's members simply sought 'the establishment of justice and peace.' The response from Russia was swift this time. Ten days later, the Soviet government replied, bluntly highlighting the organisation's rank hypocrisy: 'this League which, as you assert, has as its aim the establishment of justice and peace, has allowed full liberty to one of its Members, namely Poland, to become the disturber of peace by her aggression against Russia and the Ukraine … The Soviet Government cannot pass over in silence the attitude of the other Members of the League who are helping Poland by sending war material and instructors … [and] the direct support given at the same time to the White Guards [Army] … in Crimea.' The Council's trip to Russia was officially off.

The members met in the elegant surrounds of Palazzo Chigi, opposite a square dominated by a thirty-foot column, on top of which stands a statue of the Roman emperor Marcus Aurelius. In AD 166 he was ruler of the Roman Empire when it was ravaged by a pandemic of what may or may not have been typhus. Inauspiciously, the problem of plague in Europe was once again on the League's agenda.

Since March, when the Council had endorsed a letter from Balfour to the Red Cross urging immediate action on the typhus outbreak in Poland, there had been no change in the situation. The Red Cross had, however, replied. Balfour read out two lines of their letter to the Council: 'upon assurance from the League of Nations that food, clothing and transportation will be supplied by Governments, the [Red Cross] … shall at once formulate plans for the immediate extension of relief within the affected districts.' The Red Cross were very willing to help, if the governments of members of the League of Nations were willing to pay for it. The whole situation was of course further complicated by the fact that Poland was now at war. Balfour, in a moment of keen initiative, had formed a committee, which had discovered food, clothing and wartime medical supplies squirreled away in various places across Europe that would probably suffice. He told the Council: 'On the whole, I think we may assure the Red Cross … there will be enough of the material for which they made a demand … We shall have to inform them that the League of Nations has not the power to provide these materials, but I think while conveying that information to them we can give them the assurance that the supplies will be forthcoming.' While the Council was unable to officially be of help, for once it was actually being helpful.

The Assembly was supposed to be the flagship body of the League, the demonstration of the nations of the world settling their differences like grown-ups and together forging a peaceful future for the betterment of humanity. The problem was that it still had not met. But there was at last a rough date in the diary and a preferred location. The second weekend of November 1920 was chosen by the Council to be the first convening of the Assembly. In accordance with the League's charter – written at a time when it was unthinkable that the United States, with Wilson at the helm, would not be a member – the invitations had to come from the American president. The Council dispatched a relatively understanding note to Wilson from Rome: 'The Council would be grateful if you would inform them as soon as possible whether you would be prepared to summon the Assembly to meet at some date between the 1st and 15th November.' The Council suggested Brussels as the location. Wilson would have to convene a gathering of the Assembly, to which the United States was not invited. It was a reality that still deeply troubled him.

On the day of the League's gathering in Rome, William McAdoo wrote a full and frank letter to his father-in-law, Woodrow Wilson: 'You would be surprised, if you could mingle with the people of the country unknown, to learn how far the Republicans have succeeded in convincing them that you are responsible for the defeat of the Treaty [of Versailles] and that this defeat is due solely to your "obstinacy". It is all so grossly unfair that I never think of it without indignation but we must face the facts.'[1] McAdoo encouraged Wilson to restart debate and allow the Senate some of its reservations in the hope that the Treaty, and with it League membership for the United States, might still be passed, a notion he linked to the forthcoming election:

> Even if I desired to be President, I would, in no circumstances, permit my name to be considered if I thought that you desired to have your name placed before the Convention … I am thinking only of the welfare of the country and of the success

of the Party. If reaction, now so blatant and over confident, succeeds in winning the next election, then much that you have accomplished for the country will be lost and it is doubtful whether the League of Nations Covenant ... would survive the inhospitable and unsympathetic treatment it would receive at the hands of a reactionary Republican President.

In part, the problem was that the League was doing little to paint itself in a positive light, particularly among politicians in the United States, who viewed it at best as an organisation that meddled in other people's business and at worst as one that sought to drag the United States into every European war. Its reply to most of the questions posed to it was to emphasise its limited remit and request money and men from the major powers, or form a committee. Worse still, a war had now begun in Europe which, far from preventing, members of the League were actively participating in by aiding the Poles.

Chapter 24

The cost of peace on the frontiers

S pring is the shortest season in Waziristan. In eight weeks during
spring 1920 the snow had disappeared and temperatures now
reached highs of 48°C during the day, only dropping to 30°C
at night. According to the official record, operations in the Waziristan
campaign of 1919–20 ended on 7 May, the date that General Climo's
headquarters was dissolved. But it was an arbitrary line in the sand; some
of the tribes were still deeply hostile and both Wazirs and Mahsuds,
often in disguise, were raiding standing crops as harvest time approached,
in defiance of the British presence.

Two months previously, in late March, the Viceroy had telegrammed
Montagu that it was the opinion of the entire Indian government that
some form of permanent occupation in Waziristan was the only way
of ensuring permanent peace. The Secretary of State for India finally
replied on 11 May. Montagu opened with a reassuring, but cagey line
that he had given the proposals 'careful consideration'.[1] The delay in the
reply and the careful tone can hardly have filled the Viceroy with joy.
Montagu affirmed the British Indian Army's work to build roads and
disarm the tribes, but stated, 'I feel some doubt as to whether a really
permanent occupation will not bind you to a permanent increase in your
forces and tie up an undesirably large force.' Montagu's concern was the
same as that of the War Office in relation to Ireland: that British forces
would be needed in some corner of the Empire in the not-too-distant
future and when the moment came there would be hell to pay if there
were not enough men. He concluded his note almost cheerily, advising
the Viceroy to carry on building roads, but to 'defer permanent buildings
and accommodation as far as possible.'

If the Waziri and Mahsud leaders were waiting for an indication of
Britain's long-term commitment to Waziristan, the answer was right
in front of them. The men in uniforms would carve roads through

the rock and dust, but there would be no garrisons built to ward off the coming winter. Despite the signs that the troops would not be staying in Waziristan in significant numbers once the winter set in, two days later the Mahsud leaders assembled at Kaniguram and agreed to submit to the rule of the British government. One of their number tried to disrupt the peace plan by sending a deputation with a bribe of 1,200 Rupees.[2] Evidently it was not enough. The Wazirs were, for now, also behaving themselves. The Viceroy's now bi-weekly update on 26 May recorded that 352 rifles had been handed in during the first three weeks of May, a positive development as no villages had been required to be levelled to secure cooperation.[3] From the perspective of London, Montagu's position was completely logical and understandable, but his decision to effectively refuse to consider fully occupying Waziristan – an approach that the Viceroy had made great pains to point out was unanimously favoured in the Indian Government – was done with scant regard for the history of Britain's dealings in the region. The Viceroy later ruefully recorded that, 'As a result of hard fighting we have occupied a central and dominating position in Waziristan ... For many years ... we followed a policy of non-interference with its inhabitants ... We hoped that if we left them alone they would leave us alone. This hope has, I regret to say, proved fallacious ... We have had a campaign, more or less important, against Waziristan every four years [since 1852].'[4]

At the end of the month General Climo relinquished command of the Waziristan force. He was full of praise for the men he had led: 'To regimental officers, British and Indian, I convey the admiration of the Force and myself for their gallantry in the field ... I owe a debt of gratitude to the protective and fighting troops on whom demands have been made of greater magnitude than on any previous war or expedition on these Frontiers. Their heroism under every circumstance of fortune and weather has been splendid, of which any body of troops might be proud.'[5] Total losses up to the declared end of the campaign on 7 May were 366 dead, 1,683 wounded and 237 missing in action, the highest of any campaign against the frontier tribes.[6] General Climo was putting a brave face on a mission for which the troops on the ground had been woefully underprepared. The soldiers of the British Indian Army had been compelled to adopt the tactics of mountain warfare from their opponents and from their comrades in arms who had learned how to avoid exposure and not get shot. The assessment from the Commander-In-Chief of the whole Indian Army, Sir Charles Monro, was less charitable than that of the man in immediate command of the force. Monro was a wizened career soldier who had been in charge of the near-miraculous withdrawal of the British and Anzac troops from Gallipoli in 1916. He had witnessed near disaster before. He pointed out that Waziristan had 'merely borne out the principles of mountain warfare, which are well known from many former campaigns.'[7] In his view, the men had been underprepared and poorly trained for the task assigned to them. There was one positive outcome of the campaign, however, which was the production and printing of a pocket guide for officers undergoing training at Sandhurst, entitled *Small Wars: Their Principles and Practice*. The guide dealt with 'uncivilised' warfare and included lessons from Waziristan, although it was still no replacement for soldiers receiving actual training in how to fight an elusive enemy in inhospitable conditions, such as the rugged mountains of Waziristan.

The end of the Great War had led to a mass demobilisation of men from the British Army, but the unwelcome reality was that the force that remained was becoming overstretched across the empire. At the start of May the Viceroy informed Montagu that the maintenance of the force at Duzdap in south-east Persia (Iran), close to border of modern-day Pakistan, would soon become impossible, unless the British Indian Army began to draw on its frontier reserves: effectively the Waziristan army's back-up force. Without a railway, the only way to keep the men supplied was with camels, of which there was a 'high wastage rate'. The British soldiers in Meshed, in north-east Persia, were already scheduled to be withdrawn. In part it was a question of money. The War Office estimates did not provide for the high cost of keeping the East Persia garrison in its current form, but the Indian Government flatly refused to contribute to the cost on the basis that Persia, however close its eastern borders were, was not actually India. On 5 May the Cabinet collectively agreed to a withdrawal and Montagu was ordered to telegram the Viceroy to begin evacuating Meshed. But the Cabinet's decision had been made without any consideration for the time of year. Thesiger replied on 13 May, tersely pointing out that pulling out the force at Meshed would take about five months: 'The present is the most difficult time to carry out the withdrawal of troops from East Persia owing to lack of water and to hot wind of 120 days [the legendary *shamal*, which arrives seasonally from the north-west] which is due to begin about end of May and renders all movement extremely arduous … Withdrawal has been ordered to begin at once.'[8]

Although Montagu, as Secretary of State for India, shares much of the blame for not informing his Cabinet colleagues properly, it is surprising that there is no record of any objection from Curzon. The Foreign Secretary had, at the age of thirty, spent nearly a year travelling around Persia, and for decades had been firmly fixed on the idea that Persia was a buffer to protect India from Russia. He had even written a two-volume book on the country, its politics and geography, but at precisely the moment when his regional expertise would have been of great value in Cabinet he failed to mention the *shamal*. The result was a Cabinet spat. Churchill, as head of the War Office, informed Montagu on 26 May, 'I have seen the Viceroy's telegram … saying he can give no guarantee to reduce the period of five months estimated to be required to withdraw troops from East Persia … I have only taken a sum of [£]2,000,000 in Army Estimates for the current year to cover all charges for troops in South and East Persia … I must stipulate that any excess due to the time taken in the withdrawal of these troops from East Persia must fall on Indian revenues.'[9] Given that the Indian government had recently had to bear the entire cost of the operation in Waziristan, it was an uncharitable request. Churchill was adamant, however, informing Cabinet not long afterwards, 'expenditure on Persia is now proceeding at a rate of [£]570,00*l* per month. It is for the Cabinet to define the nature of our military obligations toward Persia or to evacuate Persia. At the present time we seem to have the advantages of neither policy and the disadvantages of both.'[10] The British soldiers in East Persia would have to make their best efforts to withdraw by the end of War Office's accounting season, regardless of the weather, or the Viceroy would have to foot the bill.

As spring turned to summer in the northern hemisphere in 1920, the uncomfortable truth was that, less than two years after the signing of the armistice that had ended the Great War, young men were once again crouching anxiously behind barbed wire listening to the sound of gunfire. The League of Nations had failed to stop the Polish-Soviet war from happening and League members were, in fact, actively aiding the aggressor. Ireland seemed to be sinking ever more into the mire, while the plans for a bright new world, in which nations like Armenia could exist in safety, seemed increasingly to be the unachievable ideal of a messianic president, destined to only have two terms in office. There was still no post-war settlement in Europe, and Germany had faced both a nationalist coup and Communist worker agitation, while the Allies who had fought together were increasingly divided.

PART THREE

Chapter 25

The call to revolution

Since the end of the war, Montagu's India Office had been supervising the administration of Mesopotamia, though the commitment was becoming a drain on resources. Despite this, Montagu was proud of what he saw as the India's Office's achievements. On 1 June, he recorded, 'Peace reigns in Mesopotamia, and law and order are effectively maintained there. Of what other area in the Middle East can the same be said?'[1]

In reality, the peace in Mesopotamia was precarious. In March the General Syrian Congress had declared Feisal king of Syria, and his brother, Abdullah, ruler of Iraq, and since then Shia and Sunni sects that had traditionally been at loggerheads had held two or three meetings a week in mosques. Gertrude Bell was sceptical of the sudden rapprochement, which she viewed as impermanent and political rather than religious, and an unwelcome development. She noted, 'There's a lot of semi-religious, semi-political preaching and reciting of poems, and the underlying thought is out with the infidel.' The same day Montagu grandly declared Mesopotamia was at peace, Gertrude Bell wrote an account of the latest incident of unrest to her father:

> It began about 10 days ago. Frank [Balfour, the governor of Baghdad] arrested a young hot head who had been making wild speeches. I think he was probably right but it is always a very delicate line of decision. Anyway next evening – last Sunday – there was a great meeting in the big mosque with the blue dome in New St, a crowd which he thought dangerous, and he sent out two armoured cars to patrol the street. One of the drivers had a brick thrown at him, drew back, and the mob made a rush at him. He fired a few shots over the heads of the people, a man was run over and the whole crowd ran like hares. The streets were empty in a second … We are in

the thick of violent agitation and we feel anxious. Not anxious
as to our safety – don't think that for a moment – but anxious
as to whether we shall get through Ramadhan [sic] without a
disturbance.[2]

A few days later, on 4 June, a group of Arabs from a nomadic tribe attacked
the town of Tell 'Afar, forty miles west of Mosul. They announced to
the residents that Sharif Abdullah was marching from Mecca to assume
his position as Emir of Mesopotamia and called on the locals to declare
their loyalty to Abdullah by 'killing the English'. They obliged. One local
official, a previously decorated British officer, two English clerks and
the crews of two armoured cars were murdered. The response from the
British administration was swift. They evicted the entire population of
Tell 'Afar and the army destroyed every single house. Bell later recorded
that she fully agreed with the decision, which in effect amounted to a
reprisal. British officials who lived in isolated towns in Iraq were aware
of the dangers, although they tended to couch them in terms that put the
British in a culturally superior light. As the British Political Officer in
Hillah once remarked, 'The Arab tribesman is of a warlike and excitable
disposition; even more ready to bring out his rifle and dagger than the
typical Irishman.'[3]

Meanwhile, the government in London was debating which Civil Service
department should manage Iraq. Montagu was keen to relinquish the India
Office's control and proposed the creation of a special department for
the Middle East, seemingly in part so the administration of Mesopotamia
did not pass to either Curzon's Foreign Office or the Colonial Office.
In normal circumstances, ministers in charge of departments were very
keen to add to their portfolios, but Mesopotamia had become the expensive,
unwanted child of Whitehall. Curzon did not want Mesopotamia either,
but he also did not want it to pass to the Colonial Office, an idea on which
Churchill seemed, to him, suspiciously keen. Curzon's suspicions were
not entirely ill-founded. Nine months later Churchill secured promotion
to Secretary of State for the Colonies.

In June 1920 Curzon opposed the notion that control of Mesopotamia
should pass to the Colonial Office, pointing out, 'the work that the Colonial
Office has done in East Africa and elsewhere, to which he [Churchill] refers
in terms of well-merited eulogy, does not bear the remotest resemblance

to that which will arise in the countries of the Middle East. In the one case we have been dealing as a rule with native tribes, commonly in a very backward state of civilisation … In the other case we shall have to manage States with an ancient history and a high conceit of their own importance.'[4] Curzon added that Churchill seemed to be 'un-acquainted with what has been passing in Mesopotamia.'

It was a rather unfair criticism of Churchill who was, at least from a military perspective, acutely conscious of what was occurring. On 12 June he pressed the Cabinet to come to a decision on military deployment, pointing out that the troops in Mesopotamia had spent months living in tents, a situation that was 'most severe upon the troops and productive both of sickness and discontent.'[5] Even with the men living in tents, the expense of the exercise was astronomical, with Churchill admitting in the same memo that, on the basis of the existing security arrangements, the combined cost of garrisoning Palestine and Mesopotamia in 1920 alone would exceed £28 million for the year. The level of expenditure was also upsetting the opposition, who tabled a debate in the House of Commons on Mesopotamia. The leader of the Opposition, former Prime Minister Herbert Asquith, gave a speech – described by Lloyd George to a friend as 'very poor stuff' – in which he called for cost-cutting measures, including a proposed withdrawal of British troops to Basra. The Prime Minister firmly rebuffed the idea, telling the House that if the British retreated to Basra, on the grounds that they could not afford to remain in Baghdad, there would be chaos and civil war.[6]

Despite Montagu's insistence that peace reigned in Iraq, the events on the ground, as witnessed by Gertrude Bell, were also being communicated to London. The official report on the situation in Mesopotamia on 12 June warned 'the Mesopotamia Arab is always a potential danger', adding that the inter-tribal dissentions, which had up to that point provided the primary safeguard against an organised uprising, were no longer a guarantee of security due to the increasing unity.[7] On 14 June Bell noted it had been 'a stormy week … there are constant meetings in mosques … The extremists are out for independence … if anyone says boo in the bazaar it shuts like an oyster. There has been practically no business done for the last fortnight. They send bags full of letters daily to all the tribes urging them to throw off the infidel yoke.' Montagu viewed such concerns as the overwrought anxieties of Europeans probably affected by sunstroke. When he circulated a report, which included a note from the Civil Commissioner in Baghdad that the plan for Iraq to become a British mandate under the League of Nations was at 'risk of disaster' without sufficient troops, he prefaced it with his own, asserting, 'It will be seen that Sir A. [T.] Wilson takes a very serious view of the military situation, the dangers of which I am inclined to think he overstates.'[8]

Bell, who witnessed the meetings in mosques, heard the rumours and sensed the rising temperature in Baghdad, was heartily relieved when Ramadan ended on 20 June with no repeat of what had happened at Tell 'Afar. She took herself on an early morning ride around Baghdad as Muslim families gathered to break the fast: 'There were numberless booths of sweetmeat sellers, merry-go-rounds with children swinging in them (much to the annoyance of my pony), groups of women all in their best clothes, and the whole as little revolutionary as anything you can imagine.'

Chapter 26

'Secret murder'

O n 1 June, the divisional commander of the RIC wrote to the Assistant Under-Secretary of the Irish administration: 'The state of this Division is steadily getting worse … the Sinn Fein method of maintaining their hold is very simple, they threaten all who oppose them and if that is not sufficient, murder them. The loyal people and law abiding people who are considerable in number are completely terrorised.'[1] Morale among the RIC was at an all-time low and the men of the force were only prevented from throwing in the towel by the strenuous efforts of senior leaders. The divisional commander warned that he could only hold the RIC together 'for a time', and that if significant support was not forthcoming the situation would be beyond retrieving. He then stated, 'I have been told the new policy and plan and I am satisfied, though I doubt its ultimate success in the main particular – the stamping out of terrorism by secret murder. I still am of the opinion that instant retaliation is the only course for this, and until it is stamped for good and all, the same situation is likely to recur.'

The admission, usually imprecisely quoted in Republican histories of the war, is nonetheless revealing. In June 1920 the RIC had apparently adopted a new policy of 'stamping out terrorism by secret murder'. In short, the Irish administration at Dublin Castle, with at least the acquiescence, if not direct support of Westminster, was now officially adopting a policy of assassinating key Republicans. The plan's existence would be strenuously denied for decades.

The following morning the Cabinet gathered at 10 Downing Street to discuss the situation in Ireland. They stopped short of immediately imposing martial law, but agreed to put in place plans to establish 'Special Tribunals' to try those accused of perpetrating the violence. The tribunals would be presided over by a judge, with no jury and no mechanism for appeal, and would be able to hand down the death penalty. The Cabinet's patience had finally snapped and Lloyd George wanted a public show of force. The Cabinet agreed to use a previously announced upcoming question in the House to state the government's new position. On 7 June, in a choreographed manoeuvre, the Prime Minister told Parliament, in response to the question of what the government was doing to bring to justice 'persons associated with crime in Ireland': 'The Government are ... strengthening the police, the Navy, and the Army in Ireland, and it will probably also be necessary for them to strengthen the law dealing with crime. It is the intention of the Government to take all necessary steps to put down the present organised campaign of murder and assassination.' The Prime Minister was preparing the ground to impose martial law in Ireland.

Events the day before had hardened Lloyd George's views. He had spent the evening of 6 June at his residence in Surrey dining with friends and the head of the police force in Ireland, who explained that he now drove with a revolver in his lap as he never knew when he might be shot at. Martial law was, in his view, a necessity.[2] Discussions continued in the garden as night fell. According to one guest, Lloyd George spoke emphatically of the need for 'strong measures' in Ireland.

In June RIC constables were encouraged to go on the offensive. Lieutenant-Colonel Gerald Smyth, accompanied by the head of the police force who had recently dined with Lloyd George, visited police constables in Listowel, County Kerry, in late June. Smyth got rather carried away in his address and told the men:

> If a police barracks is burned or if the barracks already occupied is not suitable, then the best house in the locality is to be commandeered, the occupants thrown into the gutter. Let them die there – the more the merrier. Should the order ["Hands Up"] not be immediately obeyed, shoot and shoot with effect. If the persons approaching [a patrol] carry their hands in their pockets, or are in any way suspicious looking, shoot them down. You may make mistakes occasionally and innocent persons may be shot, but that cannot be helped, and you are bound to get the right parties some time. The more you shoot, the better I will like you, and I assure you no policeman will get into trouble for shooting any man.[3]

In a demonstration of the upstanding intentions to which many rank and file RIC members still clung, the constables shouted him down, evicting him and the head of police from their barracks. But though regular RIC constables found Smyth's suggestions distasteful, he would find an altogether more receptive audience amongst the Black and Tans.

The British government was still planning on passing the Government of Ireland Bill, which would finally give Ireland home rule and devolved parliaments in the north and south. The bill's second reading in the House was the following week and, although it was hard to imagine a more irrelevant piece of legislation given prevailing conditions in Ireland, the government apparatus was pressing on with it anyway.

In the meantime, it was decided to make the bill work in the interests of the British government as much as possible. Civil servants drafted a 'suspensory clause', returning all powers to Westminster in the event that either parliament 'failed to function'. Unionist MPs – who had taken their seats in Westminster after the election in 1918, unlike the Sinn Fein members – were firmly in favour. In the words of one, the clause was 'no doubt, drastic, but it is necessary if we are to convince the Sinn-Feiners, and, indeed, a good many others, we mean business.'[4]

The bill was essentially the carrot offered to Sinn Fein, while the establishment of auxiliary mercenary units and the threat of martial law were to be the stick. The fact that limited powers handed down to a partitioned north and south were a completely unacceptable solution for almost every Republican by 1920 was largely ignored: the wheels of government had been put in motion and a bill was happening regardless. Instead of providing an incentive for Republicans, the bill simply showed how completely out of touch Westminster was with Irish sentiment. Unionists were taking every opportunity to promote their cause. On 17 June the Ulster Ex-Servicemen's Association (Belfast) sent a telegram to the King, 'We the members of The Ulster Ex-Service Men's Association hereby pledge ourselves to Assist Your Majesty's Government by all means in our power to restore law and order in Ulster. We further beg to offer the services of 3000 trained ex-servicemen and women if your Majesty's Government would accept them.'[5] His Majesty did not accept the offer of assistance, but it demonstrated that Unionist organisations were willing to defend themselves if the British government did not. They had already organised their own paramilitary groups: the Ulster

Volunteer Force (UVF) had been created in 1912 to defend against Sinn Fein, although by 1920 it was going on the offensive.

The town of Derry, according to the planned Government of Ireland Bill, was to be part of the north, a decision that would effectively trap the town's Catholic minority in a Protestant-governed land. The UVF had already been involved in street clashes and in May, armed, masked men took control of a central bridge over the River Foyle, held up traffic and assaulted Catholics. The British Army's Dorset Regiment, stationed in the town, took no action at all.

On Sunday 13 June Republicans who strayed into Unionist areas were fired on, and over the subsequent two nights there were long exchanges of revolver and rifle fire between Protestant and Catholic streets. On Friday 18 June a Unionist mob forced Catholic families from their homes in Cross Street and Union Street and then set upon the buildings, looting and destroying houses and shops. The attack lasted from 10pm on the Friday until 6am the following morning. Both streets were only a few hundred yards from the Dorset Regiment's barracks. The edition of *The Derry Journal* published in the aftermath described the Catholic areas as presenting, 'an appearance as if an avenging army had passed through them, so great was the destruction caused.' The rampage led to ten days of sporadic violence, leaving fifteen Catholics and four Protestants dead and districts protected by barricades and armed patrols. The British Army was only deployed on the streets after IRA volunteers arrived to reinforce the Catholic areas. It was a moment that was seared into the minds of the Catholic residents. The local IRA commander later summed up the sentiment in his memoirs: 'The town [of Derry] was left completely in the hands of the Orange [Protestant] mob.'

Chapter 27

The candidate

On Tuesday 8 June 1920, the Republican hopefuls and hangers-on gathered for the party's convention in Chicago. The main problem the delegates faced was a surfeit of candidates; the *Chicago Tribune* light-heartedly compared the contest to a horse race and compiled a list of thirteen 'actual starters' and sixteen 'dark horses', from which the 984 voting delegates, the majority of whom were entirely new to the process, would have to choose a potential president over the coming days. The smell of a Democratic demise was in the air and all supposedly right-minded Republicans viewed the existing occupant of the White House, politically and figuratively at the very least, as a dead man walking. Wilson was not yet dead, but he was finally walking again. The day before the Republican Convention opened, Wilson's doctor brightly informed a friend, 'The President walked to the dining-room downstairs yesterday and sat at the table for lunch – the first time since last Fall. In the past week he has been decidedly better in every way – particularly in his walking. He is in good spirits and is not as easily fatigued as formerly – mentally or physically. His condition is better and more encouraging than it has been at any time during his illness.'[1]

For what it was worth, the bookies' three favourites to secure the Republican nomination were Californian senator and former governor Hiram Johnson, former Army General Leonard Wood and Illinois Governor Frank Lowden; the best they would offer was even money on Johnson. The California senator, originally a lawyer by trade, was an ardent liberal isolationist with a gift for losing friends and alienating people in politics. Nonetheless, he habitually garnered votes. Wood was a candidate who would appeal to the Republican base today, as much as he did in 1920. An ex-army surgeon who had been awarded the Medal of Honor fighting against Apache Indians in the 1880s, he later became military governor of Cuba and was a military man through and through. When a race riot engulfed Omaha in September 1919 and 35,000 striking steel workers took to the picket lines in Gary, Indiana, Wood, as Army Chief of Staff, had sent in the troops. His methods were simple but effective. While Wood could boast of his military accomplishments, Illinois governor Frank Lowden could boast of being the epitome of the American dream. Born in a log cabin, he had become a lawyer and made himself a fortune. He was personable, but destined never to rise any higher than governor.

On 10 June the *New York Times* reported, 'Intricately interwoven and tanged in the skein of the battle of the candidates is the issue of the League of Nations ... that issue and the question of candidates cannot be separated.'[2] In simple terms, the debates about the League were about Congressional control: that was the argument advanced and forever trumpeted by Cabot Lodge and the other Republicans who opposed US membership. But more broadly, the issue at stake was the role of the United States on the world stage. Hiram Johnson was vehemently opposed to the League, which he said represented 'the chains of tyranny upon millions of people'. He told anyone who would listen that 'no reservations can cure its wickedness.'[3] Not to be outdone, Lowden claimed the League would create a super-state. Somewhat surprisingly, Leonard Wood supported the League, though with reservations. Perhaps his experience of war on the Western Front, where he had stood next to a man who was blown apart by a mortar shell, had convinced him of the need for peace. Two months before the Convention, Wood had told an audience in a speech at Harvard. 'We want to build up a strong American spirit and do all we can to get peace in the world. If we get a League of Nations with reservations, we shall be able to accomplish this'. It was, he said, a good thing to provide 'a gathering of the representatives of the nations to meet to talk things over.'[4] He thought America ought to be a force for right and peace, but was by no means a Wilsonian interventionist. In truth, not all Republicans detested the League; most of its detractors mainly detested the president's intransigence over it.

Henry Cabot Lodge gave the first keynote speech in Chicago, in which he lambasted Wilson, asserting, 'His dynasty, his heirs and assigns, or anybody that is his, must be driven from all control of the government'.[5] The entire conference was then invited to set out the Republican Party's position on the League. Given that the runners in the presidential race, let alone the delegates, held widely differing views, it was no mean feat, but the 'plank' – effectively an official party statement on the issue – trod a middle ground. Officially, the Republican Party agreed that it stood 'for agreement among the nations to preserve the peace of the world', but maintained 'this can be done without the compromise of national independence.' The wording baffled most of the newspapers, but it served to publicly unite the Republican Party in opposition to the president's position. It was largely irrelevant, as the official Republican line was one that would not have offended most Democrats.

Each of the many delegates hoping to secure the nomination was proposed by a speaker, the two most notable and well-regarded contributions coming from two women. The sister of the legendary Republican president Teddy Roosevelt spoke for Leonard Wood. Her speech was so good that one newspaper suggested that had she been a man she would instantly have given herself a platform to run. Calvin Coolidge, the earnest governor of Massachusetts who the bookies had at 8/1, was proposed by an English actress who was moonlighting from directing a Broadway play. One newspaper columnist described her four minutes at the podium as 'a refreshing oasis in the desert of turgid nominating speeches.' Warren G. Harding was seconded by a friend who was probably eyeing up his senate seat. The now-rusting metaphor of the ship of state, which had been tugged out of port for multiple nomination speeches that day, was Harding's nominator's oratorical anchor of choice. Harding was proposed as the captain who would bring 'safe and sane seamanship' and 'not a professing progressive, but a performing progressive'. It was all very much steady as she goes.

The voting process was outwardly simple: delegates casting for their chosen candidate with the loser eliminated in each round. But it was complicated by state allegiances and the influence of senior party political figures who could carry whole blocks of voters. Regardless, the first round firmly put the bookies' favourites, Wood, Lowden and Johnson, top: Wood with 287 votes, Lowden with 211 and Johnson 133. No other candidate got close to a hundred; Harding was sixth with sixty-five. Voting was an arduous process, not least because of an early June heatwave that raised the temperature inside the auditorium to over 35°C for several hours in the day. After four ballots that left Wood in front by a nose, the conference adjourned for the night. This adjournment, and the subsequent overnight politicking, was what gave Warren G. Harding the nomination.

Legend has it that Harding's nomination was decided in a smoke-filled hotel room by Republican grandees who desperately wanted to avoid a schism within the party. The two front runners had effectively nullified each other as neither Wood's nor Lowden's supporters would countenance voting for the other. The general and the boy who had fulfilled the American dream would both need to go if the party was to find a compromise candidate. Hiram Johnson was in third place and was the most divisive option. One by one, the runners were gradually eliminated. Sometime in the early morning of 9 June, Cabot Lodge – one of the senior Republican Party figures – arrived at the realisation that Harding was the most logical choice. One of the men in the room observed, 'There ain't any first raters this year ... We haven't any John Shermans or Theodore Roosevelts. We've got a lot of second raters and Warren Harding is the best of the second raters.'[6] At 3am Harding was called in and apparently received the news that he 'may be nominated tomorrow' very calmly.

When the conference delegates departed for the night, Harding was 253 votes behind the front runner, but overnight, as one newspaper reported, he was 'the man with whom they ['Republican chieftains'] hope to break the imminent deadlock.' By the seventh ballot, Harding had climbed to fourth, but it wasn't until the eighth ballot, when he secured third place and well over 100 votes, that his candidacy started to seem a genuine possibility. Lowden was the first to cave and release his supporters. The ninth ballot put Harding top, ahead of Wood, and shortly afterwards he secured the majority. Excited journalists flocked around him. When asked how he felt, Harding settled on a card-playing metaphor: 'How a fellow feels that holds a pair of eights and stays in and draws [a] full [house]'. By dint of his greatest political trait of making almost no enemies at all, an unlikely outsider had secured himself a run for the White House.

Chapter 28

Looking East

One of the founding fathers of the Russian Revolution wrote a public letter to British workers which was published in a communist newspaper on 11 June. In the letter, Lenin urged British workers to cast off the capitalist yoke and criticised the British government for its anti-Bolshevik activities. The interjection by the head of the Soviet government came at a rather awkward time, as the British had begun tentative trade talks with representatives of the Russian government, whose insistence that Britain had nothing to fear was rather undermined by Lenin's words. Negotiations were not going well anyway, not helped by the fact that one of the leaders of the Russian delegation was, in the words of Lloyd George, 'always looking over his shoulder as if he expected to be shot!'[1] Leonid Krasin, who rejoiced in the title of 'People's Commissar for Trade and Industry', did manage to escape the fate suffered by many of his erstwhile communist colleagues, later becoming British Ambassador and dying in that post. He was cremated at Golders Green and his ashes buried in Red Square, and subsequently had an ice-breaker named after him. In June 1920 he was not proving a very successful negotiator and any prospect of trade was still being held up by war.

On 13 June the impasse between the Poles and the Russians on the Ukrainian border was broken. A month after his previous failed attempt, the Russian commander, Tukhachevsky, succeeded in breaking through the Polish line. The First Cavalry Army surged through the Polish defensive positions at Samhorodok, but then the Poles rallied and closed their line again. Unlike Denikin's White Army, they refused to run at the sight of a few thousand Cossacks. The bizarre result was that the Polish line was once again intact, but an entire Russian army was rampaging at its rear. Instead of turning east and surrounding Kiev, the First Cavalry busied itself destroying lines of supply and terrifying men who believed they were sheltering miles away from the fighting. For five days the Poles in Kiev stuck it out, before having no choice but to pull back to deal with the threat behind them. By 25 June the Poles were back on home soil, where they had started in April. Lloyd's George's prophecy had come true: the Poles had been arrogant and were now getting their heads punched.

The day after the Russian cavalry split the Polish line on the Ukrainian frontier, the members of the League of Nations Council met once more, this time in St James's Palace, London. Their attentions were also focused east.

Prince Firouz of Persia, the country's Minister of Foreign Affairs, had appealed to the League at the invitation of Lord Curzon. At eight o'clock in the morning on 18 May, Soviet naval vessels had opened fire on the Persian Caspian Sea port of Enzeli. The stunned Persians had dispatched two ships under a flag of truce to try and find out why the Russians had suddenly decided to start shelling them, only to discover that it was not an accident. The official communique to the Council noted, 'The Admiral in command of this fleet stated that he had been entrusted by the Moscow government with policing the Caspian Sea, and that, as he considered that the ships and naval forces of General Denikin, which had taken refuge in Enzeli, were a source of danger to the Caspian Sea, he had undertaken this bombardment on his own initiative.'

Denikin had inherited a significant part of the former Russian Imperial Navy, which included several battleships, but the White Army's fleet on the landlocked Caspian Sea was far more modest, comprising eight armed merchant cruisers, which the British had left behind at the end of the war as they were too much trouble to dismantle and take home. In the interests of neutrality, the Persians had detained and disarmed the vessels after they arrived in Enzeli, but that did not satisfy the Russians. They demanded that the ships be handed over, and to encourage the Persians, landed 2,000 Russian marines who secured the port. The 500-strong British garrison stationed in Enzeli immediately retreated. In effect, Persia had been invaded. The action had been decided at the highest echelons of the Soviet government. A memo from Trotsky to Lenin in April 1920 asserted, 'The Caspian [Sea] must be cleared of the White Fleet at all costs. If a landing in Persian territory is required, it must be carried out.'[2] Lenin had scrawled on the margin of the note 'I fully agree'. They were events which, the Persian prince said, 'threaten to disturb the peace of the Middle East'. The Persians would not have British support, however. A week after the Russians opened fire, Cabinet had secretly agreed to evacuate Enzeli entirely and concentrate British troops further south. The main motivation was that British forces stationed at Enzeli and Tabriz, a few hundred miles to the east, were costing the Exchequer £2 million a year. It was admitted that they only remained there 'on sufferance of the Bolsheviks'.[3]

After deliberating the matter, the League of Nations Council adopted a resolution roundly condemning the Russians. It read, 'The Council considers that the Persian Government has acted in the best interests of peace and that it has rightly appealed to the fundamental principles of cooperation laid down in the [League of Nations] Covenant … The Council decides that before advising on any means by which the obligations prescribed by the Covenant shall be fulfilled, it is desirable … to await the results of the promises made by the Russian authorities. In the meantime, the Council requests the Persian representative to keep it informed of the march of events'.

At the same meeting the Council finally put to bed the plans for the trip to Russia. The Council agreed a formal declaration, stating the League's position on the matter, which laid the blame entirely on the Russians: 'The Soviet Government … states that questions of safety prevent it from receiving the Commission until the situation created by the Polish offensive has taken a more favourable turn, and thereby makes the execution of the plan impracticable. The Council of the League, which has been guided in this matter solely by high principles of peace and humanity, can do no more than note this refusal, and leave the entire responsibility with the Soviet Government.' In truth, it was not because of questions of safety that the Russians had refused the League of Nations, but questions of legitimacy. However, the Council seemingly did not want to acknowledge that any such questions even existed.

If legitimacy could be secured through persistent activity, the League would have been held in worldwide esteem. In the twelve months of its existence, the International Secretariat – effectively the League's Civil Service – had received 8,287 letters and dispatched a total of 4,728 of its own, an average of ninety a week. The Council itself had maintained its vigorous schedule of meeting once a month, in doing so allowing its members to appraise hotels and restaurants in four countries.

At the end of June 1920, six months since the first Chairman of the League of Nations Council had grandly announced the birth of a 'new world', it was clear that events had rather conspired against it. At least in Waziristan there was relative peace, but the British were now contending with open rebellion in Ireland on a scale that very few had anticipated. In addition, Iraq was increasingly on edge. The Poles and the Russians were in the middle of a full-scale war, while the Allies had still not managed to agree reparations terms with Germany and could barely agree between themselves. Meanwhile, the statesman who had been the greatest advocate of securing the peace to end all peace was largely ignored and slowly dying, and the man most likely to succeed him in the White House wanted the United States to pull back from its prominent role in world politics.

Chapter 29

A principled man

The Democratic Convention was held a few weeks after the Republican one, between 28 June and 6 July, in San Francisco. They had the advantage of knowing their opponent in advance, although many Democrats seem to have simply viewed Harding as the bogeyman. One Democrat said Harding 'represents the worst reactionary elements', a statement that was clearly untrue; Harding was a reactionary element, but he was not the worst. The Democrats could have found themselves squaring up to Johnson, but instead he was sulking in a hotel room.

The bookies' favourite was Ohio governor James Cox, who was closely followed by the President's son-in-law, McAdoo. He continued to infuriate his supporters by taking part, but doing so with the attitude of a martyr. Less than ten days before the Democratic Convention, McAdoo put out a press release: 'I am profoundly grateful to you and my other generous friends, who with such spontaneity and unselfishness, have without my solicitation advocated my nomination. To cause them disappointment distresses me deeply but I am unable to reconsider the position I have consistently maintained, namely, that I would not seek the nomination for the Presidency.'[1] Cox meanwhile was in an awkward position, as the newspapers were digging up the details of his divorce and playing it out across the front pages. Cox had been charged with cruelty to his wife, but his camp reckoned they could weather the storm as he had not been accused of infidelity and because his ex-wife had promptly gone off and married her divorce lawyer.

A. Mitchell Palmer – the Quaker who, like McAdoo, served as a member of Wilson's Cabinet – was also in the running. His stated platform for nomination was that he was a red-blooded American. One Democratic stalwart sarcastically remarked, 'We happened across Cox's headquarters wholly by accident and were astounded to discover that he, too, is an

American ... Thus encouraged we went to all camps and found that the candidates are all Americans.'[2] They may have all been Americans, but none of them were especially inspiring. The governor of New York, Al Smith, was at least interesting. He had left school at fourteen, resembled a scruffy bouncer more than a statesman in his style of dress, and had a reputation for being uncouth. Even though many Democrats blanched at the notion of his candidacy, none denied that his was a straight-shooting and extremely effective governor. In a demonstration of how wide open the race was, on 1 July, Wall Street bet-makers were still offering odds of 9/5 on McAdoo, Smith and, incredibly, Woodrow Wilson. There was no mention of putting the president on the ballot, but the Democratic National Chairman admitted in a cable to the White House that the situation at the convention was 'confused'.[3]

At 3am that morning, Wilson had called for his doctor. He told him, 'Doctor, please examine my lungs. They feel as if they have no air in them.'[4] The President and his physician sat and talked for forty-five minutes about the different Democratic candidates and the following day the president wrote a message to the convention:

> While our opponents are endeavouring to isolate us among the nations of the world, we are following the vision of the founders of the republic who promised the world the counsel and leadership of the free people of the United States in all matters that affected human liberty and the justice of law. That promise we deliberately renewed when we entered the great war for human freedom and we now keep faith with those who died in Flanders' fields to redeem it ... the course the party has taken fills me with a perfect confidence that it will go from victory to victory until the true traditions of the republic are vindicated and the world convinced not only of our strength and prowess but of our integrity and our devotion to the highest ideals.[5]

The League of Nations was as central to the Democratic convention as it had been to the Republican one. McAdoo asserted, 'We must stand squarely for ratification of the League of Nations without debilitating reservations ... The times are not propitious for equivocation or for appeals to blind passion or to doctrines of hate, or for reactionaries and those who would shut their ears to the great and swelling voice of humanity which cries aloud for the restoration of peace and good will at home and in the world.'[6] It was not a view shared by the entire convention, however. McAdoo was a die-hard Wilson and League loyalist, but many other Democrats, including James Cox, thought that at least some reservations were an acceptable compromise. The members agreed a plank which stood firmly behind Wilson on the one hand, but also left room for not doing so. It stated, 'We endorse, the president's view of our international obligations … [but] We do not oppose the acceptance of any reservations, making clearer or more specific the obligations of the United States to the League associates.'[7]

When voting finally began, delegates were hopelessly divided. McAdoo secured 266 votes, Palmer 256, Cox 134 and Smith 109. No one had put Wilson forward yet, but his spectre hung over the conference hall, metaphorically and also physically in the form of a giant portrait suspended from the ceiling, which, in the words of one party grandee, made the president look 'rather red faced and staring and frightened'.[8] The voting seemed endless. By the twelfth ballot, Smith's support had finally begun to disintegrate and Cox overtook McAdoo. Voting lasted the entire day, the convention finally adjourning at nearly 11pm on Saturday 3 July after the twenty-second ballot, having reduced the contest to a two-horse race, plus an outsider. Cox was on 430, McAdoo 372 ½, and Palmer 166 ½. The Democrats took Sunday off and resumed on Monday morning. Franklin Delano Roosevelt, in a warmly received speech that placed him as a front runner as Vice-Presidential candidate, had told the convention at its opening that the Democratic nominee, 'will not be selected at 2am in a hotel room.'[9] By the forty-first ballot, many in the hall must have been wishing for a Republican-style smoke-filled room to put them out of their misery. Cox remained in the lead on 497 ½, McAdoo second on 460 and Palmer finally out of the running with twelve. Even the front runner was still more than 228 votes from victory. Some of the delegates went back to their hotels, on the understanding that in a gentlemen's agreement their votes for their chosen candidate would still be counted in the following ballots. Two delegates from Missouri had nominated and cast votes for Woodrow Wilson, but none of the others followed suit. Eventually, hours later, there was a gradual but decisive shift to Cox. Finally, at 1.43am, the Democrats had decided on their man.

Cox gladly assented to having Franklin Roosevelt as his running mate. Roosevelt was young and handsome, and the various positions he had held, including that of Assistant Secretary to the Navy, made him a true Washington insider, all the things Cox was not.

A few weeks later the Democratic Presidential candidate and his running mate went to visit the incumbent at the White House. Wilson, Cox and Roosevelt met on the rear portico on a Sunday morning. They chatted for nearly an hour about the convention, the issues of the upcoming campaign and the League of Nations. Following the meeting, Cox informed the press: 'The president was at his best, recalling every detail we inquired about as bearing upon the international situation, and enlivening the whole conference with a humorous anecdote ... We are agreed as to the meaning and sufficiency of the Democratic platform – and to the duty of the party in the face of threatened bad faith to the world in the name of America'. He ended, 'I wish I could express to the people how deeply his devotion to principle impressed me.'[10] They were thoughtful words, but, inadvertently, the Democratic candidate had summarised the President's greatest failing: his devotion to principle in the face of all else.

Chapter 30

The enemy in the room

They arrived, in the words of one journalist, 'looking very nervous and self-conscious'. It was a deportment befitting the representatives of a vanquished nation, who for the first time were invited to join the Allies' deliberations over the post-war settlement. The central item on the agenda for the conference was to 'fix the German indemnity and methods of its payment' and therefore the Germans were in attendance.

The Allies and their former enemy convened at the Villa Fraineuse near Spa, in Belgium. The rectangular two-storey mansion had briefly given sanctuary to fleeing Emperor Wilhelm in 1918. It was a reminder how far a once-proud nation had fallen; not that many in the German delegation needed one. Many of them apparently did appear cowed, but several flatly refused to play the role of obsequent losers. A business representative who owned a chain of coal mines, Hugo Stinnes, caused upset by asserting that he intended to speak at the meetings as a matter of right, and that 'people who were not suffering from the disease of victory' would appreciate his point of view. Lloyd George did not, describing him as 'a specimen of the real jack-boot German.'[1] The British prime minister read the Germans the riot act about the abject failure to collect arms, but Dr Siemens, a lawyer on the German delegation, calmly replied, referencing Ireland: 'Even in your great country you are not always able to collect arms I understand.'[2]

The Germans also had their own ideas about reparations. The delegation collectively insisted that future payments could only be based on the economic and financial capacity of Germany, warning that a rapid increase in debt would result in a rise in inflation, which would make reparations payments – which the Allies insisted they did not want to receive in German currency – even more expensive in real terms.[3] Although it enraged the French, Lloyd George had a fair amount of sympathy with the German position and took a more pragmatic view of the reparations process. He confided in a friend, 'When one is dealing with a bankrupt estate there are two methods which require consideration – one to sell up all the assets for what they are worth and divide the proceeds, and the other to nurse the estate with a view to getting a bigger dividend later on. In dealing with the Germans we shall have to adopt the latter policy.'[4]

Germany was already in a desperate situation. Even though the main exercise of the conference at Spa was to sort out reparations, the Allies had already committed themselves to giving food aid to the German population. Without it, millions were in danger of starvation. The country's agriculture industry had been devastated by the war: the area under cultivation had decreased, and where crops, particularly cereals, were grown the yields had plummeted due to a lack of fertiliser and other inputs. The entire issue was compounded by the state having no ready cash to import food and make up the shortfall. The Germans brought with them to Spa a paper detailing their dire position: bread and cereal yields were down more than twenty percent, potatoes more than thirty; from 1913 to 1919 the total harvest of bread-making cereals fell from thirteen million to eight million tonnes; cattle stocks were also depleted. The paper bluntly concluded, 'Germany is obliged to continue the system of rationing introduced during the war ... The rations have, however, to be kept within such meagre proportions that they only yield about half the number of calories required by an adult.'[5]

The Germans did win one concession during the discussion. The Allies agreed to extend the deadline for the reduction in size of the German Army to 1 October 1920, by which time it was ordered to comprise no more than 150,000 men. They had spectacularly failed to meet their first deadline of reducing the army down to less than 200,000 men by April 1920. The penalty for failure to comply to the agreement was not monetary, but military: 'If by October 1, 1920, the German Army has not been reduced to the number of 150,000 men ... the Allies will proceed to the occupation of a further portion of German territory ... and they will not evacuate it until the day when all the above conditions have been completely carried out.'[6] The threat had a certain ring of petulance about it, but it was not an empty one: barely three months previously the French had marched into the neutral zone and occupied Frankfurt simply to teach the Germans a lesson.

The French were still pressing for a final figure for reparations, but no one could agree. They did secure the lion's share of whatever future reparations payments would be forthcoming, with the conference accepting that France would receive fifty-two percent of reparations, Britain twenty-two, Italy ten and Belgium eight.

While the Allies and the Germans were disagreeing at Spa, the League of Nations Council met for their seventh session of the year at St James's Palace, London. Balfour presided over the gathering.

The Council was presented with a new problem: the Aaland Islands. Both Finland and Sweden claimed the Baltic archipelago for themselves. The Swedish claim majored on the point that the islands' population mostly spoke Swedish and therefore deserved a chance to vote on whether they wished to remain under Finnish sovereignty. The Finns insisted that the Aaland Islands were, and always had been, part of the Republic of Finland and therefore everyone should pack up and go home. The Council decided to set up a commission to appoint three judges to look at the legalities of each side's case. To this day, the Aaland Islands still belong to Finland.

The Council had also hoped to discuss the results of the Spa conference, but was unable to do so because no meaningful conclusions had been reached. After four days of meetings everyone went home. Two days later the Supreme Allied Council wrote to the League: 'The negotiations which are at present taking place on this matter between the Allied Governments and the German Government do not, for the moment, allow the Supreme Council to give to the Council of the League any useful and precise reply.'

Chapter 31

Revolt

In July 1920 the uprising in Mesopotamia (present-day Iraq) began. For any members of the British government who still clung to the noble notion that the end of the Great War had brought peace on earth and goodwill among men, the severity and scope of the opposition to British rule in the region would forever shatter that vision. It would also bring into sharp relief the awkward fact that the Treasury could no longer afford costly wars in far-flung places that returned little to the Crown's coffers.

The small town of Rumaitha, straddling the Euphrates river roughly equidistant between Basra and Baghdad, was the site of the opening salvos. After more than 1,000 Dhawalim tribesmen routed the town's police following the arrest of their sheikh on 30 June, the local British commander cabled for reinforcements. They should have arrived within the day, along the newly-built 1m-gauge railway that linked Basra to Baghdad. They did not, because the track had been pulled up in several places and a bridge destroyed. It took several days to strengthen the town's garrison to over 300 – while an armoured train had to repair the rail track under fire – by which time they were facing an estimated 2,500 rebels. Two platoons were dispatched to halt looting in the Rumaitha bazaar and, as the culprits had come from a nearby village, the soldiers were ordered to raze it to the ground. On their return to Rumaitha, after burning the village, they were ambushed. Nearly seventy percent of the column were killed. As the casualties mounted, the remaining men fortified a small area of Rumaitha to sit it out. The occupiers were under siege.

Meanwhile, the general in charge of the British military operation in Mesopotamia was not even in the region. In an effort to escape the summer heat, he had taken a leaf out of the Government of India's book. For years, the seat of the Indian administration moved two hundred miles north every summer, from New Delhi to Simla in the cooler foothills of the Himalayas. General Haldane was in the process of shifting his entire staff across the border into the Persian hills and was decidedly irked when his presence was demanded back in Baghdad.

Barely a few days into the siege at Rumaitha, supplies of ammunition, food and water began to dwindle. Another relief force was hastily pulled together and set out by rail from Diwaniya, stopping regularly to repair the line so it could move forward. It consisted of one infantry battalion, five additional platoons and a squadron of cavalry. Less than five miles from Rumaitha, the relief force ran into 4,000 tribesmen, who had taken up positions in a dried-up canal. As the relief force came under fire, it swiftly became clear that they did not have the weight of men to break through to relieve the town and were becoming dangerously out-flanked. They were saved from the air. In the whole of Mesopotamia and Persia the British had only sixteen working planes – the dust and various mechanical problems consistently kept many aircraft grounded – but a group of Bristol Fighters from Number 6 Squadron in Basra arrived just in time and swooped down to strafe and bomb the Arab attackers. The squadron leader later recorded, 'It is not exaggeration to say that the whole column would have been massacred had it not been for the efforts of those aeroplanes.'[1] The column retreated and camped in a town thirteen miles to the north.

The British came up with a novel plan to resupply Rumaitha, British aircraft would bomb the town and hopefully shock the rebels into flight for long enough to allow the garrison to break out of their redoubt and resupply from the town's market. Number 6 Squadron's Bristol Fighters were tasked with the mission on 13 July and loaded with ordinance. A 112-lb bomb – the largest the Bristol Fighter could carry – was strapped to the aircraft designated to hit the centre of town. Haldane's second in command remarked, 'These big bombs should fairly put the wind up the Boodoos.'[2] The attack was successful and the ruse worked. Haldane gleefully telegrammed the War Office in London the following day with the news that the men holding out at Rumaitha had resupplied themselves.

Haldane began sending regular updates to British officials in London. In a typical example, he noted, 'Situation is as follows: - Yesterday an armoured train from Khidr reached Samawah … Rations and ammunition were dropped on Rumaitha by aeroplanes … Party of enemy on railway were machine-gunned by aeroplanes with good effect.' To even the most casual of readers, the updates were disturbingly similar to those the government had received twice a week on the uprising in Waziristan. Another of Britain's territories was aflame. Montagu, who had been the recipient of every single report from Waziristan, wrote to Churchill on 14 July: 'Of course I am well aware of the conditions that obtain everywhere as regards men and equipment just now, and of the great difficulties you must have to keep things going, but our people in Mesopotamia are, there is no doubt, faced with a serious situation ... we must strain every nerve to render all the men and material they have as efficient as possible.'[3]

At the start of the insurgency, General Haldane had at his command 30,000 Indian and 4,200 British troops, but because they were so spread out, he had already committed his tactical reserve. The British civil government had considered trying to raise and train local militia, but the army objected to the notion, one of the many problems being '[the] Intolerance of any sort of discipline by Arabs ... Uncertainty as to future, combined with decided menace from associating themselves with a Government which they fear may be temporary.'[4]

Suddenly fully seized of the situation, London was working to increase Haldane's available men. On the same day he received the private note from Montagu, Churchill telegrammed the general, 'The Cabinet have been exhaustively examining the situation and have come to the decision that withdrawal ... is not yet possible ... Your difficulties are appreciated and every effort will be made to complete your force in personnel.'[5] For months, the topic of conversation had been how best to draw down British forces in Iraq. Overnight, the plans were shelved. Churchill pestered India to dispatch men to bring up to strength the Indian units, while he also pushed to get a third air squadron sent to Iraq as quickly as possible. They were desperately needed, as attacks on the British were now no longer confined to the area around Rumaitha. Haldane's next telegram communicated the grave seriousness of the situation, urgently stating, 'The rising threatens to become general and may spread.'[6] Three days later Churchill informed his Cabinet colleagues that the number of British casualties had already reached 400, adding, 'Whatever the future policy may be, the rising on the Lower Euphrates should be stamped out with utmost vigour. Basra to Baghdad is the stem of the tree, and if the stem is cut through all the spreading branches, whether to Mosul or Persia, will wither.'[7]

Throughout July the disorder spread, greatly stretching the available military resources. On 22 July Lloyd George, while responding to questions in Parliament, rather awkwardly replied, 'I really do not know what the causes of the outbreak are', triggering a flurry of letters from opinionated people to newspapers, including T.E. Lawrence who wrote forcefully to *The Times* stating that the cause was nationalists demanding a 'reasonably independent' form of government.

In Iraq, the military's attempts to put down the insurgency were bordering on embarrassing. Gertrude Bell wrote to her father on 26 July: 'The military authorities seem to me all through to have [been] more inept than it's possible to conceive. The crowning scandal was the despatch two days ago of a battalion of the Manchesters from Hillah to Kifl. They were ordered to leave at 4am and left at 10, with one day's rations and water bottles. You remember that hot and barren road? Think of marching down it in July at midday! 17 miles out of Hillah they were dropping about with heat stroke.'

The Manchesters had been sent to retake Kifl, which had been overrun. Far from being an inexperienced unit, many of the men were professional soldiers, some of whom had been decorated in the Great War and had fought with General Allenby's Army in the region in 1917–18. But by midday the unit's medical officer estimated that more than half of the regiment was so affected by sunstroke they would need to rest for twenty-four hours. Instead, they had to fight. They were attacked by rebels, but put up little resistance as the victors carted off their artillery and ammunition. The Arab fighters disappeared into the heat haze as ambulances arrived from Hillah, where the column had started from, to pick up the casualties. In total, 129 soldiers were declared 'missing' and seventy-six taken prisoner, with the War Office not admitting until November that all the missing were dead. It was a depressing example of military ineptitude, but it confirmed the difficulties the British faced in putting down the rebellion, especially in the heat of summer. Bell concluded, 'Once the tribes get out on the warpath it takes all the King's horses and all the King's men to bring them to order.'

Chapter 32

Peacemaker

On the evening of 12 July the British prime minister dined in with his mistress, his golfing partner and his two private secretaries. As a summer storm howled outside, the group sat with the window open, Lloyd George revelling in the thunder and lightning. The weather, in the view of one of the party, seemed 'symbolic of the condition of the world'.[1]

It was certainly symbolic of events in Poland. The Russians, keen to press home their advantage, had launched a new offensive, beginning with a thunderous artillery barrage. Before the guns opened up, the following order was read out to the 120,000 Russian soldiers preparing to go into battle: 'The time of reckoning has come … Turn your eyes to the West. In the West the fate of the World Revolution is being decided. Over the corpse of White Poland lies the road to World Conflagration. On our bayonets we will bring happiness and peace to the toiling masses of mankind.'[2] The rulers of the toiling masses were less keen to see them liberated at bayonet point. Britain and the Allies were now supplying military aid and advisers to the Poles, while simultaneously hoping to broker a peace.

The Poles were stretched out along a 370-mile line, defended by only 80,000 men. Under the weight of the Russian advance, the line broke in the south, but the Poles successfully retreated sixty miles to take up their secondary position in a system of trenches which had been dug by the Germans in the Great War while fighting the Russians. The Poles pulled back in good order, the Russians capturing the comparatively small number of 3,000 prisoners and sixteen pieces of artillery. Tukhachevsky optimistically cabled his superiors in Moscow that the Polish army had been 'smashed' and was 'fleeing in complete disarray.' The Poles were not yet defeated, but the position was perilous. The Polish government sent an urgent message to the British Foreign Office, stating, 'Poland is at the moment engaged in a supreme struggle to preserve her existence.'[3]

The Allies' assistance was sent under the name of The Inter-Allied Mission and included considerable expertise in the form of French General Maxime Weygand, who was greeted on his arrival in Warsaw with the blunt enquiry, 'How many divisions have you brought?'[4] Lloyd George had dispatched Maurice Hankey – the Cabinet Secretary who had accompanied the prime minister to the crucial conference at San Remo – to be his personal eyes and ears. Hankey admitted that the Poles were simply ignoring the advice they were given, although he politely noted, 'It is not an agreeable task to criticise, and still less to express unhopeful views as to the future of a people whose hospitality one has enjoyed and whose confidence one has received at a moment of national anguish.'

At the same time as the Allies were sending advisors, Lord Curzon contacted the Russians to try and kick-start peace negotiations, suggesting a ceasefire along a 'minimum Polish frontier', followed by a peace conference in London to thrash out the details. On 18 July Moscow replied. Lloyd George spent the evening in the garden of his house in Cobham, heading indoors repeatedly to telephone to see if there was any news. It came at 9.30pm. The prime minister dashed into the house from the garden, reappearing breathless. The statement from the Russian government was 2,400 words long – far too long to be dictated over the telephone – but he was pleased with the gist: Russia agreed to grant an armistice if the Poles requested one. 'I don't call that unreasonable, do you?' Lloyd George enquired of a friend.[5] Not all government ministers shared his enthusiasm. The whole notion of closer relations with Russia left a bad taste in Churchill's mouth and he told his prime minister, 'It seems to me you are on the high road to embrace Bolshevism. I am going to keep off that and denounce them on all possible occasions.'[6]

The issue was greatly complicated by the fact that Poland was the original aggressor in the conflict. As the Russians had repeatedly pointed out to the League of Nations Council, it was Poland which had first mounted an offensive against Russia with the aim of gaining territory. In the drab, passive phrasing of the official minutes of the 20 July special Cabinet meeting held to discuss the subject, it was noted: 'On a general review of the problem, it was pointed out that while Poland had probably brought upon herself her present desperate situation by ill-advised attacks directly contrary to the advice of the Allies, nevertheless this did not alter the fact that, if nothing were done, Polish independence was threatened with extinction. If she disappeared and were absorbed in Soviet Russia, this might be a prelude to the union of the latter with the Bolshevist elements in Germany and the postponement of European peace.' It was a very long-winded way of admitting that if Warsaw fell to the Soviets, then half of Europe might follow.

Lloyd George was deeply embroiled in foreign policy. Despite facing the threat of strikes from coal workers at home, his two main priorities were the completion of the treaty and reparations deal with Germany and the securing of peace in Europe. His efforts concerned Churchill, who admitted, 'No man can stand the strain the PM is bearing at the present time. He really ought to hand over the international questions to the Foreign Secretary. At present, the PM is conducting the business of the Foreign Office'.[7] It was not an entirely true statement, but Lloyd George was taking centre stage in the Russian negotiations. The prime minister's view is perhaps revealed by a comment from his Private Secretary who claimed that the Foreign Office 'did not understand the necessity for achieving a Russian settlement'. Curzon himself held a high view of Poland, which he argued was 'the pivot on which our whole Eastern European policy ought to turn', but Lloyd George found dealing with the Poles personally difficult.[8]

That weekend, just before Lloyd George and Lord Riddell set off to spend a day golfing, a message arrived that the Russians had unilaterally decided they were willing to grant the Poles an armistice. It put Lloyd George in a 'high state of glee' and he paid no heed to the warnings he received that the olive branch from the Russians might be a trap. Lloyd George was not at all enamoured with the Poles' actions and thought the nation that Britain was supposed to be supporting was 'badly led'. The insistence of Polish nationalists on weakening their defences around Warsaw to protect the historically Polish region of Teschen in Silisia also baffled him. Lloyd George told one Polish representative who raised the subject with him in the final week of July, 'What is the good of worrying about Teschen when your country is in such a parlous state and when you may lose the whole of Poland?', to which the Pole replied, 'Ah well, what is life then?'[9] As they worked their way around the greens, the prime minister told his friend, 'The Poles are a most hopeless people.'

Chapter 33

The Imperial Government

'The basic fact, which cannot be ignored, is that, broadly speaking, the entire population in the South and West [of Ireland], so far as it is not actually hostile, is out of sympathy with the Government and cannot be relied upon to co-operate', stated a special report on Ireland for the British Cabinet in July 1920.[1] The British government was under pressure to act decisively. A cross-party committee of members of Parliament called on Lloyd George's government to 'show the world at large that it is deliberate and earnest in its assertion that the republican movement in Ireland should be destroyed and that the authority of the Imperial Government cannot be flouted with impunity.'[2]

There were two pressing questions: the first was how to restore order and the second was what future form of government Ireland would have. The Cabinet spent almost an entire day debating it. Even the option of negotiating with 'respectable members' of Sinn Fein was considered. Balfour wrote to his Cabinet colleagues, outlining terms that would include the scrapping of plans for a parliament in Ulster and the granting of dominion status to the rest of Ireland, but admitted, 'All through Irish history since the rebellion of 1798 the men who have been prepared to run most risks and to commit most crimes on behalf of the Ireland of their dreams are the extremists; and to them, nothing short of an Irish Republic will be really acceptable.'[3] One of the central concerns was that if Home Rule was pushed through – with its plan to create parliaments in north and south – the result would a be permanently divided Ireland, which would satisfy no one and solve nothing.

There was also no easy answer to the security problem. Martial law had first been discussed in May, but now the legal wheels were finally in motion. The Civil Service had prepared an eight-page bill which suspended the normal justice system in Ireland and replaced it with one of special military courts. Certain legal pleasantries were still undertaken. The Judge Advocate General was consulted and reported back that all that was required were circumstances that rendered martial law necessary. He helpfully informed the Chief Secretary for Ireland that, in his opinion, the circumstances presently existing in Ireland were precisely those that would legally justify the proclamation and enforcement of martial law.[4] He went on to admit, 'My knowledge of Ireland is derived only from what I read in the Press and from reviewing the Irish Courts-Martial', but his readers did not care from where his opinion was derived, only that it supported their wish that martial law be imposed on Ireland. Everyone agreed that something needed to be done. It was now thought possible that the RIC could completely disintegrate within two months. In addition, whole areas of government administration, including civil courts and the process of tax collection, had entirely ceased. In the case of taxes, the problem was two-fold: the general population refused to pay them, and it was deemed unfair to ask revenue officers to attempt to collect them as they would have to risk their lives to do so.[5]

On the evening of Monday, 19 July 1920, RIC constables Patrick Carey and James Burke were driving along a road two and a half miles outside of the town of Tuam, County Galway. They found the road blocked by felled trees. As the car slowed, they were fired upon and when the two policemen tried to exit their vehicle they were mortally wounded. Two of their colleagues in the rear seats survived the ambush. After they had expended all their ammunition, the IRA men took their rifles, set alight to the car and made them walk back to the town. Carey and Burke were the fifty-first and fifty-second policemen murdered by the Irish Volunteers since the start of the year. Early the following morning, when their bodies were recovered and returned to the Tuam barracks wrapped in white sheets, the garrison in Tuam reacted violently. A correspondent for the *Tuam Herald* later reported:

> Fully armed they marched into the streets, smashed public houses, and it is alleged looted their contents freely, dragged young men out of bed, and threatened to shoot them then and there, set fire to some of the most valuable properties ... The breaking of glass and the shooting was intermingled with the dull thuds of hand grenades ... Women and children

screamed, and some fainted. Most of them huddled together on the stairs or in the back portions of the houses and recited the Rosary. The streets remained in undisputed possession of the police, for no one dared venture abroad.[6]

By the time the two-hour rampage by the police – including the Black and Tans – had ended, the town hall and many shops, as well the houses of well-known Sinn Feiners, were ablaze and the streets strewn with glass and debris. The unofficial undertaking of what in Waziristan would have been termed 'special measures' was gradually alienating an entire population. One Roman Catholic Bishop wrote, 'They [the Black and Tans] have wrecked towns, villages, and peaceful homes … They speak of reprisals as if reprisals can justify or palliate the murder of innocent men or the destruction of property belonging to innocent people. They speak of outrages "attributed to Sinn Fein" but they do not call attention to the murder of a nation or the depopulation of a country.'[7]

The sense that what had begun as isolated Republican attacks on police was escalating into a full-blown sectarian conflict was vividly brought home by events in Belfast that same week. Until July 1920 both Catholics and Protestants had worked at the Harland and Wolff shipyard in Belfast, which had launched some of White Star Line's most iconic ocean liners, including the *Titanic*. Workers from Harland and Wolff, and another local shipyard, were called to a meeting by the Belfast Protestant Association and, in a series of fiery speeches, it was questioned whether Catholics should be permitted to work in the shipyard, given the existing political situation. Protestant workers streamed out of the meeting and hunted down Catholic workers. Some were beaten and thrown into the water. One Catholic worker recalled, 'The gates were smashed down with sledges, the vests and shirts of those at work were torn open to see if the men were wearing any Catholic emblems, and woe betide the man who was … [one man] had to swim two or three miles.'[8] That day as many as 7,500 men were expelled from their place of work. Engineering firms in the city also started getting rid of Catholic workers; one Catholic bishop estimated that in a few short weeks 10,000 men and 1,000 women had been driven from their jobs. The action triggered a wave of sectarian unrest in East Belfast. Catholic shops were looted and burned, and a Catholic church and monastery were also attacked. Eight Protestants and eleven

Catholics were killed in violence which only ended when soldiers were deployed on the streets.[9]

The readers of *The Sun* newspaper in Christchurch, New Zealand, first saw the news from Tuam on Thursday 22 July, under the headline 'Irish crimes lead to scenes of terror'.[10] The stories from the rest of the world were hardly more encouraging. Beneath the news from Tuam were the headings 'Soviet forces drawing near Warsaw', and 'War clouds in Middle East multiplying'. Two days later, a despondent prime minister conceded, 'It is very difficult to control an unfriendly population unless very violent measures are resorted to.'[11] Lloyd George was speaking about Ireland, but it could have been any one of Britain's troubled territories.

Chapter 34

The family of nations

The eighth meeting of the League of Nations Council was held in the Spanish resort of San Sebastián. Balfour having served his time in the rotating chairmanship, the Council now had a new figurehead who, appropriately, was a Spaniard. Quoñones de León opened the meeting with a sentimental speech in which he thanked the members for the honour, which had fallen to him by 'established tradition', although in truth it was a tradition less than a year old. It was, he said, 'with deep emotion' that he took on the position 'in which men of light and leading, such as M. Leon Bourgeois, Mr Balfour … have shown in the past their knowledge, authority and prestige.' He admitted that the League still had its detractors, but claimed there was 'a long and painful period of organisation. Such a period has not romantic attraction. It is like the cold grey days of winter when, nevertheless, the seed is germinating beneath the ground to give us its fruit in the splendid smiling hours of spring and summer.'[1] The fact that he was speaking at the height of summer rather wrecked the metaphor, but no one mentioned it.

Among the items on the agenda were the bills that the League was racking up for others in the painful process of its efforts to bear fruit. At their very first meeting in January, the members had debated what to do with the Saar Basin region. In an early example of the Council's decisiveness, they had established a commission to decide the frontiers, the costs of which would be borne by the government of the region. It was noted with sadness that, 'At the time, the Council … no doubt expected that the work of delimitation [deciding the borders] would be quickly completed, without involving heavy expenditure. Unfortunately, this was not the case.' The regional government was rather indignant that they should cover the cost of a commission to decide how much of their region belonged to France or Germany, and had suggested instead that the French and Germans should foot the bill. The Council agreed and revoked its first resolution, then promptly passed another. For what it was worth, the members of the Council stressed, in the passing of the new resolution, that the labours of the Delimitation Commission were not carried out under the direction of the League and therefore the Council unfortunately had 'no power to control the expenditure involved.'

The meeting was to be one of the last on the road. The Council had decided to set up a permanent home in Geneva and a few months later purchased a former hotel to become the new 'Palace of Nations'. But even though it would shortly have an established home, the League was still struggling to establish its international credibility. Balfour, in a speech responding to the new chairman's welcome, reminded the Council that the League had three enemies. The first two he defined as 'critics' and 'cynics', the latter who were 'always disposed to say that war, after all, is not a bad thing.' The third enemy were 'ill-judging friends,' who 'imagine that we are capable of carrying out at once schemes which go to the making of a new heaven and a new earth ... No genius can do this simply by the wave of a wand.'

Some of the issues were familiar. The plans to create a health organisation of the world, announced at the February meeting when the problem of the European typhus outbreak was first presented, were now coming to fruition. It had been decided to create an International Health Office to build relationships between administrative health bodies in different countries, to combat epidemics and advise the League itself in cooperation with the International Red Cross. The Council adopted a resolution to create an International Health Office, with the decision to be ratified when the full Assembly met later in the year.

But typhus was still raging across Europe. Balfour wrote a formal letter from the Council to the governments of all the nations who were members of the League. He pointed out that the Council's first appeal to deal with 'the growing menace of typhus' had met with scant success and the Council was now focused on the 'greatness and urgency of the peril'. One report shown to the members of the Council at the meeting in San Sebastián dramatically claimed that Russia was 'swept from end to end by typhus; scarcely a town or village has escaped.' What was definitely true was that two million refugees had passed through Polish disinfection stations and an untold number of people carrying the disease were simply wandering around Europe. Balfour ended the Council's letter to the League member states by appealing for a minimum of £2 million, which, he insisted, was 'urgently necessary'.

Health was not the only thing the League was attempting to manage internationally: it was also taking a keen interest in the wealth of nations. The Council had decided to convene an international financial conference. The original date set for a grand meeting was 23 July, but it was postponed at the request of the Supreme Allied Council. Crucially, the League of Nations had extended an invitation to Germany and other 'ex-enemy states' to attend the conference, but given that one of the most pressing questions of international finance was reparations, the agenda would be somewhat hamstrung if the Allies had not managed to come to an arrangement by the time it was held.

The Council cancelled the first meeting at the last minute – some of the delegates had already begun travelling to Brussels to attend – and rescheduled it for late September. Even then, there was still no agreement, as the meetings at Spa had not broken the deadlock, primarily between the British and the French. As the Council felt it could not delay the conference any longer, it announced that it would go ahead on the revised date of 23 September. The Allies were determined not to permit Germany to raise the issue of reparations, an act that would have been tantamount to pleading their case before a higher authority. As a compromise the Council agreed to inform the German government that no deviance from the set agenda would be permitted and that the deliberations of the conference would exclude any questions still under discussion between Germany and the Allies. The whole idea of the conference still presented a problem, however, as it would be difficult to assess the internal financial situation and future economic relations when, in the Council's words, 'the economic instability resulting from the war' persisted.

The issue of mandates was still up in the air and the League itself was getting frustrated. It was not concerned so much with the reality on the ground, admitting that 'the territories in question are actually being administered by the Mandatory Powers to whom it was intended to entrust them.' What troubled the Council was the legality. It was noted, 'It is not enough, however, that the Mandatory Powers should be appointed; is important that they should possess a legal title – a mere matter of form perhaps, but one which should be settled.' The former

German and Ottoman Empires were destined to be divided between the victors, but two years on from the official end of hostilities they remained occupied territories. It may have been a 'matter of form', but so-called civilised nations had made a gentleman's agreement that the war was one of defence, not territorial acquisition, and it was becoming an ever more difficult argument for the League of Nations to support, given the reality. The Council called for the Allies to get their act together and define precisely which territories would be handed to whom. The resolution stated, 'The Council decides to request the principal [Allied] Powers be so good as to (a) name the Powers to whom they have decided to allocate the Mandates ... [and] (b) to inform it as to the frontiers of the territories to come under these Mandates'.

The territories in question may have been administered by their future mandatories, but the lack of legality was a real and pressing problem. The French, who were in *de facto* control of Lebanon and Syria, had arrested and court martialled several members of the Lebanon Administrative Council, to the outrage of King Hussein of the Hedjaz, who complained on their behalf to the League of Nations that it was 'a violation of all justice and of international law'. He was only partly correct as the League Council admitted: 'His appeal is general in character, but it clearly assumes that the League is now dealing with a world in which the tragedies of the Great War have been followed by a settled Peace, of which ... the League of Nations is the appointed guardian.' The reality on the ground was that no official treaty with Turkey had yet been concluded and therefore Syria was technically an enemy country under military occupation. The minutes recorded, 'The Council have therefore informed His Majesty that it is beyond their province to intervene where, in International Law, war still continues'. In formally replying to Hussein, the Council was more guarded, noting with a hint of regret, 'the portions of territory where the events happened to which your Majesty has referred are in the military occupation of the French.' The fighting may have ended, but in legal terms the war was not over.

Five days later, the Allies finally signed the Treaty of Peace with Turkey. Known as the Treaty of Sevres, after the region of Paris where the ceremony took place, it was a complicated agreement which covered a vast area – from the Caucasus to the Sinai desert – within which were multiple peoples possessed of varying degrees of nationalist sentiment.

The victorious powers also had to contend with each other's interests and the mandates agreed with the League. The nuances of the paperwork were lost on many of those affected by the treaty. One British political officer in Iraq saw the lengthy process as a contributory factor to the unrest in Mesopotamia: 'The delay ... was extremely puzzling to the Arab tribesmen, who understood only the simple rule that what had been won by the sword should be kept by the sword. This delay allowed the idea of "self-determination" to be sedulously propagated and a general belief began to spread abroad that the British Government ... were in some indefinite way under the control of the League of Nations.'[2] Even after fifteen months of negotiation, some aspects were still outstanding. President Wilson had had four months to deliberate, but had not yet decided upon how to define Armenia's border with Turkey, so the Constantinople government had to agree to recognise Armenia as a 'free and independent state' and simultaneously 'to submit to the arbitration of the President of the United States of America the question of the frontier to be fixed between Turkey and [western] Armenia'.[3]

Even though the treaty was now formally agreed, the inconvenient truth of the matter was that the Turkish government signing it was only in control of half the country and was already facing internal nationalist opposition. A few months before, the Sultan had dissolved the Turkish parliament after its members objected to the British military openly occupying parts of Constantinople and arresting Turkish nationalist sympathisers, leaving him in sole control of the government. The treaty was not so much negotiated as presented to the Sultan, who, fairly accurately, was described by Turkish nationalists as a puppet of the British. While the Sultan had officially signed away eastern Turkey to become part of Armenia, the action was an empty gesture as Ataturk's nationalists were in complete control of Anatolia. After the Sultan dissolved the parliament in Constantinople Ataturk had set up a replacement Grand National Assembly in Ankara, even inviting nationalist deputies from the abolished Constantinople parliament to join. Ataturk's rival government, which increasingly appeared to be more legitimate than the Sultan's, roundly rejected the redrawn borders of Turkey and the entire treaty.

Although the Treaty of Sevres was now formalised, the commitment of pen to paper did not guarantee to solve the problems within Turkey, let alone the wider Middle East. Europe was also still unsolved: the Allies were nowhere near coming to an accommodation with Germany over reparations. The experience of seemingly carrying the weight of the destiny of nations on his shoulders was, as Churchill had predicted, proving very stressful for Lloyd George. He admitted he was 'very fatigued' and needed to get away. On the verge of a nervous breakdown, he wrote to his wife, 'Here I am working & worrying. It is difficult to build when there are so many people not only hindering but pulling down what you have laboriously built up.'[4]

Chapter 35

Armies and treasure

At the start of August, Gertrude Bell wrote to her father, 'My view of the matter is in a nutshell this: whatever our future policy is to be we cannot now leave the country in the state of chaos which we have created ... the situation is serious and might become very grave with any little swing in the scale.'[1]

Iraq was not the only part of the region in chaos. The French had finally smashed the Syrian uprising, capturing Damascus at the end of July, and they were not accommodating. Bell recorded: 'There's a fundamental sympathy between us and the people here and there's a fundamental hatred between the Syrians and the French ... whatever happens it means a long continuance of anger and bitterness which must to some extent react on us here. Damn the French. I wonder how often we've all said that in the last year and a half?'[2] The French did not share Bell's concerns and banished Feisal from his self-declared throne, an event which the Civil Commissioner in Baghdad, Arnold Wilson, saw as a potential opportunity, as he promptly proposed that Feisal be made Emir of Iraq. The notion of the Iraqis having their own ruler was not viewed with sympathy in many quarters of the British establishment. General Haldane thought the population of Iraq utterly ungovernable. In his mind, the causes of the uprising were simple: 'In spite of [the] obvious benefits of settled government there is among a community of semi-savage tribes a natural repugnance to ... payment of taxes, and other disadvantages appertaining to such a government ... [plus] the inevitable local grievances.'

Gertrude Bell personally liked Feisal and viewed him as a potential ruler, but it was one of the few points that she and Arnold Wilson, her superior, agreed on. Wilson saw Feisal as a man who could bring the Arabs to heel, whereas Bell saw his potential appointment as part of series of concessions to Arab demands for self-government. She had written letters advocating such a policy, but was summoned to Wilson's office for a dressing down. He demanded that she stop independently writing to the India Office. Bell told him his objections were 'quite preposterous', but agreed to acquiesce to his wishes. She wrote afterwards, 'He thanked me for my frankness and we shook hands warmly – well, you can't shake hands anything but warmly when the temp[erature] is 115°F.'[3] Wilson had also, without Bell knowing, raised his objections to her expressing her views with the India Office itself. The Secretary of State had to adhere to protocol and Bell was the recipient of cold and official rebuke from Montagu, which tersely stated, 'in the present critical state of affairs in Mesopotamia ... we should all pull together.'[4] Bell was demoralised at the treatment she received and privately questioned whether she should stay on in her post without the confidence of her superiors and when she disagreed with their entire approach. She even had moments in which she doubted her own long-held position on giving the Arabs a level of autonomy. 'In the light of the events of the last 2 months there's no getting out of the conclusion that we have made an immense failure here ... I suppose we have underestimated the fact that this country is really an inchoate mass of tribes which can't as yet be reduced to any system.'[5]

The situation was on a knife edge. By mid-August, a 10pm curfew had been imposed in Baghdad and meetings banned in mosques, while British gunboats sailed up and the down the Euphrates to shell any tribesmen who came within range. The Commissioner admitted, 'The tribes have been led to believe that it is a holy war ... The demands of rebellious leaders so far are complete expulsion of British from Mesopotamia and an "Islamic Kingdom" ... to tribes it means no Government at all, or Government by chiefs whom they can ignore at will'. Haldane, who was cheerfully carrying out 'punitive measures' across the Lower Euphrates region, where the local population was deemed to be in league with the insurgents, pointedly reminded London, 'A state of war has always legally existed in this country as no peace [was] signed. It is necessary to re-affirm this fact'.[6] He set up military courts, which handed down the death sentence for 'offences against public order'. Four men who wounded a sentry in Baghdad and stole his rifle were hanged, along with others denounced by informants. Any supposed ringleaders who were caught also received the same fate, while cavalry were dispatched to torch villages near to British-controlled towns. On 23 August *The Times* headline ran: 'Mesopotamia: A Serious War Before Us'.

Reinforcements were being rushed to Iraq and British officers sent from England as fast as possible. Upon their arrival in India they were only given time to field service their equipment, before being sent on to the front line. Within Iraq, British officials were now being targeted. In one forty-eight hour period in the second week of August, two political officers in different towns were ambushed. As a result, political officers across the country were withdrawn, several leaving their posts with nothing but the clothes they were wearing. The revolt was already beginning to shut down the apparatus of civil government, leading Bell to record, 'It's a sad business to see the whole organization crumble.'[7]

On 20 August Churchill sent a message of encouragement to General Haldane, giving the general his best wishes and informing him that by the middle of October he would receive an additional nineteen battalions from India and that he had also ordered the 55th air squadron in Constantinople to relocate to Basra with all speed, which would provide Haldane with a total of four squadrons at his disposal. The Minister for War told the top British commander in Iraq that by the end of October he 'should be possessed of effective striking forces ... to put down and punish disaffection.'[8]

In private, Churchill was far less optimistic, and with good reason. The Commissioner in Baghdad informed London on 27 August, 'Situation is still deteriorating ... encouraging our enemies and discouraging our friends ... Damage has been done to railway and Government buildings ... towns have been looted and bazaars burnt; our good name and all that word prestige stands for have I fear, suffered irreparably. Financially, the Civil Administration has been ruined, and the country has received a set-back from which it will take years to recover.'[9] Having only a few months previously discussed how to reduce the military commitment to Iraq, the British government was now funneling nearly all the available soldiers and airpower to the troubled region. Their arrival could not come soon enough. After only nine weeks of violence, the structures of government that had taken years to put in place were already falling apart.

At the end of August Churchill wrote a private note to Lloyd George: 'There is something very sinister to my mind in this Mesopotamian entanglement, coming as it does when Ireland is so great a menace ... after all the struggles of the war, just when we want to get together our slender military resources and re-establish our finances and have a little in hand in case of danger here or there, we should be compelled to go on pouring armies and treasure into these thankless deserts.'[10]

Chapter 36

Miracle on the Vistula

Poland was in peril. All foreign embassies in Warsaw had been evacuated and the Russians were marching ever closer to the capital. The defenders were in disarray. A retreating Polish soldier from the 37th Leczyca Infantry wrote, 'The heat, the lack of water, the stench of rotting corpses and the forest fires are turning into a sort of hellish torture.'[1] The line of former German trenches had broken and one Polish officer recalled, 'The fighting had an insidious quality, since there were no trenches in which to take up positions. One had to expect an attack from any quarter, and in consequence the fighting was bloodthirsty, as you either won or you perished'. The only natural barrier between the Russians and the end of Poland was the Vistula river and so the Polish commander, Jozef Pilsudski, withdrew what was left of his army to a single defensive line along the river.

Jozef Pilsudski had grown up in what is now Lithuania. Although descended from Polish nobility, his family was no longer well off, but his mother instilled in him a bitter hatred of Russia. As a young student he moved to Kharkov to study medicine, where his associations with socialists brought him to the attention of the Russian imperial government. Falsely accused of plotting to assassinate the Tsar, he was arrested in 1887 and spent five years in Siberia. From then on, he became an all-out Polish revolutionary. In the First World War he helped organise three Polish brigades to fight as part of the Austro-Hungarian army against the Russians, ending the war as a national hero who, on arrival in Warsaw in 1918, was promptly made head of state and commander of the Polish military. At the start of August 1920 his dreams of a powerful, independent Poland were in tatters.

Pilsudski spent the night of 5 August in his room, trying to devise a plan to reverse Polish fortunes. It had been a rollercoaster campaign: three months before, Polish soldiers had marched victoriously into Kiev, but now the fall of Warsaw seemed all but inevitable. In the warm darkness of the summer evening, he came up with a plan that was both brilliant and suicidal. Assuming that the Russians would concentrate all their efforts in taking Warsaw, he would leave the Polish capital guarded by the minimum number of men. When the four Russian armies were bearing down on their prize, he would strike their flank. It would be a last throw of the dice. Pilsudski calmly drafted a letter of resignation in case his gamble failed.

What he was unaware of was that the advancing Russians had stretched their limited supply lines to breaking point, even though they had successfully converted Polish railway tracks to the Russian gauge less than fifty miles from Warsaw. Many Russian soldiers, who had begun the fighting poorly clad and fed, were now in a desperate state. Polish civilians who saw them pass through villages noticed many were barefoot. The commander of the First Cavalry division, which had so successfully rampaged through the Polish rear after the breakthrough at Kiev, recorded that his men had 'reached the outer limits of human endurance', and cabled his superiors, 'In the interests of saving the cavalry, which may one day be of use to the Soviet Republic, we insist that you approve the immediate tactical withdrawal.'[2] He pulled his men back, without waiting for the reply, and the Russian advance ground to a tired halt. In the brief respite, Pilsudski discreetly transferred men south for the big push and waited.

Around 10 August a Russian soldier discovered the body of an officer of the Polish 1st Legionary division. In the inside pocket of the dead man's tunic were Pilsudski's orders for the division to prepare to attack the Russian rear as they moved towards Warsaw. It could have been completely catastrophic for the Poles, but when the find was relayed to the Russian commander, he concluded that the orders were a hoax and ordered the continuation of the advance. Two days later Tukhachevsky's men began to probe the defences around Warsaw. Much of the Polish army still seemed infected by weeks of constant retreat, unable to recognise that the fall of Warsaw would mean the end of Poland. One infantry battalion turned and ran at the first glimpse of what they thought were approaching Cossacks, only to discover they had been routed by a herd of cows. When the Polish prime minister toured the front he remarked, 'The danger loomed before us in all its grimness as we watched more and more troops, well uniformed and armed, give way to terror, unable to utter a word and seeing their

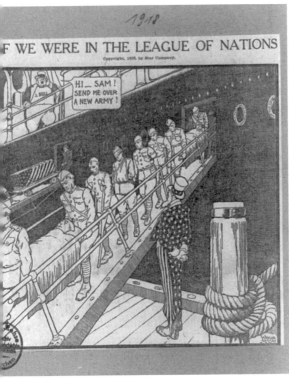

(*Above left*) 'If we were in the League of Nations', 1920 cartoon. Uncle Sam watches wounded soldiers disembarking a ship as John Bull (representing England) says. 'Hi Sam! Send me over a new Army!' The great fear of anti-League politicians was that by joining, the United States would be dragged into another European War (*Library of Congress, Prints & Photographs Division, LC-USZ62-85742*).

(*Above right*) David Lloyd George, Prime Minister of Great Britain (*Library of Congress, Prints & Photographs Division, photograph by Harris & Ewing, LC-USZ62-8054*).

(*Below*) Soldiers of the 5th Royal Gurkha Rifles on the North-West Frontier, pictured in 1923. The regiment fought throughout the 1920 campaign. (*Wikimedia Commons*).

(*Left*) Gertrude Bell, photographed alongside an RAF Sergeant in Iraq, circa 1920. (*Edwin Newman Album, San Diego Air and Space Museum Archive*).

(*Below*) DH-9A light bomber, pictured over Iraq circa 1920. The British 'instructional mission' in Southern Russia also flew the same aircraft. (*Edwin Newman Album, San Diego Air and Space Museum Archive*).

(*Above left*) Prince Feisal, who would be invited by the British to become king of Iraq. (*Wikimedia Commons*).

(*Above right*) The first posed image of President Woodrow Wilson following his stroke, taken in June 1920. He had only just started walking again. His wife stands at his side holding the paper still while he adds his signature. (*Library of Congress, Prints & Photographs Division, photograph by Harris & Ewing, LC-DIG-ppmsca-13425*).

(*Right*) Walther von Lüttwitz (centre) speaking with the German government's Minister of Defence prior to the Kapp Putsch. (*Bundesarchiv, Bild 183-1989-0718-501/CC-BY-SA 3.0*).

(*Above*) Men of the Marinebrigade Ehrhardt Freikorps unit in Berlin, pictured in the Pariser Platz with the Brandenburg gate visible in the distance, March 1920. (*Bundesarchiv, Bild 183-H25109 / CC-BY-SA 3.0*).

(*Below left*) Ronald Storrs, 'the first military governor of Jerusalem since Pontius Pilate'. (*Library of Congress, Prints & Photographs Division, LC-DIG-ggbain-37185*).

(*Below right*) Nebi Musa procession, April 1920. (*Wikimedia Commons*).

(*Above*) Victorious Polish troops in Kiev, May 1920. (*Wikimedia Commons*).

(*Below left*) Warren G. Harding, pictured with his wife, autumn 1920. (*Library of Congress, Prints & Photographs Division, photograph by Harris & Ewing, LC-USZ62-95939*).

(*Below right*) James Cox and Franklin Roosevelt at the White House, ahead of their post-nomination meeting with President Wilson on Sunday 18 July 1920. (*Library of Congress, Prints & Photographs Division, LC-DIG-ppmsca-33569*).

Harding addressing a crowd on the front porch of his house in Marion, Ohio at the start of campaign. (*Wikimedia Commons*).

(*Above*) Polish defenders manning a machine gun near Milosna, August 1920. (*Wikimedia Commons*).

(*Left*) General Anton Denikin, commander of the White Army at the start of 1920. (*Wikimedia Commons*).

(*Above left*) Charles Francis (back right) with members of his platoon, pictured in 1917. Three years later the Royal Scots Fusiliers were sent to Novorossiysk to aid the evacuation of Denikin's White Army. (*Kindly supplied by Roger Francis and the Francis family*).

(*Above right*) RIC, accompanied by a military armoured car, leaving Limerick on patrol, circa 1920. (*Hogan-Wilson Collection, National Library of Ireland*).

(*Below*) British soldiers carrying out a reprisal in Meelin, County Cork, thought to be January 1921. (*National Library of Ireland*).

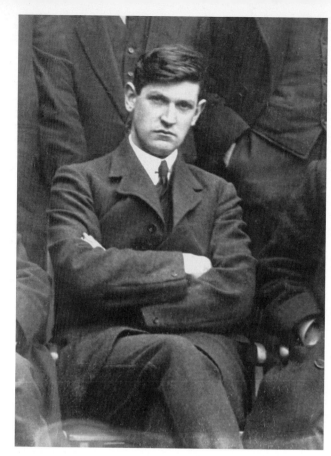

(*Left*) Michael Collins, IRA leader and finance minister for the breakaway Irish Parliament. (*Wikimedia Commons*).

(*Below*) The devastation in the centre of the city of Cork, December 1920. The blackened building on the right is the City Hall. (*National Library of Ireland*).

only chance in flight.'³ They were in fact little better equipped than the Russians they faced, and many were similarly fighting barefoot. The wave of desertions was stopped by two divisional commanders who implemented an effective and very Russian-style solution to halting the propensity of their men to turn and run. They set up a cordon of military police behind the front line, ready to machine-gun any deserting troops. There would be no retreat from Warsaw. Russian advance units were now only twelve miles from the suburbs and the churches were full of trapped residents and refugees who had gathered to pray for a miracle of deliverance.

On 16 August the Russians discovered a weak point in the Polish defensive line at the small town of Plonsk, which was defended only by Polish sailors and civilian volunteers. They were quickly overpowered by Russian infantry, who threatened to create a puncture in the line, such as had precipitated the flight from Kiev a few months previously. At the last moment, the Polish 1st Light Horse regiment arrived. One cavalryman wrote, 'As the church towers of Plonsk came into sight, we heard the rattle of machine guns … like a hurricane the whole regiment galloped into the broad street leading to the market square … we charged into the throng carrying everything before us like a whirlwind.'⁴ The Russian advance was halted.

The same day, Pilsudski made his move. He took personal command of three of the five divisions he had placed, ready to launch a counterattack into the flank of the advancing Russians. In total, he had just over 50,000 infantry, 3,500 cavalry and 160 field guns. He ordered them to ignore their own flanks and just attack. For a whole day the Poles advanced, virtually unchallenged. It seemed too good to be true. Pilsudski later wrote, 'Was I dreaming now that five divisions were merrily marching unopposed over the same area they were so recently abandoning to the enemy in the deadly terror of the retreat … at last I heard the sound of life, a sound of reality, the sound of guns coming somewhere from the north. So the enemy was there after all!'⁵ The Polish attack was a spectacular success. Pilsudski's gamble had paid off.

Tukhachevsky, the Russian commander, was completely oblivious to the fact that his army had been scythed in two and had moved his headquarters forward to be closer to the front for the final advance on Warsaw. He received early reports of the Polish offensive on 17 August, but did not remember the crumpled orders discovered in the dead Polish officer's tunic barely a week earlier. Meanwhile, the officer's former regiment, the 1st Legionary Infantry, had advanced thirty miles on the first day and over twenty miles on the second, with the men pausing to sleep for only three hours before pressing on. In less than two weeks, the regiment travelled nearly 280 miles and captured over 12,000 prisoners with the loss of only 250 dead or wounded. Instead of fighting to take Warsaw, the Russians were now retreating and an entire army was encircled. One Red Army general admitted, 'The catastrophe assumed proportions even more grandiose than the Poles could possibly have hoped for.'

The extent of the Polish success was barely realised outside of Poland. On 22 August Lloyd George was ensconced in a villa near Lucerne, Switzerland, with the Italian prime minister, attempting to hammer out a memorandum on the Allied position on Russia and Poland without any regard for the French. The day after the Italian and British prime ministers had agreed the wording of their memorandum, news of the Polish success reached them, which 'entirely changed the aspect of affairs'.[6]

The Russian retreat had turned into a rout. When Pilsudski's counterattack ended on 25 August, 50,000 Russians had been taken prisoner, 25,000 killed and at least 30,000 had fled into East Prussia and been interned. In his report to London from the Allied military mission in Poland, Major General Sir Percy Radcliffe described it as 'a victory as complete and dramatic in the annals of war', which he personally put down to the lack of quality of the Red Army, describing them as 'a Jew-led rabble of untrained peasants.'[7] Tukhachevsky, who had previously escaped from Germany's highest security prisoner-of-war camp, managed to escape sanction for the Russian defeat, which would, in all likelihood, have meant facing a firing squad. The dejected Russian general later asserted, 'There can be no doubt that if we had been victorious on the Vistula, the revolutionary fires would have reached the entire continent.'[8] For a further seven weeks the ragged but victorious Polish army pushed on, breaking a final attempt by the Russians to halt their advance, until, under pressure from Britain and France, they finally agreed to a ceasefire. They had regained nearly all the territory previously lost.

Chapter 37

Non-cooperation

Revolutionary fires were smouldering elsewhere in the East. On 1 August 1920 a series of strikes and processions started across India: the non-cooperation movement against British rule had begun. The instigator of the unrest was a fifty-year-old bespectacled Hindu Indian by the name of Mohandas Karamchand Gandhi. Although the world would come to know him as a wizened acetic, dressed in only a traditional Indian *dhoti*, he was a British-educated lawyer who had once worked at chambers in London wearing a three-piece suit and tie with a starched collar; he had also served as an officer in the British army. He was Indian, but he knew the British system, and its weaknesses, inside out. In a few short decades his unswerving leadership would bring about the independence of India after nearly two centuries of British control.

There were several facets to the non-cooperation movement, which included the surrendering of all titles and honours bestowed on Indians by the British government, the boycotting of schools, councils and colleges, and an attempt to bring the cotton industry to its knees by not buying British-spun cloth. Gandhi practiced what he preached, and when the movement began a letter landed on the Viceroy's desk. It was from Gandhi, enclosing the *Kaisar-i-Hind* medal he had been awarded in 1915 for his role in creating an Indian ambulance corps while serving as a sergeant major in the British Army in South Africa. Gandhi wrote, 'I venture to return these medals in pursuance of the scheme of non-cooperation, inaugurated today in connection with [the] Khilafat Movement. Valuable as these honours have been to me, I cannot wear them with an easy conscience so long as my Musselman [Muslim] countrymen have to labour under a wrong done to their religious sentiments.'[1]

Officially, Gandhi was citing the trigger for the movement as the British disregard for Indian Muslim concerns over the Treaty of Peace with Turkey. Indian Muslims had campaigned (under the banner of the

Khilafat movement) for Britain not to abolish the Ottoman Empire's Muslim figurehead and also to keep custodianship of Muslim holy sites. The Treaty of Sevres tore apart the land that had been a Muslim Caliphate and gave custodianship of Medina and Mecca to Hussein as King of Hedjaz, while the third holiest site in Islam, the Haram al-Sharif (the Temple Mount) in Jerusalem, was part of a British mandate. In truth, the non-cooperation movement was more about Indian grievances, but Gandhi was simply making the most of a rare opportunity to unite Hindu and Muslim Indian opposition to the British.

The announcement of non-cooperation should not have come as a surprise to the Viceroy. A few months before Gandhi had written to the British politician in charge of India stating, 'The peace terms [with Turkey] and your Excellency's defence of them have given the Mussalmans of India a shock from which it will be difficult to recover. The terms violate ministerial pledges and utterly disregard Mussalman sentiment ... Mussalmans and Hindus have lost faith in British justice and honour.'[2] Gandhi then threatened to instigate non-cooperation if compromises were not forthcoming, openly claiming, 'It is the right recognised from times immemorial of the subject to refuse to assist a ruler who misrules.'

Gandhi had not always had such a low view of the British. At the outbreak of war, he had told Indians, 'We are, above all, British citizens of the Great British Empire. Fighting as the British are at present in a righteous cause for the good and glory of human dignity and civilisation ... our duty is clear: to do our best to support the British, to fight with our life and property.'[3] But British actions following the end of the conflict, in which many Indian soldiers had given their lives, were convincing millions of Indians that they were anything but citizens of an empire which bestowed upon them human dignity.

Special measures introduced in wartime allowed the internment of suspects and suspended the normal process of law. But instead of allowing the legislation to expire six months after the end of hostilities, as had been originally planned, the British brought in new legislation – the Rowlett Acts – which extended the special powers of indefinite detention and imprisonment without trial. The result was mass protests. In Amritsar in Punjab, in northern India, the protests turned violent and on 10 April 1919 several foreign nationals were killed by mobs and a Christian missionary was badly beaten. Three days later a crowd of 10,000 men, women and children defied a ban on public gatherings and congregated in an enclosed area by the city walls. The local British commander sealed off the only exit and, without warning, ordered his men to open fire. The soldiers fired until they ran out of ammunition, leaving 379 dead and over 1,000 wounded. The British commander was hauled over the coals in an official report, ordered to resign and publicly criticised by Churchill, but members of the House of Lords awarded him a sword engraved with the motto 'Saviour of the Punjab'. Many in the British public shared the Lords' view and a fund set up by sympathisers raised large amounts for the disgraced Brigadier General.

In January 1920 the British responded to calls for autonomy by passing the Government of India Act, which increased Indian participation. The Act formerly entrusted Indian elected representatives 'with a definite share in the Government and points the way to full responsible Government hereafter'. A few Indian representatives were delighted. One sycophantic message sent to Montagu following the announcement of self-rule read, '[We] Indians [are] gratified by our Magna Carta generously conferred by Parliament … You, members of Government, Indian Secretary of State, have earned lasting gratitude of Indian people.'[4] But the majority of Indian campaigners were demanding more than just a democratic input into decision making: they were calling for full self-government. Prime Minister Lloyd George had no truck with such notions, bluntly asserting, 'If Britain withdrew her strong hand, nothing would ensue [in India] except division, strife, conflict and anarchy.'[5]

Gandhi was attempting to bridge division and, through promoting non-violence, avoid conflict, but he was very happy to incite strife and anarchy. He toured different regions of India throughout August, encouraging officials and those who worked for the British-run establishment to resign their posts. He was not above strong-arm tactics. During a visit to Madras he refused to eat or speak with his hosts until he had received four 'non-cooperation' resignations from officials. Resignations were widespread, but not extensive. In Sindh, nineteen clerks, eight teachers and ten magistrates resigned their posts, but their action hardly brought the process of government to a standstill. On 27 August the Viceroy telegrammed Montagu, 'Gandhi's speeches have contained nothing exceptionally violent, though [they are] inherently seditious and disloyal ... Generally speaking, non-co-operation [has been] nominally adopted in principle by most Provincial Committees, but [is] not likely to be taken up in practice'.[6] For now, there was enough division for the British to continue to rule, but the non-cooperation movement was just the beginning.

Chapter 38

Tranquillity at home

Warren G. Harding and his team decided to run a 'front porch' campaign. The description is misleading. Rather than meeting the electorate on their front porches, Harding instead planned not to leave his own. Voters – including women, who for the first time, were permitted to vote in all states following the passage of the 19th Amendment – could come to him. In preparation, he replaced the grass in front of his family house in Marion, Ohio, with gravel and the Republican machine laid on special buses and trains to bring people to listen. Thousands visited Harding's house during the course of the campaign.

Harding's team made excellent use of new media to make up for their fact that their candidate was not going on the road, and Harding recorded gramophone speeches to be played on radio and at state fares and other events. It may have been to his advantage that he was not touring the country pressing flesh. As Harding's national publicity campaign director admitted to a friend, 'Harding is pathetically without color [sic], atmosphere, ideas or knowledge about affairs generally … an ignoramus, a sonorous fraud, a sounding brass'.[1] But he sounded off about the right things. He had two election slogans. The first, 'Return to normalcy', was, as he phrased it in one famous speech, the need for America 'to steady down, to get squarely on our feet'. Harding was advocating a return to a pre-war world, which now seemed in the eyes of many to have been an idyllic time. His second slogan was a reaction to Wilson's interventionism. It was simple and catchy: 'America first'. The slogan itself was not new – it had been utilised in a number of past campaigns, even by Democrats – but in Harding's hands 'America first' became a mantra for self-serving isolationism. As Harding told voters: 'Let us stop to consider that tranquillity at home is more precious than peace abroad.' 'America first' featured heavily on Republican campaign posters in the 1920 election. In one, it was emblazoned beneath the picture of a rather youthful-looking Harding clutching a billowing Stars and Stripes.

On 24 August he held his largest rally yet outside his home. There were celebrities who came to endorse him, a fifty-piece brass band and even a specially composed song, which included the rather forced line, 'We're here to make a fuss, Mr. Harding you're the man for us.'[2]

Harding was indeed the man for many people, especially women. The young woman who had given birth to the daughter he never saw, and who was now looked after by a professional nanny for $20 a week, was not the only 'other' woman in his life. Harding was effectively blackmailed by one former lover, Carrie Philipps, who lived in Marion. The Republican machine removed her and her surprisingly obliging husband from the scene by paying for them to take a tour of China, Japan and Korea for the entirety of the campaign, costing the party an estimated $20,000. It did not put an end to the rumours, however. When journalists visited the home of one of Harding's neighbours, a widow, an eight-year-old girl proudly took the newspapermen to see the presidential candidate's toothbrush: 'He always stays here when Mrs Harding goes away', she told them.[3]

Harding's speech to those gathered outside his home on 24 August was solemn in comparison to the festive occasion engendered by the band and the celebrities. In it he slammed the notion of internationalism. Although Harding liked to campaign on domestic issues – the higher cost of living, jobs and immigration – the obvious campaign move was to present himself as running more against Wilson than against Cox; by tarring all Democrats with the same brush. A desire for world peace was interventionism, not altruism, and concern for the wider world was symptomatic of a person who was un-American. In his speech, Harding asserted, 'Some of our people lately have been wishing to become citizens of the world. Not so long ago since, I met a fine, elderly daughter of [the state of] Virginia who would have been justified in boasting of her origin … but was shocked to hear her say, "I am no longer American. I am a citizen of the world." Frankly, I am not so universal. I rejoice to be an American and love the name, the land, the people and the flag.'[4] As if to prove the final point, Harding had installed a new flagpole outside his house and could often be seen personally lowering the Star Spangled Banner each evening and running it up the pole the following morning. But Harding still avoided taking an official position on the League of Nations. Anti-League hardliners within the party were pushing him to come out once and for all and declare whether or not a US administration under his lead would become a member, but Harding prevaricated. Conscious of the need to not alienate Republican voters who saw the League, despite all its failings, as a good idea, Harding initially promised he 'would take all that is good and excise all that is bad'.

The Democratic position was at least clearer. Wilson had endorsed Cox, and Cox stated in his opening campaign speech, 'The first duty of the new administration will be the ratification of the treaty ... The League of Nations is in operation. The question is whether we shall or shall not join. As the Democratic candidate I favour going in.'[5] There was nuance to the Democrat position. Cox himself favoured reservations and early on in the campaign promised to leave 'at the first evidence of bad faith', but in the noise of the campaign, the Democrats were simply painting themselves as pro-League, in contrast to the Republicans who, overwhelmingly, were not. On 18 August Roosevelt was forced into answering claims that Great Britain, by virtue of its dominions, would have six votes in the Assembly to the United States' one, and the candidate for vice president resorted to claiming that Cuba, Haiti, Panama and much of Central America would vote with their 'big brother'. The Democrats' argument already seemed weak, but the other problem was the front man proposing it. Franklin Roosevelt was largely adored by the Democratic press and public – and made the most of it, travelling 18,000 miles and giving an average of seven speeches a day in the campaign – but even one pro-Democrat paper admitted his running mate Cox was a 'man of mediocre ability and unimpeachable party regularity.' In contrast, Harding looked vaguely interesting. Roosevelt got caught up in the crowds and adulation, but when he enquired about planning for a Democrat administration he was brought soundly back down to earth by his campaign financial manager who bluntly told him, 'You're not going to [make it to] Washington ... I've been getting around in the crowds. They'll vote for you, but they won't vote for Cox and the League.'[6]

Chapter 39

Dark ages of chaos

The uprising in Iraq was not an isolated event and compounded British fears about their colonies. The gravity of the situation was noted in a formal message from the government of India to the Cabinet: 'We must recognise that we are fighting in Mesopotamia not a constitutional question as to the future government of Mesopotamia, but for the very existence of civilisation in the Middle East. If we are driven out, only anarchy can supervene.'[1] This fact was not lost on the populations of Britain's other colonies. Gandhi wrote an article in the Bombay journal *Young India* in September, which also found its way into the in-trays of concerned Cabinet members: 'England finds Mesopotamia a tough job. The oil of Mosul may feed the fire she has so wantonly lighted and burn her fingers badly. The newspapers say the Arabs do not like the presence of the Indian soldier in their midst. I do not wonder ... Whatever the fate of non-cooperation, I wish that not a single Indian will offer his services for Mesopotamia.'[2] Gandhi's urging presented a problem, because the vast majority of the force available in Iraq was Indian. The government of India responded by alerting London to '[the] danger anticipated from continued deployment of Indian troops outside India', and it was suggested that Indian soldiers might be more willing to be sent to Palestine instead.[3] In practice it was nothing more than wishful thinking. Haldane was in desperate need of men and the only men available were Indian, and so they were sent.

In the absence of sufficient men on the ground to pin down the rebels, aircraft took centre stage. They flew along the railway lines, strafing the bands of rebels who tore up the track as fast as the British could repair it, while also bombing towns and villages. A.T. Wilson, the Baghdad Civil Commissioner, in a moment of apparently absent-minded musing, telegrammed London remarking that one of the reasons for the British administration's loss of popularity was 'the use of aeroplanes against recalcitrants'. The remark drew a storm of protest from the Air Ministry and resulted in a formal communication, which pointed out that prior to the uprising aircraft had not been used against the population. It also quoted at some length messages from the commissioner himself advocating and praising the deployment of aircraft against the rebels. The damning indictment ended, 'In preparing this Memorandum, the Air Staff realise that the last telegram of the Civil Commissioner has been sent at a time of grave anxiety and possible depression, but they are unwilling to allow it to remain on record.'[4]

Churchill was a strong advocate of the use of aircraft and even encour-aged the head of the Air Ministry to expedite 'experimental work on gas bombs, especially mustard gas, which would inflict punishment upon recalcitrant natives without inflicting grave injury upon them.'[5] Historians have since leaped upon his remark as advocating the use of chemical weapons (true) but have typically quoted his statement in truncated form, without admitting the complicated fact that victims of mustard gas poisoning did typically survive, although they suffered vile symptoms and often permanent damage to their health. Whatever Churchill's true intention, it is clear that he was seeking an end to the war, and quickly.

Gertrude Bell wrote to her stepmother: 'The war drags on and it's a supremely difficult task to do anything … The problem is the future. The tribes don't want to form part of a unified state; the towns can't do without it … We've practically come to the collapse of society here … The credit of European civilization is gone … It may be that the world has now to sink back into dark ages of chaos, out of which it will evolve something, perhaps no better than what it had.'[6] Reinforcements were on their way, but that did not change the situation on the ground. At the start of September Erbil was entirely evacuated of British staff and soldiers. The British did not want to risk another Rumaitha.[7] Haldane's hand was growing stronger, however, and nineteen battalions as well as two new air squadrons were expected to go into action in the autumn, when the temperature would also be cooler. The waiting was uncomfortable. As Bell recalled, 'Sep.[tember] is a disagreeable month. The air is very still and rather sticky … and the dust hangs in long, low lines over the world.'[8] But there seemed to be cause for optimism too: 'I begin to see daylight with regard to the pacification here. I think it's daylight', although she noted, 'Reprisals on our part seem to me to be pointless.' Even without the full strength of reinforcements, the rebellion itself was being gradually beaten down through brutal measures. The *Najaf* newspaper narrated that the British 'attacked the houses of the sheikhs, burned them and their contents. They killed many men, horses, and livestock ... the officers had no other interest but in exterminating us.'[9]

But the rebellion had, in part, succeeded. The British government, mindful, in the words of Churchill, that 'all troops sent to Mesopotamia increase the risks in the theatres from which they have to be withdrawn', agreed to grant a level of autonomy to Iraq.[10] In the context of other rebellions it was remarkable compromise. General Haldane, and many others, viewed any indigenous government as anathema and cabled Churchill, describing the uprising as anarchical and religious and insisting 'peace can only come by the sword'. Continuing the military campaign and introducing the possibility of self-government were, in his view, 'quite incompatible'.[11] Bell herself admitted, 'The agitation has succeeded. No one, not even H.M.G. [His Majesty's Government], would have thought of giving the Arabs such a free hand as we shall now give them – as a result of the rebellions!'[12]

In truth, Britain could not afford Iraq to be in a constant state of ferment. The government had been planning to save money by drawing down the number of troops in the region and instead had been forced to reinforce them by the thousands. The Indian troops, who were the ones primarily being sent, were beginning to accept less kindly their role as policemen of Britain's conquests, while the issue of Ireland rumbled on. If Iraq could be placated, Whitehall was willing to finally give in to the urgings from 'Arabists' like Bell and permit the natives to start running some of their own affairs. A worried Winston Churchill summed up the general situation in a note on 30 September: 'The local trouble [in Mesopotamia] is only part of a general agitation against the British Empire and all it stands for.'[13]

Summer 1920 had brought about an escalation in Ireland and a full-blown revolt in Iraq. The non-cooperation movement in India illustrated Churchill's concern that it was the idea of British rule, not just particular British-run administrations, that were now being questioned. There had at least been one positive turn of events that summer, in the form of the miraculous Polish victory against the Russians, but that unexpected ray of sunshine could not dispel the general gloom.

Although the Treaty of Sevres had been signed, there was no solution to the problem of protecting Armenia – either from the Allies or the League of Nations – and Harding's presidential campaign appeared to be surging ahead, largely because the Republican platform was proposing to put 'America first' and, in the process, damn the League and all that it represented.

PART FOUR

Chapter 40

Balbriggan

On 11 September Lloyd George resorted to his Welsh mother tongue to describe the most pressing concern of his premiership: 'Ireland is a hells broth. Potas y Diafol [Devil's broth]. I dare say there is a good deal of damnable business on both sides. This is inevitable & may end in forcing the moderate men on both sides to seek a settlement.'[1] Sadly, moderate men seemed few and far between, and some of the least moderate men were those the British government had employed to restore order in Ireland.

The town of Balbriggan is located twenty miles north of Dublin, perched on the coast looking out towards the squally Irish Sea. During one night in September reprisals by Black and Tans would force the majority of the population to flee their homes, leaving the town, in the words of one former British prime minister, looking like one from Belgium during the Great War.

The RIC District Inspector and his brother spent the evening of 20 September off duty, drinking in a pub in Balbriggan. Sometime around 9pm they were shot at. The District Inspector was killed and his brother seriously injured. News of the shootings spread fast and, around 11pm, lorries full of armed men rolled into the town. They were stationed in a barracks just three miles up the road. The Black and Tans first looted and trashed pubs in the town and then ran through the streets smashing windows, setting buildings alight and firing their weapons. Most of the town's residents fled, many into the surrounding fields where they watched their houses and businesses burning on into the night. Two men known to be involved with the IRA were dragged from their homes: James Lawless, a barber, and John Gibbons, a young dairy farmer. They were questioned at the local RIC barracks in the town and, according to some reports, were subjected to a mock execution; put up against a wall before shots were fired close to where they stood. As they were escorted back into the town by a group of Black and Tans, they stopped close to Gibbons' home and their escort started to beat them over the head. Their battered bodies were found the next morning. Nineteen houses in Balbriggan, four pubs and a stocking factory had all been burned. The Black and Tans had also wrecked a further thirty houses during their four-hour rampage through the town.

Although the reprisal at Balbriggan garnered significant attention because of the town's proximity to Dublin, it was only one of many in September. The day after events at Balbriggan, on the other side of Ireland in County Clare, as many as sixty IRA men ambushed a patrol of six Black and Tans, opening fire from less than thirty metres away with hollow-point bullets. The dead were 'a gruesome sight', recorded one the Volunteers.[2] Black and Tans, along with their RIC colleagues, first went to Milltown Malbay, where they destroyed eight houses and killed an old man driving a hay cart, then on to Ennistymon, where they shot a man believed to have taken part in the ambush, and set fire to houses and shops. The final reprisal took place at another village, where the policemen torched the town hall and several houses, including one in which the Volunteer leader who had coordinated the ambush at the start of the day was burned alive. One Volunteer later recalled, 'RIC, Black and Tans and military – all went berserk in their orgy of destruction, becoming frightfully drunk in the process.'[3]

The wave of reprisals was now being criticised, even in the London Press. *The Times* reported, 'Day by the day the tidings from Ireland grow worse. Accounts of arson and destruction by the military … must fill English readers with a sense of shame.' The paper concluded, 'The name of England is being sullied throughout the Empire and throughout the world by this savagery for which the government can longer escape, however much they may seek to disclaim responsibility.'[4] Some critics were even more forthright, with one British First World War General, who had commanded soldiers at the Somme, writing in a Manchester paper, 'I don't think any truthful or sane person can avoid the conclusion that the [British] authorities are deliberately encouraging … reprisals and "counter murder" by the armed forces of the Crown.'[5] Even some of the forces of the Crown, who were themselves in the firing line, were shocked. One British Army officer serving in Ireland wrote to his superiors in the final week of September, complaining about the Black and Tans,

'We are importing crowds of undisciplined men who are just terrorizing the country.'[6]

Lloyd George never publicly condoned the reprisals, but there are strong indications that, privately, he was very much for the policy. In a conversation with the former British Foreign Secretary, Lord Grey, in autumn 1920, he apparently 'strongly defended the murder reprisals', claiming that they had been resorted to in 'difficult times' in Ireland 'from time immemorial.'[7] In a conversation with a politician in September 1920, he remarked, 'You cannot, in the exciting state of Ireland, punish a policeman who shoots a man whom he has every reason to suspect has connived with the police murders. This kind of thing can only be met by reprisals.'[8] When he met up with Field Marshall and MP, Sir Henry Wilson – who would later be assassinated by the IRA – Lloyd George was made to squirm by Wilson, who stated his objections to reprisals being carried out unofficially. Wilson recorded in his diary on 29 September that he told Lloyd George, 'It was the business of Government to govern. If these [IRA] men ought to be murdered, then the Government ought to murder them.'[9] The prime minister replied, stating that no government could take responsibility for such a thing. In his personal communications, Lloyd George was clearly conflicted by the situation in Ireland, but he supported the system of reprisals, which, by autumn 1920, was increasingly becoming the typical response to IRA attacks from British law enforcement on the ground.

At the end of September Black and Tans were deployed for the first time in the historic east coast town of Drogheda, just fourteen miles north of Balbriggan. The local RIC initially refused to work with the men being sent to assist them. The new arrivals lost no time in ensuring that the locals were aware of the changing of the guard and posted a notice around the town. It read: 'Drogheda Beware! If in the town of Drogheda or its vicinity a policeman is shot, five of the leading Sinn Feiners will be shot. It is not coercion – it is an eye for an eye. We are not drink-maddened savages as we have been described in the Dublin rags. We are not out for loot. We are inoffensive to women. We are as humane as other Christians, but we have restrained ourselves too long … Stop the shooting of police, or we will lay low every house that smells of Sinn Fein. Remember Balbriggan. (By order) Black and Tans.'[10]

Chapter 41

The invasion of Armenia

O n 8 October the Armenian government dispatched an urgent message to the United States. 'The Armenian government in this moment of crisis appeals in the name of the entire Armenian people to all the civilised peoples of the world and to their governments to protest decisively against the sinister intent of the Turkish Nationalists, and it fervently begs for assistance.'[1] The Armenian nation was fighting for its very life.

Early on the morning of 13 September the Armenians guarding the crucial mountain passes had been caught by surprise when five Turkish battalions advanced. Most of the Armenian soldiers were asleep. They fell back in disarray and only narrowly avoided encirclement. The Turks halted and it seemed that the action might simply have been a limited statement of intent against Armenian plans to recover lost land to the west. In fact, Ataturk had decided to eliminate the Armenian threat altogether. On 26 September the Turkish nationalist commander on the eastern front, General Karabekir, telegrammed his leader to confirm that a full offensive would begin two days later: 'I am marching against the Armenian army. Our preparations are complete, I trust that, with the help of Allah, we will be victorious.'[2] In the first days of the advance, the Turks swept all before them and Armenians retreated from the city of Sarikamish, leaving behind most of their stores intact. But the Turks did not press home their immediate advantage. Concerned about possible British intervention, or even action from Russia, they halted again.

The Russian position was complicated. On one hand, they were actively supporting Ataturk and the rival nationalist government he had set up in Ankara with weapons and money, but a few months previously they had been negotiating with the Armenian government. A crowd of incensed Armenians living in neighbouring Georgia descended on the Russian Mission in Tiflis until a Soviet spokesman appeared on the balcony.

He assured them, 'We have recognised, we do recognise, and we shall continue to recognise the independence of Armenia so long as this is the will of the working people.'[3] When Armenian diplomats visited their Russian opposite numbers in Georgia, their concerns received a lukewarm response. In a two-hour meeting, the Soviet envoy explained that by agreeing to the Treaty of Sevres, the Armenians had set out their stall in the Allied camp, 'naively expecting' that they would be given the former Armenian regions inside eastern Turkey. As the Armenians had massed what forces they had on their western border, anticipating having to take the regions granted to them by the treaty with force, the Turkish nationalist offensive was, in the view of Russia, simply a response to Armenian designs on their territory. The Soviet representative then offered his country as a mediator. For now, Russia was pretending to be a neutral observer.

The Armenian government had grossly underestimated the capabilities of Ataturk's army. Having heard reports of mass desertions and internal opposition within the eastern region of Turkey, they assumed it would only be a matter of time before Ataturk and his rival Ankara government aligned with Constantinople and accepted the terms of the Treaty of Sevres. Now, though, they panicked. Martial law was instituted and every man under age of thirty-five was ordered to take up arms. Deserters would be publicly hanged. The small Armenian army was stretched over a 400-mile-long defensive front. Although it had a well-trained officer corps who had been through the Russian army system, the soldiers themselves were typically ill-disciplined and inexperienced conscripts. They were also poorly equipped: the British had sent uniforms and guns to the Armenians, but many of the gifted Ross rifles were in very poor condition and unusable. The Armenian army was the last destination of all the military cast-offs in the region. They had been sent broken rifles by the Greeks and five million rounds of ammunition from the defeated White Army, most of which was rusted and useless. Due to a lack of horses, army transport was provided by ox carts and most soldiers were barely fed.

On the final day of September the Armenian representatives met with British and French diplomats. The Armenians claimed that the Turkish offensive constituted a threat to the entire Treaty of Sevres. They received sympathy and the promise of future surplus military equipment. On 3 October the British Chief Commissioner in the region, Colonel C.B.

Stokes, travelled to Armenia to meet the prime minister, who he criticised for his previous attempts to court the Soviets. Privately, he was alive to the danger, however, and after visiting the ceasefire line, messaged his superiors in London: 'In view of [the] very creditable manner in which Armenia is doing her utmost to meet [the] very serious danger which threatens her, and bearing in mind probable consequences to our position in [the] Middle East if Turks and Bolsheviks succeed in joining hands across Armenia, I trust His Majesty's Government will carefully consider every possible means of assisting'.[4] The Foreign Office was not considering anything of the sort. The chief of the Eastern section noted in a memo, 'We receive a "supreme appeal" from the Armenians about once a month. We are usually unable to do anything, but Armenia continues to exist. I am not sure that these attacks are not exaggerated.'[5]

As the threat of a renewed Turkish offensive loomed, the Armenian government turned to its other great protector and dispatched an urgent message to the United States. American diplomats were not just unresponsive, they were downright hostile. In response to the Armenian plea for help in early October, the US High Commissioner in Constantinople reported, 'The Armenians may desire to have it appear that the Turks are attacking to force our President to act more rapidly on the boundary question and to get aid.'[6] The Armenians even wrote to the League of Nations, outlining their concerns that the Turks were striving to combine with the Bolsheviks. The British organised the supply of some fuel oil, but no further arms and, other than that, their pleas fell on deaf ears. By mid-October, the Assistant Secretary at the British Foreign Office remarked that it was 'more convenient not to answer' the continued calls for help from the Armenian government. The Foreign Office mulled over the idea of lodging a formal protest with the Soviets, just in case they were planning something, but Curzon replied, 'I don't see the good.'[7]

The Armenians now accepted the Soviet offer to broker a truce, with the intention of using it to buy time. If negotiations could hold off a Turkish advance, the arrival of winter would make renewed attacks impossible. Snowfall would also seal the mountain passes on Armenia's border with Azerbaijan and keep her safe from any potential Russian attack. On 13 October negotiations began between the Armenians and the Soviets, although a note of caution was sounded in an editorial by one Armenian newspaper, which warned 'The Bolsheviks today are the allies of our historic enemies, the Turks'.[8] The Soviets were offering to secure Turkish withdrawal and recognise the independent Armenian Republic. In exchange, the Russians wanted agreement on a territorial swap on their nearest border and permission to transit Soviet armed forces through Armenia at will. By 28 October, with all sides apparently getting on remarkably well, a draft protocol of understanding had been prepared. If the deal seemed too good to be true to the Armenian delegation, that was because it was. The Russians were planning the 'Sovietization' of Armenia.

In the meantime, the Turks had restarted their offensive. Some units were using Russian-supplied ammunition and there were even reports of small detachments of Red Army advisors providing assistance to the Turkish nationalists. The Armenians were well aware of the Russian hypocrisy and one representative sent a further urgent message to the British Chief Commissioner: 'I am sure that Great Britain will not allow the young Republic of Armenia to be annihilated and that she will take measures to save [the] Armenians.'[9]

The day before the draft protocol between Armenia and the Soviets was signed, the League of Nations Council gathered in Brussels for their final meeting before the inaugural session of the full Assembly the following month. Their time was mostly taken up with preparations for the big event, but they did collectively agree to condemn 'the acts of aggression of which Armenia has been the victim at the hands of Turkish nationalist troops.' The League passed on to the Supreme Allied Council the Armenians' request for financial assistance and military aid. The letter lamented that, 'The League of Nations itself is powerless to deal with bandits who know no allegiance to any organised government.'[10] It was a slightly unfair description of Ataturk's nationalists, who had their own parliamentary assembly and, if nothing else, were determined to become the recognised and organised government of the whole of Turkey. The Council again raised the suggestion of Armenia becoming a mandate, but concluded that the only interim solution was to again appeal to the Allies, 'In the hope that the Four Powers may be able to take some steps to alleviate the position of this unhappy people.'

Chapter 42

The final furlong

With one month to go until the election, Warren G. Harding finally nailed his colours to the mast regarding the League of Nations. He slammed Wilson, who he said 'favours going into the Paris League,' adding, 'I favour staying out.'[1] Four days later, as news of the apparent recovery in Wilson's health reached London, the president's doctor received a note from the British prime minister. It read: 'I would like to take this opportunity of congratulating you on having pulled through your distinguished patient. He has had a hard time but history will recognize the part he has played in the realisation of a great ideal.'[2] Even though the evidence on the campaign trail was that the voters overwhelmingly did not care for that 'great ideal', the Democrats' candidate for the vice presidency still eloquently advocated it right up to the day before voters went to the polls. Franklin Roosevelt told an audience in New York State that the decision before them was 'whether we are to join the other forty odd nations in the great working of the League of Nations that will serve to end war for all time or whether we will turn our backs on them.'[3] The American public had a pretty good idea of which option they preferred.

It was not just the Democrats' policies that left them trailing. They were also out of step with technology. Harding's team made great use of new media in their campaign. Even if their candidate was not leaving his front porch, his message could reach anywhere. They utilised phonograph recordings and newsreels, although one showing Harding playing golf led to the campaign receiving hundreds of letters of complaint, stating that it was a rich man's sport. In response, the campaign swiftly organised a baseball game in which the Chicago Cubs, whose owner was a Harding supporter, played a local team. Harding donned a Cub's jersey and threw the first three pitches of the game, telling the press afterwards, in a not-so-thinly veiled criticism of the president and his supporters, 'You can't win a ball game with a one-man team. I am opposing a one-man play for the nation.'⁴ A film crew was based almost permanently at his home and captured Harding editing his newspaper and driving his father around in a horse and carriage. The screen editor of the *Syracuse Herald* wrote, 'Senator Harding is almost a two to one choice among the moving picture patrons of Syracuse.'⁵ In media terms, the Republican campaign was trouncing the Democrats, and Harding barely had to leave his house. Harding did undertake a brief tour of the Midwest, but out of choice rather than necessity.

One of the key midwestern states was Ohio. And it was here that the ugly and persistent racial divide in America was plainly exposed in the election of 1920. As a result of post-war migration and the application of the 19th Amendment granting women the right to vote, Ohio's black population theoretically held the balance of power in the state. In October *The New York Times* ran a lead story with the warning, 'These black migrants from south of the Mason and Dixon line do not begin to compare in intelligence to the Northern negroes.' The pro-Democrat paper added, 'Many are illiterate, but they are being coddled by Republicans who have had them and their women folk herded to the registration places.'⁶

The Republicans were hardly 'herding' black voters to the registration booth, but the Republican candidate was at least willing to listen to their concerns. Two black church delegations visited Harding at his home in September, and Harding talked with them as he did his other visitors. Such actions fed rumours, and there was even an accusation that Harding had 'negro blood in his veins', which appeared on thousands of pamphlets, in all likelihood funded by Democrats. Cox himself even repeated the rumour in private conversations with voters. Harding was swarthy and appeared to be courting the new-found black vote, and that was all the evidence needed. But while Harding may have been sympathetic to the black cause, there was no suggestion of the abolition of segregation laws, even though a Republican advert in one black newspaper claimed the party stood for 'Freedom and Equal Opportunity'. On 9 October Harding told an Oklahoma journalist, 'I would not be fit to be President of the United States if I did not tell you in the south precisely the same I would say in the north. I want you to know that I believe in equality before the law ... You cannot give one right to a white man and deny the same right to a black man, but, while I stand for that particular principle, I want you in Oklahoma to know that does not mean the white man and the black man must be made to experience the enjoyment of their rights in each other's company.'[7] To modern ears, such sentiments sound like an endorsement of racism, but even the idea of equal rights for blacks was still seen in many quarters as progressive.

Most Democrats in Ohio took a much more strident stance over the 'Negro problem', which had the potential to swing their candidate's state. After all, Ohio was the state for which Cox, the Democratic candidate, was governor and Harding, the Republican candidate, a senator. The Democratic State Committee urged 'the attention of all [white] men and women' to counter 'the threat of Negro domination in Ohio.' The Committee noted with horror that 'Negro' newspapers (evidently the *New York Times* was wrong in its assumption of illiteracy) were 'openly predicting that full social equality will be ensured them [blacks] by the election of Republican candidates.'[8] Despite the race scaremongering, Harding would go on to decisively win Ohio with nearly sixty percent of the vote, though full social equality for blacks did not follow.

The League of Nations was not the only polarising issue. Prohibition was still a point of debate, but it only troubled Cox because he changed his mind. Having begun as a 'wet', his travels across eighteen states in under a month saw him shift his position, claiming to a woman he met in North Dakota, 'I have always voted Dry.' Harding, meanwhile, stuck to his line of not being prohibitionist and never pretending to be, and – although it exercised a vocal minority – the issue proved to be far less a feature of the campaign than the debates over the League. Cox, who had initially vacillated between the reservation and non-reservation wing, campaigned firmly for the League, although he moderated his message when in the presence of less receptive Democratic audiences.

On 30 October, with the vote only two days away, Cox gave five speeches and told a crowd of three thousand loyalists that the League of Nations was being brought down by the 'basest conspiracy of the ages', while criticising his opponent's position which represented 'cheap and spurious patriotism.' For the whole campaign, however, he was dogged by his own shadow. Cox himself was utterly unspectacular, awkwardly outshone by Roosevelt, his younger, more dynamic deputy, and prone to ineffective action. One Republican newspaperman recorded, 'I think the picture the public has [of Cox] is that of a game young lightweight prize fighter, dancing about'.[9] Cox gave the truthful impression of activity. In total during the campaign he went to thirty-six states, gave close to four hundred speeches, and even had his car pulled over for speeding. But he was faced with an opponent who revelled in being viewed as steady and immovable, a perception Harding reinforced by his refusal to leave his front porch. The Democrats' strategy simply played to Harding's strengths. By the end of the October the bookmakers had a Harding victory at 7/1 on.

Chapter 43

The coming messiah

As the sun set over Baghdad on the early evening of 11 October, an expectant crowd of notables, diplomats, soldiers and their partners gathered at the train station to witness the arrival of Iraq's first High Commissioner. Seventeen guns outside the city fired a salute, but the wind blew the sound the wrong way so the throng at the station were surprised by the arrival of the train. In a pristine white uniform, Sir Percy Cox stepped from the carriage and saluted as a band quickly struck up 'God Save the King'. 'I thought as he stood there,' Gertrude Bell later recalled, 'in his white and gold lace, with his air of fine and simple dignity, that there had never been an arrival more momentous – never anyone on whom more conflicting emotions were centred, hopes, doubts and fears'.[1] A famous Baghdad orator read out an address of welcome, to which the new High Commissioner replied (in Arabic) that he had come by order of His Majesty to set up an Arab government under the guidance of Great Britain. Sir Percy Cox had been given the task of saving Iraq.

The same day that the British government's official peacemaker arrived, General Haldane carried on as he had always wished and launched his first major offensive south of Hillah. Until mid-October he had spent his time fighting fires without sufficient forces. Three months since the uprising had begun, the British were finally able to get on the front foot. At the heart of the uprising were the southern towns of Kabala – the location of a historic Shia shrine – and Najaf, which had a combined population of 600,000. In a leaf taken out of the Waziristan playbook, the people of both cities were ordered to hand over their weapons and pay a fine. When they refused, Haldane set about neutralising each in turn.

The British first obliterated the villages surrounding Kabala in a show of force. The leader of Number 6 Squadron later narrated the process adopted for pacifying Arab villages, explaining how the aircraft would time their arrival with the troop column. First, the air force would bomb and strafe the village, putting the inhabitants to flight, after which all the village livestock would be driven out and the soldiers would torch everything that was left. The squadron leader stated that 'this had a most salutary effect on the tribes'[2]. Kabala fell within forty-eight hours, when the British threatened to block the canal that supplied the city's water. The rebels who had not laid down their weapons, or quietly gone home, retreated and holed up in the citadel of Najaf.

For Najaf, Haldane reserved a special spectacle. Instead of attacking, the British amassed around the battlements as if it were the ancient city of Jericho. At 10am on 16 October five British and Indian battalions, plus three batteries of field artillery, lined up east of the town's walls, while ten aircraft performed a menacing fly past. Later that day British lancers entered Najaf unopposed. Within two days the revolutionary leaders had handed themselves over. Although an utterly forgotten episode of British history, the fall of Najaf is still remembered in the city, which today houses a museum to the uprising of 1920, including statues of some of the rebels and a cache of weapons that escaped confiscation.

In Baghdad, Sir Percy Cox was faced with the challenge of creating a 'native' government from scratch. Unlike in India, there was not a wealth of talented, well-trained indigenous civil servants who had begrudgingly been allowed to attend English schools. The High Commissioner had to approach figures in the community, while also being mindful of the normally antagonistic relationship between Sunni and Shia, and invite them to take up positions of power within the establishment, in the hope that once inside the glass house they would desist from throwing stones. The initial plan was to create a Council of State to conduct the administration of Iraq under the control of the High Commissioner until elections for a National Assembly could be held. It was a difficult balancing act, and Cox was acutely aware of this fact. His own response to the summary of the plan was: 'We might perhaps avoid use of [the] word "control" by saying "we will conduct administration in *association* [emphasis added] with the High Commissioner.'[3] The proposals for the new government came in for criticism, not least in the Arab press, as Bell admitted: 'One of the papers says quite rightly, that we had promised an Arab Govt with British advisers and had set up a British Govt with Arab advisers. That's a perfectly fair statement. But let us now turn to another mandated province – Palestine. The same general principles should apply there as here, it seems to me; yet [there is] … a British Govt with native advisers'. Rather prophetically, she noted, 'Sometime or other, probably with the help of Egypt, Arab Palestine will throw off the Zionist yoke. And the fault will be ours for if there's any lesson which Mesopotamia has given us the opportunity of learning it is that you can't safely protest one thing and do another.'[4]

Gertrude Bell found herself thrust into the centre of the new administration and brought in as a trusted adviser to 'Sir Percy'. Shortly after his appointment she diffused the first crisis when several notables came to her to complain that they felt deeply insulted as they had not been permitted to shake the High Commissioner's hand upon his arrival at the station. One 'furious old Shi'ah [sic] of distinction' told Bell, 'We came in love and obedience … and when we tried to get near His Excellency we were pushed away.'[5] In most British eyes it was an irksome complaint, but Bell was aware of the long-term damage such an insult to the honour of community figures could cause and took immediate action. Without asking for permission, Bell drafted an invitation to all the notables of Baghdad to meet the High Commissioner the following morning and made a list of those with whom he should arrange private audiences to make up for his unrecognised slight. Sir Percy Cox agreed instantly to Bell's suggestions and from that moment on she became his Oriental Secretary.

The British approach still left them in real control in Iraq, but it was a move in the right direction for Bell, who was delighted when the High Commissioner finally persuaded the Naqib of Baghdad – the most important regional Sunni religious leader – to agree to form a provisional government in late October. She wrote, 'The first success is scored and no one but Sir Percy could have done it. Indeed that even he should have induced the Naqib to take a hand in public affairs is nothing short of a miracle. Sir Percy's delight and satisfaction was only equal to ours and we all sat (for) half an hour bubbling over with joy.'[6]

While Arabs and British rejoiced in Baghdad, the residents of the southern port city of Basra were less impressed. When Sir Percy Cox visited the city in the final week of October, he reported he 'found no enthusiasm for [the] idea of a national government. The merchants and people of Basrah [sic] itself have grown rich, their trade is prospering; they fully appreciate the advantages of British administration and have no desire for material change.' Even the Arab population was largely aware of their leaders' total inexperience in running a modern government and the High Commissioner wrote to London that it was only 'a few older and a number of ambitious and visionary young men who believe that, if we were not here, they could run the administration.' Cox concluded, 'They have in great measure been disabused of these illusions, partly by our vigorous repressive measures, and partly by recent benevolent announcement [of the creation of an Arab administration] by His Majesty's Government, which have taken the wind out of their sails.'[7]

Chapter 44

'In Mountjoy jail one Monday morning'

K evin Barry joined the Volunteers in Dublin at the age of fifteen, while still at school. Three years later, in 1920, he became the first member of the IRA to be executed by the British.

In late September Barry's group of Volunteers planned to hold up a British army truck on its regular morning run to pick up bread from a bakery on Upper Church Street for a barracks in Dublin. The aim was to steal the escorting soldiers' weapons. The day of the ambush, Barry was due to sit his first-year exams at medical school, which he had started the year before. The operation initially went well, the Volunteers obeying the orders of their commander that 'there was to be no shooting'.[1] The five British soldiers in the truck laid down their weapons, although one of them is thought to have fired a warning shot. The Volunteers then opened fire. Barry's revolver jammed and he dived under the truck to dislodge the jam, only to find that the rest of his group of Volunteers had fled. Barry was captured, while three of the British soldiers died, one at the scene and two later in hospital. All were between nineteen and twenty years of age.

Barry was taken to a nearby barracks, handcuffed and interrogated. When he refused to give any more information than his name, occupation and address, his interrogators – two sergeants and two officers – fetched a bayonet. In a signed affidavit, Barry wrote afterwards:

> When it was brought in the sergeant was ordered by the same officer to point the bayonet at my stomach ... The sergeant then said that he would run the bayonet into me if I did not tell ... The same officer then said to me that if I persisted in my attitude he would turn me out to the men in the barrack square, and he supposed I knew what that meant with the men in their present temper. I said nothing. He ordered the sergeants to put

me face down on the floor and twist my arm ... When I lay on the floor, one of the sergeants knelt on my back, the other two placed one foot each on my back and left shoulder, and the man who knelt on me twisted my right arm, holding it by the wrist with one hand, while he held my hair with the other to pull back my head. The arm was twisted from the elbow joint. This continued, to the best of my judgment, for five minutes. It was very painful ... I still persisted in refusing to answer these questions.[2]

Throughout his internment, Barry refused to divulge the names of any other Volunteers.

On 20 October Barry was tried in a military court for the murder of one of the soldiers, Private Marshall Whitehead. He was convicted of murder, despite the fact that eye witnesses testified that he had been armed with a .38 Mauser Parabellum revolver and that the bullets recovered from the body of the man he was alleged to have shot were of a .45 calibre. The Judge Advocate General – the senior legal representative for the Army – informed the nine British officers on the panel that they only had to be satisfied that Barry was part of the group who had fired on the British soldiers to make him guilty in the eyes of the court. The conviction caused a storm of protest in the Irish newspapers, as Barry was only eighteen years and nine months old when he was sentenced to death. His case came up at a conference of government ministers in Westminster on 28 October, chaired by Lloyd George, after repeated calls for the government to reduce the severity of Barry's sentence. The minutes record, 'It was pointed out ... that three [British] soldiers had been murdered in the raid in question ... and it was precisely young and irresponsible men of this [Barry's] type who were the main cause of the present disturbances in Ireland.' The conference agreed 'they could not recommend any commutation of the death penalty.'[3]

Four days later, on Monday 1 November, Kevin Barry was hanged at Mountjoy jail. Before his sentence was carried out, Barry reportedly told a friend, 'It is nothing, to give one's life for Ireland. I'm not the first and maybe I won't be the last. What's my life compared with the cause?' The priest who administered Barry's final mass later wrote to his mother that Barry was 'one of the bravest and best boys I have ever known.

His death was one of the most holy, and your dear boy is waiting for you now, beyond the reach of sorrow or trial.'[4] His story was immediately turned into an independence ballad, later sung at concerts by sympathetic musicians, including Leonard Cohen. It ends with the verse:

> Another martyr for old Ireland, Another murder for the crown, Whose brutal laws may kill the Irish, But can't keep their spirit down. Lads like Barry are no cowards. From the foe they will not fly. Lads like Barry will free Ireland, For her sake they'll live and die.

Although Barry was barely older than some of the British soldiers who had been killed, his treatment at the hands of British officers, his conviction in a military court and the fact that he was the first Irish Republican executed since the Easter Rising of 1916, made him a martyr for the Republican cause. In mid-October, several weeks before his hanging, a group of Catholic bishops lamented the 'countless indiscriminate raids and arrests in the darkness of night, prolonged imprisonments without trial ... the burning of houses and town halls, factories, creameries and crops ... all perpetrated by the forces of the crown who have established a reign of frightfulness.'[5] The execution of Kevin Barry was seared into Irish memories at the start of the violent autumn of 1920, which was shortly to lead to the single bloodiest event of the war in Ireland.

Meanwhile, the British prime minister had been forced to move house. At the advice of the secret service, Lloyd George had relocated to the home of a friend in Barnet, north London, as a result of death threats from Sinn Fein. He was remarkably sanguine about the risk and frequently remarked that he was second on Sinn Fein's hit list, after the Ulster Unionist leader Edward Carson. He also seemed to have recovered somewhat from the exhaustion and melancholy which had dogged him over the summer, with a friend recalling how one evening 'he devoted himself to singing Welsh hymns with much gusto, and to see and hear him one would never have thought that he was burdened with so many serious problems, and that he was – so it was alleged – being stalked by assassins.'[6]

By the end of October, the situation in Ireland was nearing crisis point. The impact of events was not lost on other members of the

British government, as Edwin Montagu remarked, 'A campaign [in India] similar to the Sinn Fein campaign in Ireland would be almost impossible to deal with except by punishment and revenge, certainly not by prevention.' As Secretary of State for India, he was one of the few in the British establishment who appeared willing to connect the dots between events that were happening around the world. In Iraq, the uprising had finally been quelled, but the success of the carrot and stick approach of self-government, in tandem with a remorseless military campaign was a strategy that could not be replicated in Ireland. Flattening the villages of Cork and Clare from the air was unconscionable, while Home Rule was dead in the water. There seemed no end in sight to the violence.

Chapter 45

The end of the White Army

For seven months the White Army had been stuck on the Crimean Peninsula. The 10,000-strong rabble that had arrived after the frantic retreat from Novorossiysk had gradually grown as it attracted the other defeated elements of the forces that had once fought to uphold the throne of the Tsar, but every attempt to break out from the spit of land failed.

Following the departure of Denikin, they had a new commander. General Baron Pyotr Nikolayevich Wrangel was a former Cossack cavalry officer, with family ties close enough to German nobility to rejoice in the appellation of 'Baron'. He was strikingly tall, with an elongated face that appropriately gave him a supercilious air. In most photographs he is pictured in a *kubanka*, a sheepskin hat that was part of the Cossack uniform. He was not entirely against the notion of revolution. Before the Soviets overthrew Tsar Nicholas II, Wrangel had discussed the state of the administration with other high-ranking officers who went as far as proposing a coup to replace the Tsar who was making 'fatal mistakes'. In the event, they were too late and found themselves fighting and failing to stem the tide of a communist takeover.

In Wrangel's view, the Russian nationalists had been betrayed twice: first, when Western powers stopped arming the White Army, and again when each in turn began overtures with the Soviets to attempt to secure trade agreements with Russia. He later wrote in his memoirs: 'England opened the way, Italy followed and then France.'[1] In simply economic terms, Russia was an untapped resource, and now that the hostilities with Poland were over, securing a trade deal seemed a much more realistic prospect, especially as Russia would be in need of foreign exchange. As Lloyd George admitted, 'Russia before the war was one of the great exporters of grain. She has other things we want – oil and flax. It is most important that we should have peace in the East and that the Russian supply should become available for the rest of Europe.'[2] The British had been negotiating since the spring, when they had abandoned Denikin to his fate on the shores of Novorossiysk. The French were late to the party because they had been the only nation to recognise the 'Government of South Russia', which none of the White Army's other allies felt necessary to do as it basically consisted of a collection of self-important, self-appointed men in Sevastopol, headed by Wrangel. In November 1920 the French rescinded their recognition and, in a far more telling blow, announced that they were to stop shipping food to Wrangel's army. The French had only ever sent the supplies on 'humane grounds' anyway. The die had been cast and the Bolsheviks were now firmly in power.

Faced with the prospect of his army starving to death, Wrangel acknowledged that he had no option but to quit the Crimea. He refused to give up hope, however, recording in his diary, 'At this moment, when circumstances compel me to leave the Crimea, I must consider if and how I can use my Army on the territories which are still occupied [by the Soviets]'.[3] In truth, his optimistic attitude may have been closer to denial than hope. Even after his army had been evacuated, Wrangel refused to let it be stood down and he forever clung to the possibility of a reversal of fortunes. In March 1921 a British envoy in Constantinople, where most of his soldiers eventually ended up, reported to London, 'General Wrangel may be expected vigorously to oppose any suggestions to disband his formations, as he contends that it is particularly desirable that his army, which is the only anti-Bolshevik force, should be ready to benefit from … events.'[4]

Wrangel was also being encouraged to quit Crimea by an advancing Bolshevik army that had been steadily marching forward and was now threatening his last defensive line. On 11 November the British Cabinet held a special meeting to discuss the situation. They concluded that Sevastopol could fall within a week.[5] Refusing to have a repeat of Novorossiysk, the Cabinet agreed only to help evacuate British nationals. Churchill violently objected, insisting that it would result in 'the massacre of the civilians in the Crimea'. He was overruled, but his objection was recorded in the minutes. The British, having formally ended their support of the nationalist cause, were determined to be 'strictly neutral', but it was a difficult part to play convincingly. Even though Wrangel had an embarrassing army, he still possessed an impressive maritime force, which included a dreadnaught battleship and several submarines. It was the potential threat posed by the submarines that caused the most concern, leading the commander-in-chief of the Mediterranean fleet to enquire whether the Admiralty wanted them destroyed. He received a reply that neatly expressed the British predicament: 'It has been decided that no action should be taken against General Wrangel's submarines while they remain at Sevastopol, even if they turn "Red". Previous orders that Red submarines met with at sea are to be treated as hostile, hold good.'[6]

The British were still trying to negotiate a trade agreement with Russia and it was decided that firing upon Bolsheviks was likely to affect negotiations, even if any action were done in the name of protecting civilians. There was a debate raging about whether preconditions should be, or already had been, attached in the previous negotiations. At the end of June, the government had dispatched a letter to Russia, stating that 'the fundamental condition' of any agreement was that Russia would refrain 'from military action or propaganda against British interests or the British Empire.'[7] But the letter had also left Britain, in the words of Lloyd George, 'bound in honour if we can agree to details'.

There was a fiery Cabinet meeting on 17 November. The general consensus was that if there had been preconditions, the Russians had flagrantly flouted them. In the opinion of some of those present, that was sufficient proof that such efforts were worthless. Curzon, ever with one eye on the region he had once ruled as Viceroy, insisted, 'The Russian menace in the East is incomparably greater than anything else that has happened in my time to the British Empire ... from Moscow to Tashkent conspiracies worked by Bolshevik agents and paid for by Bolshevik gold are going on ... You will find that after the trading agreement all this will go on just the same.'[8] Remarkably, it was the prime minister who intervened, defending the actions of the Bolsheviks and effectively using the same argument that Russia had presented to the League of Nations: 'We organised a military mission to Poland,' Lloyd George pointed out. 'The only way in which we can justify ourselves is [to say] that the agreement was not in force and their case is that there has been no agreement.' In the end, realpolitik won out. Britain was going through an economic depression at home, unemployment was rising and Russia was willing to pay for goods in gold. The prime minister concluded the meeting, 'I have heard predictions about the fall of the Soviet Government for the last two years. Denikin … Wrangel, all have collapsed but I cannot see any immediate prospect for the collapse of the Soviet Government.'

The withdrawal from the peninsula began in the second week of November. By 15 November all the British subjects who wished to leave had been transferred to Royal Navy vessels, with the commander-in-chief of the Mediterranean fleet reporting, '58,000 refugees are now on board ships at Modn (opposite Constantinople) and possibly another 15,000 may yet arrive. Men are reported to be quiet despite intense discomfort and privations, and the conditions on board ships are naturally extremely bad.'[9] When they reached Constantinople, conditions were little better. The refugees lived in crowded camps, at risk of disease and initially some of them even stayed on the ships they had arrived in. Churchill lobbied Cabinet to spend £80,000 on refugee relief and was grudgingly given £20,000, on the basis that if nothing was done, there might be an outbreak of 'pestilence'.

The functioning warships of Wrangel's navy slipped out to sea and took shelter at Constantinople, where they stayed impounded for three months until the French permanently interned them in Bizerte, in Tunisia, where they rusted away to uselessness. General Wrangel himself fled aboard his dreadnaught and for a while stayed on a yacht in Constantinople harbour, before moving to Eastern Europe and finally to Belgium, where he lived out the rest of his days working as an engineer, still clinging to the false hope the Soviet takeover would be short lived.

Chapter 46

Casting votes

Steady rain cascaded from a drab November sky on election morning in Marion, Ohio. But it did not put off the voters. Harding was the eleventh person to cast his vote at his local polling station on 2 November and posed afterwards for a picture for the newspapers. When photographers asked him to hold up a ballot paper he quipped, 'But I can't vote for myself more than once.'[1] He then went off to play golf with a friend, despite the weather.

President Wilson had voted by post on 30 October, so was not at a polling station to witness the historic sight of women voting for the first time across the whole of the United States. There has been much debate about the impact of the women's vote in 1920, but the more nuanced truth is that women did not vote as a block any more than men did. Wealth and class proved far stronger factors than gender when it came to the ballot box. There were several recorded instances of violence and intimidation against black men and women, but they were no more than generally isolated incidents. Most of the intimidation of black voters had been more subtle and had taken place for weeks beforehand. Nearly 26 million people voted – a new record – but by the early evening a Republican newspaper in New York was already calling the election for Harding. He won with a record 60.2 percent of the popular vote, more than seven million votes ahead of his Democratic rival James Cox. Woodrow Wilson's Secretary said, 'It wasn't a landslide, it was an earthquake.'

Wilson himself reacted better than anyone had expected. His doctor noted, 'All who saw the President in the days immediately following the election felt that he looked stronger than he had looked for some time.'[2] He was seen laughing and joking, but there was 'an impression impossible to describe, but which clearly indicated yearning love for his country and a sense of his own helplessness to "do anything about it." For a long time, the ill, closeted president had ignored the grim truth that his political career was ended. Now his successor had been elected, even his frail eyes could see the writing on the wall.

Harding's victory statement to the press invoked the blessing of the Almighty and attempted to be self-deprecating: 'I am happy to utter my gratitude, but I am not exultant. It is not a personal victory. It is a renewed expression of confident Americanism.' Congratulations poured in, although one Republican grandee tempered his compliments with a criticism of the decision to damn Wilson and the League together, 'The abandonment by some of the most prominent Republicans of the League of Nations, which they helped to construct, has been successful. People have succumbed to the confusion wrought by these distinguished men and the misrepresentation of those who would not and did not understand the League of Nations.'[3]

The League of Nations itself was enthusiastically preparing for the inaugural gathering of its Assembly in Geneva, the occasion which had been so many months in the planning. The day after Harding became the president in waiting, a group of British ministers debated which representative should be dispatched to fly the flag at the upcoming Assembly meeting of the League. There were several arguments in favour of the prime minister attending, not least because the Assembly planned to discuss several subjects where 'his presence might be desirable'. One of the subjects was the proposal of German membership, although Leon Bourgeois had personally informed Lloyd George that if Germany joined, France would leave instantly. More relevant was the question of disarmament, which, it was admitted, was 'particularly thorny … at the present time.'[4] Theoretically, if the League were to succeed in its goal of ending all wars, then there would need to be some form of collective disarmament. While no one expected every nation to beat their swords into ploughshares immediately, in the euphoric moments of the League's conception, it had been hoped something constructive might be achieved. However, the United States, Russia and Germany were not and would not, for the foreseeable future, be members of the League, and two of the three had, for the last hundred years, been habitually guilty of declaring war in all directions. In principle, the idea of disarmament was on the table, but in typical understatement, it was noted that it was 'doubtful … whether much progress can be made at the forthcoming

[Assembly] meeting.' It was decided that Balfour would go in the prime minister's stead.

The city was a sight to behold: 'Thousands of people had poured into Geneva from every quarter of the globe and turned every one of the big hotels around the Lake into centres of infinitely varied life.'[5] The British delegation commandeered the five storeys of the Hotel Beau Rivage and draped Union Jacks from the balconies. The French defiantly flew the Tricolour from the Hotel des Bergues, 400m further along the lakeside promenade. They would be there for some time, as the Assembly's session was to last several weeks.

To begin with, when it opened on 15 November, proceedings were dull, dealing with internal procedure, the rules of the Assembly and its relationship to the Council, and the setting up of various committees. There was even a lengthy debate about how the Assembly should vote on matters, which was decided by a vote. Typhus was still a problem in Poland and across Eastern Europe. At its last public meeting before the gathering of the Assembly, the Council had admitted that its call for funds to deal with the epidemic had been unsuccessful, noting that many countries had 'failed to respond' to the appeal and that 'the funds necessary to begin the campaign [against the epidemic] had not yet been fully collected.' The representative from the then independent state of Nawanagar, which in 1948 was subsumed into India, spoke eloquently of the need for action: 'I beseech you to rise again now in aid, not of one people alone, but of the many peoples attacked by a foul pestilence … It is not a matter alone of the disease and death of unhappy men, women and children in a central plague spot in Europe. It is a matter of grave and enduring social unrest and economic disruption'.[6] The Assembly resolved to do more, voted to affirm the action already taken by the Council and approved a telegram to various governments calling for the donation of £2 million.

Money was a problem, as not all the members were paying their dues. At the time of the Assembly meeting, many countries' second payments were proving hard to extract. Only seven members had paid their expected contributions in full: eight had paid in part and twenty-eight had paid nothing at all. In total, the League was short of 5 ½ million francs. The salary of the Secretary General of the League's Secretariat – effectively its top civil servant – was repeatedly called into question, leading Balfour to step and defend it (the post happened to be held by an Eton-educated British diplomat, Sir Eric Drummond). Balfour asserted, 'Those criticisms are ill-founded, and it will be a very evil day for this Assembly if they pronounce to the world that the salary it gives its chief official is too high, though it is far lower than that which great firms, great men of business, give to the brains which make those businesses profitable.'[7] No one disputed that the League was proving expensive: in its second fiscal period from 1 April–31 December 1920 the direct costs of the League totalled over 3.2 million francs, including 200,000 francs on furniture and fittings, 70,000 francs on books and periodicals, and the first gathering of the Assembly itself, which was eventually costed out at the neat figure of half a million.

A significant moment of embarrassment occurred when one representative demanded to discuss 'why intervention was not made in the war between Poland and Soviet Russia'. The lack of mention of the topic at the Assembly was, he claimed, a 'policy of hush-up'.[8] Leon Bourgeois, the original Chairman of the Council, responded by insisting that he could not speak on its behalf, but then did so anyway, 'I would point out that neither Poland nor the Soviet government asked the Council to intervene.'[9] He then went on to speculate that the League was not asked because 'it was clear its intervention would be of no avail,' adding that, 'At the time the Council of the League of Nations had, at the request of the [Allied] Supreme Council, tried to carry out an inquiry in Russia ... [but] Even moral intervention was rejected.' He neglected to mention two facts, now apparently erased from the collective memory: that Poland had started the war and that Great Britain and France (both Council Members) had supported and supplied her throughout.

In his closing speech to the Assembly, the newly appointed President of the Council, the Belgian politician Paul Hymans, asserted, 'The League of Nations has found itself; it works; it acts; it lives, and it has the will to live.'[10] It was not a view shared by the editor of the British *Daily Herald Newspaper*, who wrote, 'Eighteen months ago, when the League was born, there were very many who looked forward to the meeting of its Assembly as a historic event of profound significance. Today, there are very few who do not see it as a sorry farce.'[11] That judgement was most obvious when it came to the question of Armenia.

Chapter 47

The death of a nation

On 1 November the US Commissioner in Constantinople cabled his superiors in Washington: 'I am inclined to doubt the importance of the reported attack of the [Turkish] Nationalists on the Armenians ... I desire to warn the [State] Department in advance not to take these reports too seriously.'[1] His inclination was wrong. The Turkish nationalists had decided to end their ceasefire and resume the offensive in Armenia. When an Armenian diplomat was dispatched to London, he attempted in advance to secure a meeting with Curzon. A Foreign Office minion informed the Armenians that the Foreign Secretary was likely to be 'too busy'. When he visited on 12 November the Armenian emissary was fobbed off with a meeting with the Assistant Secretary, who bluntly made it 'quite clear that it was wholly out of the question that HMG [Her Majesty's Government] should send any military aid of any kind or accept a mandate or do anything whatsoever to render assistance'.[2] The British appeared to be washing their hands of Armenia.

The day before the Armenian diplomat's fruitless meeting, the Turkish nationalists had offered an armistice. But they demanded that the Armenians agree to sign before seeing the terms. There was a brief truce, but after a debate in the Armenian Parliament, the government refused and insisted it would continue to fight. The perilous nature of the situation was privately summed up by Montagu in a memorandum to Cabinet: 'Armenia is helpless unless the Bolsheviks help her. Turkey has practically ceased to exist and the combination of Islam with Bolshevism is an increasing menace and peril to British interests.'[3] The Bolsheviks were not planning to help. They were planning to take over. On 6 November a Communist Party Committee leader in the Caucasus recorded, 'Soviet revolution in Armenia means a breach in the front that capitalist Britain is erecting against us ... a Soviet coup in Armenia will serve as the first step towards the creation of a Soviet federation in the Caucasus'.[4] The Soviets, who were claiming to offer themselves as peacemakers in Armenia, were only doing so to achieve their own aims.

As their army fell apart, the Armenian government finally gave in, and on 18 November agreed to accept the Turkish demands. They had to give up all the territory the nationalists had acquired and hand over weapons and ammunition to the Turks. Among other conditions, the Armenians were forced to renounce the Treaty of Sevres, permanently giving up the lands in eastern Turkey that the Allies had bequeathed to them a few months before, subject to the boundaries being defined by President Wilson. In regards to Armenia, the Treaty of Sevres was now not worth the paper it was written on, which was exactly what Ataturk's nationalists wanted. Already, they had regained the areas of eastern Turkey that had been stripped from them following the end of the war. Their next step would be to try and force Britain and the other powers to accept the new reality on the ground.

Two days later, the situation in Armenia was debated at the Assembly of the League of Nations. Senator Henri Lafontaine of Belgium gave a passionate address to the Assembly, bluntly asserting, 'In time of peace Armenia is dying, a nation of a million inhabitants being destroyed under the eyes of the League of Nations which comprises forty-one States, with their armies numbering millions'.[5] The Assembly decided to create a special committee to examine the situation in Armenia, much to the disgust of one delegate, who lambasted the other members: 'We are told Armenia is suffering; she is in her agony and is appealing for help. These appeals reach us here. What solution is proposed to us? A committee. When there is in the house a sick person on the point of the death, do we send for a doctor? … No Gentlemen, we pause on the threshold and say: "A committee".'[6]

The Assembly did also adopt a resolution on 22 November, but it simply called, once again, for Allied governments to intervene 'in order to put an end in the shortest time possible to the horrors of the Armenian tragedy', suggesting that Armenia could still become a mandate, if any of the Powers were willing.[7] The resolution was supported by Balfour, the British representative, but he pointed out, 'Good intentions by themselves are perfectly useless, unless means can be found for carrying them into effect.'[8] As well as calling upon the Allies, the League also again wrote to the president of the United States, making clear that the re-proposed mandate was not trying to make the United States 'assume obligations' but simply wanted to offer 'the possibility of undertaking a task of such high humanitarian importance.'[9]

The League received a swift and revealing reply from the president, in which he admitted, 'I am without authorization to offer or employ military forces of the United States in any project for the relief of Armenia, and any material contributions would require the authorization of Congress which is not now in session and whose action I could not forecast.' Wilson could not offer men or money, but in the spirit of international peace, which he had strived for all his life, he offered the only thing he had left: 'I am willing ... to use my good offices and to proffer my personal mediation ... to end the hostilities now being waged against the Armenian people and to bring peace'. The news of his offer was joyously related to the League, as it seemed that the talk might eventually lead to material support, backed by the perceived clout of the president as peacemaker. The League, in a moment of blind optimism, messaged the British Foreign Office to ask if, in their opinion, Armenia would be able to defend herself if she received competent military advisers, along with supplies of munitions, clothing and food. When the question was received, one Foreign Office representative sarcastically noted privately, 'I do not believe that a wilderness of advisors or any amount of supplies would save Armenia'.[10]

On the night of 28 November Soviet regiments crossed the Armenian border. A pre-prepared announcement was released the following day: 'By the will and desire of the insurgent labouring people of Armenia, the Armenian Communist (Bolshevik) Party declares Armenia from this day a Socialist Soviet Republic.'[11] There were Soviet sympathisers in Armenia, but they were outnumbered by those who were deeply distrustful of Russia. The Armenian government had only ever really turned east because its pleas to the west had gone unanswered. In a foretaste for what would happen in later years to multiple states across Eastern Europe, the Soviets had manufactured a situation that allowed them to claim they were invading, not as an act of war but as an act of peace. Colonel Stokes, the British Chief Commissioner in the region, urgently telegraphed the Foreign Office in London with a statement of the blindingly obvious:

'My information is that this is not a spontaneous rising, but one organised by the Russian Bolsheviks'.[12]

The Armenian government had just lost the western half of its country to the Turks and now the Soviets were advancing from the east. Armenian soldiers simply gave up and joined the ranks of the advancing Russians. In an effort to retain some level of autonomy, the government agreed to align with Russia. An official agreement was signed on 2 December proclaiming Armenia as an Independent Socialist Soviet Republic. Its independence was underlined by the demand that the lead ministers resign and hand over power to a Russian-appointed Commissar. The Republic of Armenia was no more.

The new Chairman of the League of Nations Council touched on Armenia in his closing speech at the end of the first Assembly. He stated: 'The heart-rending condition of Armenia has been brought to our notice. For a long time the Great Powers have been preoccupied with the Armenian problem and they have been unable to solve it ... We have not found a mandatory, but at least we have succeeded in finding a mediator [President Wilson] ... Armenia is much in our thoughts and we earnestly desire to save her. It is our duty to work for this end.'[13] His words may have been genuine, but in reality the League was too late. Although the Allies, and particularly Great Britain, were arguably more responsible for the situation in Armenia than the League, the latter's total failure to achieve any meaningful action disgusted Lloyd George. He told a friend, 'The League of Nations is, I regret to say, deceptive and dangerous. They cannot even protect a little nation like Armenia. They do nothing but pass useless resolutions.'[14]

Chapter 48

Democracy and oil

T he Council of State of the first officially Arab-led government of
Mesopotamia convened for its inaugural meeting on 2 November.
Gertrude Bell was over the moon: 'If we can make them work
together and find their own salvation for themselves, what a fine thing it
will be. I see visions and dream dreams. But as we say in Arabic countless
times a day "Through the presence of His Excellency the Representative
of the King, and with the help of the Great Government, all please God,
must be well!".'[1]

Bell was a remarkable diplomat, linguist and Oriental expert, but
her perspective could occasionally be clouded by her own emotional
investment in the country she loved. She wavered between despondency
and joyous hope, sometimes in the space of a few short weeks as events
unfolded. While she was delighted by the prospect of some degree of Arab
own rule, British politicians in London were interested in other matters.
Now that the large-scale, organised uprising had been quelled attention
once more turned to oil.

The minister in charge of the government's Petroleum Department
wrote an urgent note to the Cabinet in mid-November: 'The serious
world shortage of oil and the almost complete dependence of this
country on supplies under foreign control compel me to press the
Cabinet for an immediate decision in regard to the method of operation
of the oil deposits of Mesopotamia.' He went on to admit, 'Whilst no
actual development can take place until the future administration of
Mesopotamia is decided, it is of great importance to have our policy
determined beforehand, so that valuable time may not be lost later.'[2]
The French were still being difficult, even though Millerand and Lloyd
George had agreed a memorandum on Mesopotamian oil at San Remo
in April. Having agreed the construction of the pipeline in exchange for
a share of revenues, they then suddenly demanded that Britain provide

specifics regarding the location of the fields where the wells would be sunk. The minister viewed this request as utter lunacy, replying that it was impossible to provide such specifics because 'many of the oil zones have not yet been discovered.' In any event, the British had still not decided whether the drilling and extraction of oil was to be paid for directly by government funding, by the government employing a commercial company, or by a private enterprise, with the government making money by taking royalties. Opinion was leaning towards using a private company, which had been the original plan until Lloyd George had intervened to halt it in January of 1920. Five months of uncertainty had been followed by four months of violent revolt, which had conspired to put the plans to extract Iraq's oil back by almost a year.

There were still concerns over security. General Haldane had only been able to put down the strongest elements of the revolt once reinforcements had arrived from India. Until that point in October, British actions had been severely limited. The arrival of men and aircraft had changed the nature of British actions, from defensive rescue missions to save isolated garrisons to offensive reprisals, but Haldane would not have that level of force at his disposable forever. It was never intended that the divisions fast-tracked to Mesopotamia would stay there indefinitely, it was simply too costly. A week into November Bell noted, 'Already India is clamouring for the return of the divisions she lent us. Very soon the force won't be here.'[3] Her view was that the British should 'patch up matters and leave them to the Arab Govt [sic] to settle', but she admitted that if British troops were withdrawn, the Arab government, such as it was, had none if its own. The result would be 'a chaotic local independence; but the rest of the country will suffer for it.' For Bell, it proved the point she had been making for years: 'If we had been setting up native institutions in the midst of order instead of in the midst of disorder, the task would have been incomparably easier.'

Haldane's view was a lot less nuanced: 'There can be no security for the future peace of Mesopotamia unless the punishment awarded were such as would discourage a repetition of this foolish outbreak.'[4] He also had little time for political solutions, writing, 'The period of negotiations, under all circumstances apt to be lengthy, is approaching … The Arab is cunning, but not as a rule clever, and [British] political officers, whom one might expect to understand the workings of his mind, are constantly at fault in their predictions.'[5] Among the 'political officers' he had no time for was Gertrude Bell, who he noted, 'Wrote to me on 30th June that the horizon was unclouded, and that the country gave every evidence of settling down. On that very date the trouble began'. Haldane blamed the political officers for demanding troops be 'sent hither and thither', claiming, 'The affair in which the Manchester Regiment had heavy losses was brought about by such pressure.' In fact, as Gertrude Bell had recounted at the time, the heavy losses that the Manchester Regiment experienced in the foolish march in the heat of a July summer were entirely the result of the ineptitude of the military commanders. Haldane did admit how close the whole affair had been, writing, 'Yes, I have had an anxious time, far exceeding anything experienced in France and Belgium, where it was bad enough at times [Hadane been a commander at Ypres on the Western Front]. At one time, and indeed for some weeks, our position was precarious and we might have been within an ace of losing Mesopotamia.' Both the politicians and generals were united in their desire to prevent a repeat.

The Council of State was only intended as a stop-gap measure ahead of the creation of an elected National Assembly, but now the idea of a national figurehead was gaining serious traction. Britain was going to gain Mesopotamia as a mandate and it was only viable if it was fiscally sustainable; and it was only fiscally sustainable if it did not require constant military expenditure. The appointment of a national figurehead would be an apparent answer to Arab demands for their own leadership, while also fulfilling the official mandate criteria of 'tutelage'. More importantly, it might lead to a settled security situation. The Naqib, who headed up the Council of State, was old and ill, therefore the most likely front-runner was, and always had been, Hussein's son Feisal. He was one of the few candidates who was likely to be acceptable to the majority of Arabs in Mesopotamia as well as the British. Feisal was well known to the British, having fought with and led an Arab guerrilla army against the Ottomans during the war, while at the same time his nationalist antics against the French in Syria burnished his credentials with the Arabs and upset the British less than the French would have liked.

Mesopotamia was not isolated from events taking place elsewhere. Near the end of the month, Bell wrote to her father, 'The news of the defeat of [General] Wrangel [in Crimea] and the final union between the

Turks and Bolshevists [in Armenia] has made a great impression here.'[6] As she phrased it in another letter home, 'The truth is that Asia, from the Mediterranean to the Indian frontier, is now such a devil's cauldron that it's impossible to feel convinced that we shall save Mesopotamia from the general confusion.'[7] Feisal seemed to offer a potential ray of hope.

Chapter 49

Bloody Sunday

In early November Winston Churchill called for a special Cabinet meeting to discuss the situation in Ireland. Attached to his request was a memo outlining his own thoughts. It was marked 'SECRET' with good reason. In the first point, he firmly defended reprisals: 'I cannot feel it right to punish the troops when goaded in the most brutal manner and finding no redress, they take action on their own account.'[1] He slammed the courts martial handed down, stating, 'It is not fair on the troops, it is not fair on the officers who command them.' Churchill said that he was receiving 'very strong' representations from military authorities that 'reprisals within strictly defined limits should be authorized [sic] by the Government and regulated by responsible officers.' He went on to propose a system of compulsory identity cards, on the basis that members of the IRA would not dare apply for them and therefore 'a system of sweeps and roundings up in large areas would … lead to the arrest of many men now being sought in vain.'

Almost exactly the same day, his Cabinet colleague Edwin Montagu wrote a memo calling for a 'discussion of Irish affairs', adding, 'I confess I am inclined to gloomy pessimism on the subject.'[2] But Montagu took the absolute opposition position to Churchill. As Secretary of State for India he was not party to most of the discussions over Ireland, so was not aware of the details, but was appalled by what he had heard about reprisals: 'I notice that uniformed men, undeterred, continue to commit reprisals, and I hear accounts of the "black and tan" officers as being wholly undisciplined, shooting and burning indiscriminately … I am told that they have every reason to believe that the Government has encouraged them in the action.' He wrote that he had heard reprisals were 'carefully planned', noting with open disgust, 'Terror is answered by terror, crime by crime, blood by blood. I feel a growing conviction that even if the murder gang in Ireland can be destroyed by this process …

[the younger generation] is entering upon manhood and public life with murder and revenge in their hearts.' It was a remarkable memorandum coming from a Cabinet minister, effectively accusing his own government of state-sponsored terror. He blamed the IRA for murders and outrages, but said the forces of the Crown were also guilty of outrages. Montagu concluded, 'If this is the situation on both sides, has not the time come for immediate negotiation?'

The IRA shootings and the army reprisals were the brutal public face of the war in Ireland. But there was also an unseen element: the work of the British security services to quietly bring down Sinn Fein. The operations in 1920 were nothing compared to the scale or complexity of the efforts undertaken by British intelligence against the IRA during 'The Troubles' in the latter part of the twentieth century, but there was an awareness that clandestine methods could succeed where the blunt instrument of uniformed men patrolling the streets was failing.

At the start of the year, British Army Intelligence in Ireland recruited around twenty army officers to undertake clandestine operations against the IRA. They received training in London and staggered their arrival in Dublin, where, under aliases, they took jobs and gradually built up contacts. Some of them were experienced spies who had worked for British military intelligence in Egypt and Palestine. They were quietly compiling a hit list of Republican leaders. They successfully assassinated an Irish Treasury Official connected to the IRA, but were then exposed through a series of unfortunate coincidences. One of the intelligence officers involved in the assassination admitted, when drunk, to a local girl what he had done and she told an IRA informant. Several other officers were exposed when their landlady unwittingly revealed to another informant that several of her British guests went out late at night, despite the official curfew. The IRA pieced together the identities of many of the spies and by November was ready to fight back. Michael Collins, the famous Republican leader who was Minister for Finance for the breakaway Irish government and the IRA's Director of Intelligence, wrote to the commander of the IRA Dublin Brigade on 17 November: '[I] have established addresses of the particular ones. Arrangements should now be made about the matter.'[3] The 21st was, he stated, 'A most suitable date and day I think.'

On Sunday morning, 21 November, IRA hit squads assembled across Dublin for a simultaneous attack. Fourteen men were killed by the hit squads, but they were not all involved in British Intelligence. In the eyes of the IRA, those targeted were nothing more than British spies and assassins, but in the eyes of the military they were regular combatants, murdered in cold blood. As Lloyd George phrased it: 'These men were soldiers, and took a soldier's risk.'[4]

The city was on edge as news of the killings spread, but a planned Gaelic football game between Dublin and Tipperary went ahead at Croke Park Stadium that afternoon, a little later than scheduled. While the game was underway, three armoured cars and multiple military lorries rumbled down Jones Road and pulled up outside the stadium where 5,000 spectators were watching the game. What happened next has been a point of contention for a century. The Irish account states that Black and Tans dismounted from the trucks, entered the stadium and opened fire without provocation. In the space of ninety seconds they fired 228 rounds. One of the Dublin players recalled, 'We ran, we didn't know where we were going, but we ran to the centre of the field and we didn't realize we could see the bullets [hitting].'[5] Thirteen people were killed and sixty more were injured. Among the dead was one of the Dublin players, an IRA man named Michael Hogan. Even the closed-door British Army inquiry, the proceedings of which were kept secret for decades, concluded no order to open fire had been given and that the action was unjustified.[6]

The official British version of events maintained that members of the IRA, who were definitely in the crowd, opened fire first. The fact of the matter was that British forces had deliberately shot at a massed crowd of civilians, causing panic. Two more people were killed in the crush of bodies as men, women and children ran for their lives. The crowds fleeing down one of the roads away from the stadium were greeted by the sight of an armoured car driving towards them, firing its machine gun into the air. Ambulance drivers directed to the scene recounted what they witnessed when they reached Croke Park. One told the inquiry, 'When we arrived there we found a man inside the gates, dead. We placed him in the ambulance and saw that his leg was badly shattered. On the opposite side of the field we found a woman. She was dead.'[7] The woman was twenty-six-year-old Jane Boyle. She worked at a local butchers and had been due to marry her fiancé, a Dublin motor mechanic, five days later. Her brother was summoned as a witness to the official inquiry, but a lawyer for the family refused to let him appear and told the hearing, 'I decline to produce witnesses on the ground[s] that this is not a public inquisition … I protest against an inquiry held behind closed doors into a tragedy which is one of the most awful in the annals of our country.'[8] The events of 21 November became known as the first 'Bloody Sunday' in Irish history.

Chapter 50

Old World, New World

The President's doctor was adamant: whatever Wilson's own ambitions might be, medically, his voice would not stand the strain of an extended period of public speaking. Reluctantly, the president agreed. Wilson would not deliver his final State of the Union address in person. Instead, he wrote down his remarks and sent them to Congress to be read out on 7 December. He began by quoting Lincoln, asserting that it was 'by faith alone' that the world could be 'lifted out of its present confusion and despair'. Winston Churchill had been right when he had remarked at dinner with Lloyd George in Paris eleven months previously that the 'old world' would wag its tail. The peace that had supposedly been won through the greatest slaughter humanity had ever witnessed had never begun. There had been another war in Europe and uprisings in Asia and the Middle East, while the Bolshevik menace cast a shadow over the entire globe. 'The old world', the president wrote, 'is just now suffering from a wanton rejection of the principle of democracy and a substitution of the principle of autocracy ... forces of chaos and tyranny ... are playing so disastrous a part in the fortunes of the free peoples of more than one part of the world ... This is the time of all others when Democracy should prove its purity and its spiritual power to prevail. It is surely the manifest destiny of the United States to lead in the attempt to make this spirit prevail.'[1]

Wilson did not openly criticise the man who was shortly to take his place in the Oval Office, but the first part of his speech was a lament for the new world as he had once imagined it and an implicit criticism of everything his successor stood for. What saddened the president was not just the course of events, but being forced to sit on the sidelines and watch as his own nation turned its back on the ideals that he considered to be those of America. 'The United States', he asserted, 'cannot refuse this role of champion without putting the stigma of rejection upon the great and devoted men who brought its government into existence.' Wilson might have added that in refusing to take on the role of 'champion', the United States was also rejecting him.

Ten days later members of the American Committee for the Independence of Armenia visited President-elect Warren G. Harding at his home in Ohio. They were meeting Harding to ask him to approve a memorandum that they hoped would go to the White House and from there on to the Allied Supreme Council. It stated America's continued interest in a 'self-governing and free state' of Armenia and called on the Allies to enforce the Treaty of Sevres. Harding humoured them and intimated that he would not oppose it. The humanitarian lobbyists sent the text on to the president. They waited a month before receiving a reply from Wilson's secretary: 'While the President did not feel justified in acting on the suggestion made in your letter, he is not unmindful of the issue involved in the present serious plight of Armenia, or of the necessity of the most generous spirit of co-operation among the Powers in the effort to preserve the independence of the Armenian people.'[2] The sad truth of the matter was that Wilson, once the head of state who had spearheaded the drive for a new, equitable and peaceable world, knew that he was now a lone voice crying in the wilderness.

As Wilson was putting pen to paper to compose his final State of the Union address, European officials were gathering once more to try and conclude a post-war settlement. The meeting between the Allies and the Germans at Spa in July had still not solved the issue of reparations. For most of history, the winners in any war had immediately stripped bare the conquered through loot and pillage, but in an age of armistices and treaties, with the League of Nations watching on, such blatant tactics were no longer acceptable. Instead, payback for German aggression was to be extracted over an extended period of time. But it was no good simply demanding money if Germany could not, or would not, hand it over. The situation was further complicated by the fact that the Allies did not actually want German money. Germany had abandoned the Gold Standard at the start of the Great War so, from 1914 onwards, its currency no longer had a definitive value in precious metal and the *Papiermark*, which had replaced the gold-linked Mark, had depreciated quickly. The Allies therefore wanted reparations to be paid in gold, or in a foreign currency which was backed by gold, or in raw materials.

Such a process could only be worked out with the agreement of the conquered nation and so, much to the chagrin of the French, two years after the war had ended, the final total of reparations and the details of how Germany would pay had still not been agreed. Germany had started delivering coal shipments, but already these were below quota. The plan was that the value of the shipments would eventually be deducted from the overall sum Germany had to pay, but still there was no agreement on an actual figure.

After the failure to come to terms at Spa, the Allies and Germany had consented to set up a special commission, with a delegation from each nation, which would meet to try and thrash out a solution. The British civil servant in the room was Sir John Bradbury. He had previously been Private Secretary to Lloyd George's predecessor, Herbert Asquith, and subsequently Permanent Secretary to the Treasury. The Cabinet informed him that one of his primary objectives was to 'undertake a thorough investigation into the subject of Germany's capacity to pay.'[3] Even though it was years since the war had ended, the instructions to Sir John Bradbury revealed the often-overlooked truth that the Allies were still actually uncertain whether the German government could even afford anything like the size of payment the Allies were planning on demanding.

The entire exercise was to some extent one of smoke and mirrors. Political opinion demanded that Germany be forced to pay an extra-ordinary sum that would be seen in the Allied countries as a fair recompense. Political reality demanded that the final sum should be something Germany could feasibly pay. In the words of the head of the German delegation at the Brussels meetings, 'immeasurable damage,' would result 'if a theoretical amount were to be demanded without regard to actual possibilities'.[4] This would, he said, 'drive Germany into despair.' The situation was further complicated by the perspectives of different British representatives. Having initially favoured 'an elastic scheme' of reparations, the British Ambassador to Berlin suddenly changed his mind in Brussels and pushed for a final figure. Far from being deliberately difficult, the German delegation was being the most practical and level headed in Brussels. They wanted to secure a loan from America to stabilise the *Papiermark* and thus halt the depreciation, which, if it continued on its current course, would make every single cash reparations payment increasingly expensive. The push to nail down a total left German concerns about financing and payment methods ignored, leading the head of the German delegation to cable Berlin, 'The car has now attained a high speed thanks to the pressure of some Allied representatives, and it cannot be stopped without injury; it only remains to guide it cautiously down its dangerous course.'[5] The first gathering of the special commission closed just before Christmas, with all the major issues over German reparations still unresolved.

Progress was however being made as far as German disarmament was concerned. A memorandum by the British General Staff, circulated by Churchill in late December, stated that the German government was on course to finally meet its target of reducing its army to 100,000 men by the start of 1921. He noted, 'From a military point of view, the disarmament of Germany has been carried [out] sufficiently far to prevent any fear of an organised aggressive military operation on her part in the near future', adding, 'There is no doubt that Bolshevism, and not Germany, is at present the danger to peace in Europe.'[6]

Chapter 51

Friends and enemies

The British government were still hoping that the offer of trade with Soviet Russia would secure a new peace and potentially tame the Bolshevist threat to some degree. Now that the White Army had been routed from its last redoubt on the Crimean peninsula, the awkward complication of British assistance being provided to pro-Tsarist forces was removed from the equation, while along the Polish-Russian border there was an uneasy truce; neither Russia nor Poland was currently capable of another full-scale war. The Russian economy was in a dire state and the course of events seemingly opened the way for a potential trade deal with Britain. Curzon remained deeply sceptical. The British had received 'political assurances' from Russia, which, in Curzon's view, 'Should neither be evaded, nor whittled away, nor should evaporate in misty generalities, leading to indefinite procrastination'.[1] He clearly stated his concern on 13 December: 'I was afraid that unless we were very much on the alert the Russians might get their Trade Agreement, while we should lose what is in my view, our sole *quid pro quo*, *viz.*, the cessation of Soviet hostilities and propaganda both at home and in the East.' Negotiations were moving towards a position of accepting Russian demands to agree a trade deal and then to hold a later conference to agree obligations on 'activity in the East'. The idea appalled Curzon, who wrote, 'I once again plead with my colleagues not to allow ourselves to be cheated by these tactics.'

Simultaneously, Britain was reconsidering its position on Turkey and the hard-won Treaty of Sevres appeared to be going out of the window. Churchill was pushing for a rapprochement, with support from Montagu at the India Office. In Churchill's view, it was impossible for Britain to maintain its position in the Near East and India except on a basis of friendly relations with Turkey.[2] Lloyd George objected against making a definite shift to attempt to woo Ataturk. But the issue was debated at length ten days later and the conclusion of the 13 December Cabinet meeting was that an opportunity had arisen to arrive at 'an understanding with the Turks and making the conditions of the Treaty of Sevres less heavy on them.'[3] In view of Britain's reduced resources – a situation brought to the fore due to events in Mesopotamia – Churchill pushed for a pragmatic foreign policy, noting:

> The only way we can exert influence in the Middle East and safeguard our enormous and varied interests there, is by dividing up the local Powers so that if we have some opponents, we have also at any rate some friends. This is what we have always done in the whole of our past history … When Russia was our enemy, Turkey was our friend, when Turkey was our enemy, Russia was our friend. We have been accustomed to utilise to the full the division between the Arab and the Turk … Now we are out of joint with the whole lot at once.[4]

If Britain showed a willingness to bend what had been agreed at the Treaty of Sevres and accept Kemal Ataturk and his nationalist Turkish government, it would at least give Britain one friend in the Middle East. The hope was also that it would lure Turkey away from the Bolshevik orbit and result in Britain creating a buffer between Soviet expansionism and British oil interests in Persia and Mesopotamia.

In July the Soviets had organised the first Congress of the Peoples of the East, held in Soviet-controlled Azerbaijan. The alarming invitation to 'the enslaved peoples of Persia, Armenia and Turkey', printed in a Russian newspaper, read as follows: 'Peasants of Anatolia! The English, Italian and French governments have kept Constantinople under the fire of their guns; they have imprisoned the Sultan, have forced him to agree to the dismemberment of purely Turkish territory … you are urgently called to the colours under Kemal [Ataturk] Pasha, in order to fight the foreign invasion'.[5] It was exactly the kind of propaganda the British wanted to see stopped.

Ataturk meanwhile was carefully managing relations with the Soviets and accepting Soviet financial aid. A Russian consul visiting eastern Turkey in September 1920 took with him one million gold roubles, money which helped to fight the Armenians. The great British fear was that with

Turkey aligned to the Soviet Russia, Persia and even Mesopotamia was open to attack from the Turks, or the Soviets, or a Communist fifth column. The fears were a gross exaggeration of the reality, but contained enough elements of truth to cause concern. When a formerly 'wildly nationalist' Baghdad newspaper suddenly and suspiciously became strongly pro-Bolshevist in December, the newly-appointed Iraqi Minister of Interior suggested that action should be taken. Bell recorded, 'He thinks it should be suppressed and I believe he's right.'[6] The perceived Communist threat was something that the whole British administration in Mesopotamia was alive to, although Sir Percy Cox was fairly sanguine about it. He remarked to Gertrude Bell on one long car journey, 'It will be a pity, won't it, if this Bolshevist business queers our pitch just when the country has got the first chance it ever had.'[7]

Ataturk was merely playing along with the Soviets to secure his own interests, the official Turkish Communist party being a case in point. A few months before, he had admitted in a private telegram to one of the other leaders of the Turkish revolutionaries that Communism 'was being diffused in our country from internal and external sources … and unless necessary measures were taken, the peace and unity of the Turkish people would be put in jeopardy. Thus it was concluded that the wisest step would be to get some friends to form a communist party under the guidance of the government.'[8]

On the evening of 21 December, Lloyd George met with Leonid Krasin, the Russian trade negotiator. As well as the propaganda problem, there was also another issue of Soviet 'debt' to British subjects. At the outbreak of the revolution, the property of the wealthy had been seized across Russia and 'returned' to the people. Some of those who lost out were British, and one aggrieved woman had written to Winston Churchill earlier that month. Mrs Blanche Lunn proposed that before any trade was resumed with Russia, the Soviet government ought to be made to pay back what they had 'robbed' British subjects of:

> I am a widow, with a lame delicate daughter, and my small fortune was invested in a cotton mill near Moscow. This was taken over by the Bolsheviks in 1917, and has been worked for their benefit ever since. I have had to give up my home … and my daughter is trying to earn her own living. My only son

came from Russia … He was wounded in France and after the Armistice he volunteered to join General Denikin's forces in South Russia, returning and being demobilised this year … Is it too late for anything to be done for us? I know there are hundreds of British subjects living now in this country in poverty, who were turned out of Russia with nothing more than they could carry, and only enough money to pay their fares home, the rest of their possessions being appropriated by the Bolsheviks. These are not Tzarist [sic] debts but Bolshevik debts, and ought to be paid by them. It is not pleasant to read that "M. Krassin [sic] is paying twenty-two guineas per week for his flat".[9]

Krasin was adamant, however, that there would be no settlement of 'debts' until a date had been set for a political conference, which would only happen once the basis of a trade deal had been agreed. He was also concerned that once the Russians paid for British goods, payments were liable to be held up in the courts. British creditors who, like Blanche Lunn, had had their Russian assets seized, were already lining up lawyers to take the government to court to recover their losses if Russian money reached Britain. In the face of the long list of roadblocks, the Cabinet concluded that 'at present an agreement was improbable'. They even decided on the political line to present to the electorate. If negotiations broke down it was 'desirable they should fail on an issue like hostile propaganda, which could be popularly understood, rather than on more technical questions affecting payment'.[10]

Chapter 52

Independent minded

Since the riots eight months before, an uneasy peace had been maintained in Palestine. But there were still causes for concern in the country that was to become another of Britain's mandates under the League of Nations. An 18 December memorandum by the military staff outlining the future risks in Palestine stated, 'The country has not yet settled down under the current Administration ... Riots are likely to break out in large towns such as Jerusalem, Jaffa, Haifa, Nablus &c. There is strong feeling between the Arabs and Jews, as the former are under the impression that their land is to be forcibly taken away under the British mandate and given to the Jews.'[1]

There were 9,800 British and a further 19,000 Indian troops stationed there in December, but many were already being withdrawn and it was planned to have only 9,000 British and 6,000 Indian troops in Palestine by the end of January 1921. Reducing the garrison was an 'urgent necessity' but the threat of potential disorder was a major concern. Churchill added his own note to the memo by the military staff, stating dejectedly, 'So far as the security of the Empire is concerned, we are the weaker, rather than the stronger, by the occupation of Palestine.' His view was shared by Field Marshal Sir Henry Wilson, the highest ranking British soldier in the Middle East, who would later be assassinated by IRA gunmen. Wilson stated, 'The problem of Palestine is exactly the same ... as the problem of Ireland, namely two peoples living in a small country hating each other like hell.'[2] From the Field Marshal's perspective, there was no point in the British being there at all: 'The best thing we can do is to clear out of Jewland as soon as we can and let the Jews run the country'.

Since the *Nebi Musa* riots in April, the situation in Palestine had been relatively calm. There had been Arab protests and strikes, but nothing on the scale of the violence over Easter. In contrast to Iraq, Palestine was as calm as a millpond. The proposal to withdraw the entire British position in Iraq to Basra to reduce military expenditure, while maintaining soldiers in Palestine, greatly angered Gertrude Bell, who thought that it showed a favouritism towards Palestine: 'What makes me also pretty rabid,' she wrote to her father, 'is that we are cheerfully paying for two Divisions in Palestine. That tiny country, with its comparatively high stage of civilization, could be held by a few thousand gendarmes under British officers. We keep two Divisions there in order to carry out our iniquitous policy of making it a home for the Jews.'[3]

Gertrude Bell's strong objections exemplify a rift within the British administration over the policy towards Palestine. The perception that decision makers in Westminster were pro-Jewish had not been helped by the appointment of Sir Herbert Samuel as High Commissioner, replacing Ronald Storrs, in June 1920. Storrs wrote an upbeat note to his successor, congratulating him on the appointment and remarking that a 'great adventure' awaited him. In truth, however, Storrs thought the appointment of Herbert Samuel to be 'mad'.[4] First of all, Herbert Samuel was a Jew, and secondly, at the very least, had Zionist sympathies. In 1915, when Ottoman Turkey had entered the war, he had penned a memo to the then Foreign Secretary outlining a proposal to conquer Palestine and establish a Jewish state. His appointment as High Commissioner seemed to be such a coup for the Zionist cause that when it was announced, Chaim Weizmann had written to his wife, 'Well my darling, our trials have come to an end.'[5] In practice, Samuel was far more even handed than either side had expected. But because he was a Jew and a known Zionist sympathiser, his appointment was, understandably, never accepted by Arab representatives. One organisation sent a formal message of complaint to the British administration the week before he arrived, which summed up the general Arab sentiment: 'Sir Herbert Samuel [is] regarded as a Zionist leader, and his appointment as [the] first step in [the] formation of [a] Zionist national home in the midst of Arab people contrary to their wishes. Inhabitants cannot recognise him, and Muslim-Christian Society cannot accept responsibility for riots or other disturbances of peace.'[6] In December 1920 Palestine was enjoying an unsteady peace, but the following year there would be a renewed outbreak of communal violence.

At the same time as the British were sanctioning a trial of Arab self-government in Iraq and debating the future of Palestine, India was going to the polls. The subjects of British India had been represented in the Imperial Legislative Council for decades, but with only very limited influence on policy (it largely extended to being permitted to ask questions about it, but not actually alter anything). The most significant change of the 1919 Government of India Act had been to devolve some powers to regional Provincial Councils and to create a new Central Legislative Assembly, which was effectively a lower elected house with 105 members and which equally represented British Indian subjects. However, it was hardly the bright new dawn of Indian democracy. In addition, even though it could be termed a 'general election', there was no universal suffrage as only around one million people, out of the total population of 250 million, were eligible to vote in the polls that took place throughout November and December. Many opponents of British rule, unsurprisingly, opposed the elections. In line with his programme of non-cooperation which he had launched in August, Gandhi lobbied for a boycott.

Gandhi's non-cooperation movement had not brought the country to a standstill, but his actions were being watched carefully. He was attempting to gain a following among students, who he encouraged to quit British education establishments. On 5 December the Indian 'Home Department' reported that Gandhi's visit to schools in Varanasi, in Uttar Pradesh, had not brought about a mass exodus of students: 'According to present information not many students are prepared to follow him into [the] wilderness. We would be surprised if even 5 or 1 percent leave … None, so far, actually have'.[7] Other higher education establishments across the country were reporting reduced attendance, but there was no wave of desertion. Gandhi had opened his own 'National University' in Surat, but this was deemed a school 'for propagandism rather than instruction.'[8] In a speech in Allahabad in December, Gandhi denounced the government – which now included elected representatives from across the whole country – as 'satanic', but stronger rhetoric could not hide the fact that his efforts to create a mass movement against the British were faltering. In the northern region of Punjab, locals were boycotting established courts and foreign goods, and were refusing to sign up for the army if it meant service in Mesopotamia, but the movement was only active in the towns. British officials reported, 'Attempts [are] being made to spread non-cooperation among villages, but, in [the] opinion of officers touring districts, [are] shallow and unreal, and people know nothing about it and do not care.'[9]

They added, '[The] General feeling [is] that Gandhi and party have lost influence through campaign against schools.' Gandhi's calls for a new India did resonate among the young educated elite, but it was they who had the most to lose.

Voters were not swayed by the calls for a boycott and across India anti-British agitators had to adopt different tactics. In Bombay turnout was around fifteen percent. Supporters of the non-cooperation movement had cycled around districts, informing electors that the vote had been cancelled at the last minute, while also spreading rumours that the elections were intended as a way of increasing taxes. They may have been partly responsible for the low turnout, but another cause was the 'General lack of organisation and zeal on [the] part of candidates.'[10] The lethargy was not universal. Turnout in districts of Madras varied from forty to seventy percent. In one Muslim district, an illiterate 'coolie' was elected to the legislative council unopposed, a development noted in the report from the government of India to the British Cabinet with open contempt, which pointed out 'the new Council will contain several unsuitable members.' In Punjab, leaders of the non-cooperation movement resorted to strong-arm tactics. Turnout in rural areas, which voted a few days earlier, averaged around thirty-six percent, but in the region's two major cities, Lahore and Amritsar, the votes held on 8 December were a failure. In Amritsar, where the year previously 379 peaceful protestors had been massacred by the British, non-cooperation leaders employed hooligans to rampage through the streets, while in Lahore, voters, candidates and officials were all intimidated.

The split between Hindu and Muslim opposition to British rule appeared to be widening and non-cooperation only seemed to be working where it was being brought about through the threat of violence, which went against everything Gandhi had hoped for. The English language weekly newspaper, *The Pioneer Mail*, reported on 17 December, 'Whatever may be said to the contrary by certain Extremist newspapers which are naturally anxious to keep up the illusion of a great wave of non-co-operation sweeping across the country, there can be no doubt that Mr. Gandhi's programme has hitherto failed to gain any substantial or conspicuous success. Intimidation, moral and physical, may have prevented a certain number of voters from going to the polls, but the abstentions were due in the main to sheer apathy'. The assessment by the British was that 'Gandhi is regarded with veneration, but his [non-cooperation] programme is regarded with tolerance extended to children's games.'

Opposition to British rule was still divided. Earlier in the year Gandhi had aligned himself with the Muslim *Khalifat* movement to attempt to unite Hindus and Muslims against British rule. Increasingly, *Khalifat* leaders appeared to be shifting away from Gandhi's desire for the independence movement to be non-violent. He was even being denounced within the movement. Muhammed Ali Jinnah was a Muslim political campaigner who would go on to found the modern state of Pakistan. In the final week of December, Jinnah addressed university students at Fergusson College, Bombay. He told them that he was a believer in non-cooperation, but said that Gandhi's efforts were 'premature' and that the programme was 'harmful and impractical in the present state of political consciousness'.[11] Achieving independence for India would take nearly another three decades.

Chapter 53

A city on fire

A clandestine war was being fought in the southern Irish city of Cork. British forces manned checkpoints in the winding maze of streets, stopping and searching indiscriminately, while IRA Volunteers organised covert 'patrols' in the hope of launching a hit and run attack. Most of the time they waited in vain. A Cork university student, Michael O'Donoghue, who was a member of the Volunteers in the city, recalled, 'We spent hours hovering around waiting to have a crack at the military party from the prison, who occasionally slipped out for an adventurous "refresher" at the local hostelry.'[1] Each time the Volunteers went out, they had to pick up and then drop off weapons at hidden caches to avoid being caught in possession. The risks were not insignificant. A Liberal Member of Parliament, whose constituency was in Durham, but who had been born in Ireland, asked the government in the House of Commons on 9 December how many people had been shot in Ireland for refusing to halt when ordered. The Chief Secretary for Ireland responded, 'The number of persons fired at in Ireland since the 1st January last for failing to halt when challenged is, approximately, 200, and the numbers killed and wounded are 41 and 43, respectively.'[2] The next day, martial law was declared in counties across southern Ireland, which included Cork, Kerry, Limerick and Tipperary. Anyone found carrying firearms could now face the death penalty, as could anyone taking part in 'insurrection'. Henceforth they would be considered guilty of waging war against the King.

Lloyd George played golf on the afternoon of Saturday 11 December in north London. When it came to Ireland, the prime minister told his friend and golfing partner that the gunmen were being 'got under' and suggested that before long he would be able to negotiate.[3] He could not have anticipated what would happen in Cork that very evening.

At the usual time of 8pm, a group of British Auxiliaries left their barracks in a lorry. Their routine had been observed. By leaving each night at the same time and driving the same route, they had left themselves vulnerable to attack. Six IRA men waited with grenades and pistols at a tight bend. One grenade landed inside the lorry and then the ambushers opened fire. One Auxiliary died and eleven others were seriously wounded. The IRA men dispersed and ran off. Michael O'Donoghue, who was at home when the raid happened, recalled, 'From the moment we heard of the bloody ambush of the Auxies [sic] that night we had a peculiar sense of impending tragedy, a foreboding that something terrible was going to happen.'

The Irish cause was gaining publicity, and even organisations within Britain were questioning the official narrative. The League of Nations Union – the popular group set up in Britain to support the ideals of the League of Nations – sent a special envoy to find out more. George Mallory was a world-famous climber, who would later die on his third attempt to reach the summit of Everest. His selection as envoy was primarily down to his personal connections to one of the key leaders of the Union, and the fact that he was getting itchy feet working as a schoolteacher while preparations were underway for the next assault on the mountain, so he had volunteered. Remarkably, he received an all-access pass to the IRA: a leading member wrote on the back of a photograph of Mallory, 'Mr G. Mallory is anxious to have first-hand information as to acts of oppression and terror. I shall be glad if he can be assisted.'[4] Mallory was taken around Dublin and, by a stroke of perverse luck, was dragged from his bed when British security forces raided his lodgings in the middle of the night. He had always had sympathy with the Irish cause, having climbed the mountains of Snowdonia with an Irish friend who became an IRA gun-runner, but his experiences in Ireland left him in no doubt. He wrote afterwards, 'There has been wrong on both sides, but national aspirations, a passionate idealism, is to be found only on one side. It is to this fate that Irishmen appeal when they exclaim "If only the people of England knew. If only they would come and see."'[5]

The violent night of 11 December only got worse. The reinforcements on the scene of the IRA ambush evicted the occupants of nearby houses and then burned them to the ground. Uniformed men roamed the streets, looting shops, firing into the air and setting trams and buildings on fire. As the Cork Opera House spilled its audience onto the pavement in the late evening, the civilians, in town for a night out, quickly realised that something was happening. A young woman who had gone to watch Gilbert and Sullivan's *The Gondoliers* with her fiancé recalled, 'We left the Opera House as planned and turned along the quay towards St Patrick's street ... Almost immediately we could hear the shouting and smell the burning.'[6] When firemen went to tackle the blazes they saw British forces pouring petrol on fires. Firemen were shot at by drunk Black and Tans and later reported that British forces had cut their hoses as they tried to tackle the various conflagrations now spreading across the centre of Cork. The city's library was engulfed and firefighters could not attempt to douse the flames attacking the City Hall as Auxiliaries refused to grant them access to a fire hydrant nearby.

As dawn broke, the extent of the devastation was revealed. One Sinn Fein activist wandered the streets aghast: 'Last night in Cork was such a night of destruction and terror as we have not yet had. An orgy of destruction and ruin: the calm sky frosty red – red as blood with the burning city, and the pale cold stars looking down on the scene of desolation and frightfulness. The finest premises in the city are destroyed'.[7] The *Irish Times* assessed in its report the following day that an area of five acres had been completely devastated. One of the Auxiliaries, a former British soldier, wrote to his girlfriend: 'You will have read all about Cork. Suffice to say I was there and very actively involved to boot until dawn on Sunday. I just escaped the ambush ... but later arrived as a reinforcement. We took sweet revenge.'[8]

The official reaction from the British government was at first one of complete denial. The Chief Secretary for Ireland later claimed in the House that there was 'no evidence' the fires had been started by forces of the Crown and alleged that Sinn Feiners were responsible, to jeers from the opposition benches. A commission of members of the British Labour Party was already in Cork on a research mission in early December and started making immediate enquiries. Some of the group wrote a damning note to Lloyd George: 'The statements made by the Chief Secretary of the House of Commons confirming the burning of Cork are greatly inaccurate. The parliamentary members of the Labour Commission who visited Cork yesterday are convinced that the fires were the work of Crown Forces ... We, therefore demand independent inquiries into [the] recent incidents in Cork. If the government refuse, the British public will draw its own conclusions.'[9]

In Ireland there was almost universal outrage, but the Roman Catholic Bishop of Cork laid the blame at the feet of the IRA. At midday mass on the Sunday after the burnings, he condemned the destruction, but said it was caused by a 'murderous ambush' and then threatened to 'issue a decree of excommunication against anyone who, after this notice, shall take part in an ambush or a kidnapping or attempted murder or arson.'[10] His comments drew widespread condemnation. The burning of Cork created one of the most powerful images of the conflict in Ireland, which the *Illustrated London News* printed across its entire front page a week later on 18 December: it shows a sombre crowd staring at the blackened shell of the City Hall, grey smoke still lifting into a leaden sky.

Five days later the Government of Ireland Act passed into law. It officially partitioned Ireland, giving 'Home Rule' to one parliament in Belfast and another in Dublin. In Ulster, the legislation was welcomed, not because the Protestant majority wanted a parliament, but because it guaranteed that the north could not be subsumed into a united, independent Ireland. Lloyd George viewed it as part of a 'double policy' to 'crush murder and make peace with moderates', a policy which, behind the scenes, he was secretly pursuing.[11] The go-between was a Catholic Irish Archbishop from Australia, whose nephew had been killed on Bloody Sunday. He passed messages between the British government and Irish representatives, including Michael Collins.

Lloyd George insisted that the IRA lay down its weapons before any truce could start, a position Michael Collins and other leaders refused to countenance. The IRA leader also admitted that he would not be able to make his men give up their guns. Simultaneously, British military commanders were claiming that the hardline approach was working. At an afternoon Cabinet meeting dedicated entirely to Ireland on 29 December, the general in overall command of British forces in Ireland stated the military situation was 'improving', in part because of the implementation of martial law, which he wanted to impose across the whole country.[12] The struggle within Lloyd George's own mind is revealed in his comments in the meeting. He told the Cabinet that 'all kinds of attempts' had been made to secure a truce and asked the generals present, 'If there was a chance of patching up some kind of truce ... could they keep their men in hand?', pointedly adding that there had been 'a good deal of drunkenness' amongst the Black and Tans. Remarkably, the prime minister was openly suggesting that if he managed to broker a cessation of hostilities, it would most likely be wrecked by the auxiliary forces the government had sent to Ireland to maintain law and order. The idea of a truce was anathema to several of the military commanders, one of whom told the Cabinet that the IRA would simply use the time to reorganise and that 'they would certainly regard a truce as a sign of weakness.'

At the same meeting the Cabinet heard that an army inquiry into the burning of Cork had found that the burnings had been carried out by Auxiliaries. The official minute taker recorded, 'The opinion was expressed that the effect of publishing the Report ... would be disastrous to the Government's whole policy in Ireland.' There would be no truce in Ireland in 1920 and the inquiry into the burning of Cork would be suppressed for years.

Chapter 54

Winter in Baghdad

'It has been bitterly cold this week,' wrote Gertrude Bell in the first days of December, 'I find oil stoves are [an] insufficient means of keeping out [the] frost and shall be glad when it's a little warmer.'[1] The cold was not the only nagging problem. Edwin Montagu, the Secretary of State for India, who, despite his every effort to get rid of the responsibility, was still technically in departmental charge of Mesopotamia, cabled Sir Percy Cox on 1 December. His tone was apologetic: 'I am very reluctant to trouble you with financial difficulties in the midst of your other urgent preoccupations. But the situation here is really serious in view of universal and often unreasoning demand for economy in all directions … It would greatly assist me if you could estimate roughly what is the smallest number of troops, British and Indian, with which you think it would be possible to carry on during [the] next financial year provided general conditions do not appreciably deteriorate'.[2] If the High Commissioner had ever harboured any illusions about what the priorities were in Whitehall, they were at least instantly debunked: Montagu's department even seemed to follow a budget-based calendar.

In December 1920 there were a total of 18,000 British and 85,000 Indian troops in Mesopotamia and Persia, who collectively cost the taxpayer £30 million a year. After the start of the revolt, the garrison had been increased by a further 22,000. Although General Radcliffe, the Director of Military Operations in the region, had some sympathy with the British taxpayer, who he said 'may be pardoned for wanting to know what he is getting for his 20 or 30 millions a year', he had no sympathy for notional economy drives. In a message to Churchill on 7 December, he tersely noted that. in the previous year, 'Great pressure was being brought on the military authorities to reduce this figure [the number of troops]', adding, 'it is clear that we ran things too fine and that a great disaster was only narrowly avoided'.[3] In effect, the army was telling the government 'I told you so.'

On 13 December the Cabinet debated the Mesopotamia problem and concluded that even a reduced budget of £25 million a year was unaffordable. The suggestion, which Lloyd George himself had stood up in the House of Commons in June and insisted would lead to 'chaos', was suddenly back on the table: perhaps it was feasible to just station British troops in Basra in the south to guard Iraq's oil and leave the rest of the country well alone. The idea had its attractions, not least that the cost of the number of troops needed was estimated at only about £8 million. Churchill was all in favour. The proposal had been resurrected by the War Office and Churchill himself was actively exploring the decidedly optimistic idea that the whole of Iraq could be controlled from the air by eight Royal Air Force squadrons working in tandem with armoured cars on the ground. Montagu sent an enquiring message to Percy Cox.

The High Commissioner dispatched a remarkably restrained official reply on 20 December, in which he suggested that if the War Office proposal to pull back to Basra were accepted 'we should before long either have to withdraw altogether or reconquer the country'.[4] Clearly not wanting to appear obstructive, he intimated that such a move might be possible two years into the future, but in the present circumstances the proposition was 'not a practicable one'. He also added, although no one seemed to care, that such a proposition was not in keeping with Great Britain's commitment to the League of Nations to take on Iraq as a mandate. Gertrude Bell was considerably less restrained when she found out, describing the idea as 'preposterous', writing, 'Can you imagine Great Britain content to remain at Basrah [sic] in a perpetual state of war? Of course not.'[5]

Cox's rebuff of the communique from London was backed up by his senior military commander, General Haldane. The general had never flinched from a robust exchange of views and cabled Churchill that Basra was the 'most unhealthy part of the country', expanding on his objection by stating that such a withdrawal would require considerable time and thought to put in place. While General Haldane and Percy Cox disagreed on the idea of letting the Arabs govern themselves, they were firmly united in the view that retreating to Basra was not an option. Churchill was not impressed. He added his own note to Haldane's telegram supporting Cox, suggesting, 'I fear we shall find ourselves confronted with a very stubborn resistance from all those on the spot, both military and civil.'[6]

In the face of 'resistance' from the men on the ground, Churchill took matters into his own hands. On 23 December he telegrammed Haldane and effectively ordered him to start taking the idea seriously. He angrily informed the general, 'The Cabinet regard the necessity for the early reduction of expenditure by the withdrawal of military forces as entirely over-ruling any consideration for the internal security of the country … the time required for organising local forces in the evacuated area need not to be taken into consideration by you.' Churchill had grossly overstepped the mark and when his telegram came to light, it triggered an almighty Cabinet row.

Montagu crossed swords with Churchill and backed Cox and Haldane: 'As I understand it, no decision has yet been taken by His Majesty's Government. I do not therefore know what it is to which the Secretary of State for War fears that the authorities on the spot will offer "a very stubborn resistance" to. I presume that, until a policy has been laid down, it is their duty to say what they think and not what they are wanted to think.'[7] He then went as far as to privately contact Percy Cox, to make sure he was aware that the Cabinet had not yet decided upon withdrawal. Curzon was even angrier. In reference to Churchill's domineering message to Haldane, he wrote, 'I read those remarks with amazement, because I could neither imagine the Cabinet arriving at any such decision, nor could I in the Minutes of the meeting … find the smallest trace of it.'[8] In ministerial terms, he was effectively calling Churchill a liar.

The Cabinet's internal hostilities were briefly suspended over Christmas, but the litany of problems besieging the government – Iraq and Ireland foremost among them – dampened the festive cheer. Christmas at 10 Downing Street was, 'Rather a gloomy proceeding, strongly impregnated with the atmosphere of the offices downstairs – the sort of Christmas a shopkeeper spends when he eats his Christmas dinner on the counter surrounded by his goods.'[9] Bell spent Christmas day quietly at home penning letters to her family. In one, she pondered the future: 'I've been feeling a good deal lately how much the Arabs here who are our friends want us to give them a lead … they ask me again anxiously what I think would be best for the country … I feel quite clear in my own mind that there is only one workable solution, a son of the Sharif and for choice Faisal [sic]; very very much the first choice.'[10] She was not the only one toying with Feisal as the solution to the long-term security problems in Iraq.

Percy Cox and his predecessor had both suggested to Cabinet that Feisal should made de facto ruler of Mesopotamia, but suddenly it was being taken seriously. Montagu contacted Cox again, this time asking for details on how Feisal 'candidature' would be accepted by the different parties within Iraq.[11] A few days later Cox replied, affirming that such a solution was his preferred option. He wrote, 'My belief, and that of those of my staff on whose judgement I rely [among whom was Bell], is that such an announcement of a fait accompli would be a welcome relief to majority of people of Mesopotamia, and that it would have [the] support of moderate element[s] among Nationalists, while it would take the wind out of the sails of the young extremists, who want to get rid of the mandate altogether.' Nine months before, Feisal had declared himself King of Syria and then been unceremoniously ousted by the French. Now, at the end of 1920, as a way of hopefully pacifying their future mandate, the British were preparing to offer him the throne of Iraq.

Chapter 55

Storm clouds

The start of the new year in 1921 was an anxious moment for Gertrude Bell. She wrote, 'Upon my soul I'm glad I don't know what this year is going to bring. I don't think I ever woke on a first of January with such feelings of apprehension ... For the truth is there's little that promises well.' It was not just events in Iraq that seemed to bode ill. Bell noted, 'When I read the Irish news I wonder we've the face to set [ourselves] up as a guide to anyone in statecraft or administration. As for statecraft I really think you might search our history from end to end without finding poorer masters of it than Lloyd George and Winston Churchill.'[1]

The two men had been together as the sun set on 1920. The prime minister and his mistress had gathered with Winston Churchill and a few friends at a fellow parliamentarian's mansion in Kent for New Year's festivities. The evening's entertainment was supplied by Lloyd George's private secretary, who had brought with him gramophone records of campaign speeches made by Warren G. Harding. Together, the group sat and listened, while Lloyd George and Churchill amused everyone by taking turns shouting insults at the president-elect down the horn of the gramophone. Churchill railed against the 'platitudes' spouted by Americans, who he said barely got beyond, 'The sun shone yesterday and upon this great and glorious country. It shines to-day and will shine to-morrow.'[2] Lloyd George was, above all, concerned, and told the gathering, 'If this was to be the outcome of the League of Nations propaganda', he was 'sorry for the world and in particular for America.'

When Harding was inaugurated a few months later, his address contained a few emollient lines, but it was also unflinching in its assertion of American primacy:

> Our eyes never will be blind to a developing menace, our ears never deaf to the call of civilization ... But America, our America,

the America builded on the foundation laid by the inspired fathers, can be a party to no permanent military alliance. It can enter into no political commitments, nor assume any economic obligations which will subject our decisions to any other than our own authority ... a world supergovernment is contrary to everything we cherish ... This is not selfishness, it is sanctity. It is not aloofness, it is security. It is not suspicion of others, it is patriotic adherence to the things which made us what we are.[3]

The United States never joined the League of Nations. Warren G. Harding himself died in office in August 1923 of a heart attack, aged fifty-seven. His body was laid to rest at a state funeral. After his death, a series of scandals exposed the extent of the corruption within the Harding administration. Not only had he promoted a number of completely unqualified friends to important positions, some of them were found to have engaged in bribery and embezzlement. Eventually, details of his extra-marital affairs also became known, along with efforts of Republican Party figures to keep them hidden during his time in office. His legacy, such as it was, was one of scandal.

War in Ireland dragged on for another seven months after the end of 1920. Lloyd George, whose attempts to secure a truce in December 1920 had been rejected by the IRA, continued to push for a negotiated suspension of hostilities. He confided to a friend in April 1921, 'The question is whether I can see Michael Collins. No doubt he is the head and front of the movement. If I could see him, a settlement might be possible. The question is whether the British people would be willing for us to negotiate with the head of a band of murderers.'[4] Despite the perceived risk of alienating public opinion, negotiations between representatives from the breakaway Irish government and London went ahead. On Saturday, 9 July 1921 a message went out to divisional Volunteer commanders: 'In view of the conversations now being entered into by our Government with the Government of Great Britain, and in pursuance of mutual conversations, active operations by our forces will be suspended as from noon, Monday, 11 July.'[5] With the exception of a few aberrations, violence subsided, the British forces reined back their patrols and the use of stop and search, and in December, Michael Collins travelled to London to meet with Lloyd George.

Partition was already an established fact as a result of the Government of Ireland Act passed in 1920, and Lloyd George was adamant that

Ireland could not become an independent republic. What the British were willing to offer was dominion status – effectively giving southern Ireland the same level of independence as Australia – and a guarantee that all British troops would withdraw from Ireland. The proposal Collins took back to Dublin was criticised by those who wanted nothing short of independence and when he and the delegation departed again for London, they planned to return with the draft for the breakaway parliament to debate. Lloyd George, under internal pressure to get a deal, gave Collins an ultimatum: agree the treaty or go to war with the British government. At 2.20am on 6 December 1921, the Anglo-Irish peace treaty was signed. Ireland, under the name of the Irish Free State, had been granted near total independence. The result did not satisfy many die-hard independence campaigners because Ireland remained part of the Commonwealth, and Ireland itself remained partitioned. To them, Ireland was free in name only. Lloyd George's forced compromise was destined to fail.

In Iraq, however, the political gamble paid off in the short term. Gertrude Bell was sat in the front row of the audience on the early morning of Tuesday, 23 August 1921, when Feisal bin Hussein bin Ali al-Hashemi strode past a British guard of honour towards a raised stage set up in the historic town of Sammara, north of Baghdad. Following a poll in which ninety-six percent of those who voted had chosen Feisal, Iraq had democratically elected its first king. Somehow, the irony of the process was utterly lost on most of the participants. After Feisal was announced as monarch, a British military band struck up 'God Save the King' – in absence of an Iraqi national anthem, it was only thing which seemed appropriate – and the audience stood. A delighted Bell wrote to her stepmother, 'I'm glad I've lived to take part in this.'[6] That year, Iraq became a nation in its own right as a British mandate and Bell helped to officially map out the new country's borders.

Winston Churchill's desire for Great Britain to welcome Turkey back into the fold did not materialise entirely as he had planned. Ataturk signed an official treaty with the Soviets in 1921 and, aided by supplies of Soviet gold and armaments, fought against the Greeks to take back disputed territory. The decisive moment came in autumn 1922 when he laid claim to the historical region of Thrace on the Anatolian peninsula and with it, the capital, Constantinople. As Ataturk advanced, Lloyd George, with the support of Winston Churchill, ordered British troops to stand and fight. But the British Cabinet was deeply divided and public opinion, along with Britain's Allies, was strongly against starting another war. Lloyd George was forced to back down. An armistice with Turkey was hastily signed, handing over control of Constantinople to Ataturk, while the Sultan fled on a British warship to Malta. It was one crisis too many for Lloyd George who, having the lost the backing of the majority of his Cabinet, was forced to resign as prime minister. His golfing partner, Lord Riddell, visited him that afternoon. Riddell found Lloyd George sat by the fire in his secretary's room, making notes for a speech he was scheduled to give that weekend. He told his friend that he was glad it was over, as 'one cannot work properly when one feels that one may be stabbed in the back at any moment.'[7] Despite the immediacy of the betrayal, Lloyd George was already fondly viewing his premiership. He stood, walked around the room, and then shook hands heartily with Riddell: 'It has been a wonderful time', he said.[8]

In the autumn of 1922 Britain and the Allies began negotiating the Treaty of Lausanne, which replaced the stillborn Treaty of Sevres. The new treaty, signed in July 1923, recognised the boundaries of the modern state of Turkey and made no mention of Armenia.

In March 1921 the months of deliberation and debate throughout 1920 bore fruit and Great Britain became the first country to sign a trade deal with Soviet Russia. Seven years later, diplomatic relations were suspended and the trade agreement was terminated after British secret services discovered that the official Russian trade organisation in London was a front for a spy ring. The British government published a thirty-two-page dossier, detailing secret messages discovered in a raid on the premises and Soviet propaganda efforts against British interests overseas. If Lord Curzon had been able to communicate from the grave, the by-then-deceased statesmen would have rejoiced in informing the government that he had been right all along.

Waziristan meanwhile enjoyed one of the longest extended periods without a war for a century. The peace was ended in 1936, when a local religious leader managed to unite the Wazirs and Mahsuds to launch a *jihad* against the British. After one open engagement, they turned to guerrilla tactics. In the first six months the campaign cost the British Exchequer over a million pounds, and in the three years of operations a total of 61,000 British and Indian troops were deployed to fight in the rugged mountains. They adopted the same tactics as their predecessors had in 1920: razing villages and using air attacks to pacify opposition. A British captain who served in the conflict later wrote, 'The core of our problem in the army was to face battle on an elusive and mobile enemy ... while he flitted and sniped, rushed and ran away, we felt as if we were using a crowbar to swat wasps.'[9] It was a depressingly familiar observation.

The year 1921 also saw the conclusion of a reparations deal between the Allies and Germany. The final figure settled on was £6.6 billion. The eye-wateringly high sum was broken up into three different rated bonds – so that payment of around two thirds of the total was initially deferred – leaving Germany to pay around £100 million a year, in addition to twenty-six per cent of the value of its exports and a first lump-sum payment of £50 million, due by August 1921. The German government had little option other than to accept the payment schedule presented, as it was accompanied by the threat that, if they refused, the Allies would simply occupy the Ruhr industrial region, the source of almost all of Germany's coal, iron and steel. Germany made its first payment, but missed subsequent ones and the French occupied the Ruhr anyway in 1923.

Domestically, the German government's programme of money printing to finance foreign currency purchases backfired spectacularly, and the value of the *Papiermark* fell dramatically, triggering hyperinflation. On 4 May 1923 Adolf Hitler addressed a crowd of supporters in Munich. Three years since the Nazi Party had emptied its coffers to stage Hitler's address to a disruptive audience in a Munich hall in February 1920, the Party had grown to more than 50,000 members. In his speech, Hitler railed against the situation in Germany, asserting that 'Reparations are nothing but a "legal device" intended to bring a state to its knees with a facade of legality, to destroy the fabric of a nation ... If you want to free yourselves from the "obligation to provide reparations", you cannot possibly do this by endless compliance. The only way is to have the strength of will to one day tear up the Treaty of Versailles and to develop instead the ability to defend our nation and ultimately to attack its enemies.'[10] He would do just that when he finally came to power.

In 1920 the world was already heading towards another global conflict, while the largest empire in history had begun its decline. Those who had hoped that the year would usher in a new era of peace, prosperity and goodwill among men would never see that vision become reality.

Afterword

The events of the year 1920 cast a long shadow. In the unclouded vision of hindsight, the response of the British government to movements for independence in Ireland and Iraq seems hubristic at best. But the leaders who navigated the ship of state had been born into a world where the sun never set on the British Empire. To even begin to imagine the fading of that hard-won glory and the Empire's decline was a leap of imagination bordering on heresy.

Far from being peaceful, the world after the Great War was full of conflict. Nations fought nations and British subjects fought against their overlords, while a battle of ideologies was also waged through diplomacy and war. The leaders of Russia made no secret of their plan to 'Sovietise' Europe and that threat was uppermost in the minds of many European politicians, even while they faced more immediate dangers closer to home. The reprisals conducted by British forces in Ireland were reprehensible, but in comparison to Waziristan, Ireland achieved a victory. The end result of the Irish War of Independence was that the British government granted southern Ireland dominion status, offered to pull out all British forces and hand over power to an Irish government. It was short of true independence, but in Waziristan the legacy of the uprising against the British was scorched earth and flattened homes. The Irishman who had negotiated the end to hostilities with Britain, Michael Collins, was assassinated by a fellow Republican in 1922 as the Irish independence movement split and fought against itself. Southern Ireland remained neutral throughout the Second World War and within a few decades of the end of the war, sectarian violence broke out in Northern Ireland. The so-called 'Troubles' would last for thirty years and leave more than 3,500 dead.

King Feisal successfully passed on the throne to one of his sons, but the Iraq he bequeathed upon his death was a divided, troubled country: technically independent, but still tied by treaty to Great Britain, with a monarch and a parliament, and which held ten elections and appointed fifty different cabinets in the first thirty-three years of its existence.

In 1958, the monarchy was overthrown in a military coup and, two years later, a law was passed ending the granting of drilling concessions to any foreign company, a prelude to full nationalisation. Until then, the majority of Iraq's oil had been extracted by Western-owned companies for Western markets. The stipulation in the original agreement at San Remo in 1920 that Iraq's 'native interests' were to be granted a twenty percent share in future oil development was never adhered to, due to objections from shareholders in the drilling companies. Ten years later, another military coup brought the Ba'ath Party to power. Among the party's up-and-coming leaders was an Iraqi Arab from Tikrit named Saddam Hussein.

Great Britain's other League of Nations' mandate, Palestine, proved to be a nightmare for the British government. From 1936 to 1939 the British faced a full-scale Arab revolt, which led them to effectively rescind the Balfour Declaration and to place strict limits on Jewish immigration. Even when the full horror of Hitler's Holocaust became known after the Second World War, the British administration refused to lessen the restrictions in the face of Arab opposition. The result was that Jewish armed groups turned to terrorism, the most high-profile attack being the 1946 bombing of the British administration headquarters at the King David Hotel in Jerusalem, which left ninety-one dead. The following year, the British announced their intention to relinquish the mandate and to lay the problem of Palestine at the feet of the United Nations, the global intergovernmental organisation which was the spiritual successor to the League. The UN proposed the partitioning of Palestine into two states – one Jewish and one Arab – but the tipping point had already been passed. As the British readied themselves to evacuate, one British civil servant pointedly and accurately remarked, 'By the time the United Nations arrives, Palestine will be up in smoke.' The first Arab-Israeli war resulted in the establishment of the state of Israel and Palestine has never found lasting peace since.

Poland endured the ignominy of being invaded simultaneously by Germany and Soviet Russia at the start of the Second World War, and at the end of the conflict the country was occupied by a Soviet troops that stayed until 1993. Soviet ambitions also extended to Afghanistan, where Soviet troops fought a nine-year war, ending in a Russian withdrawal in 1989. The efforts of Western nations to counter the 'Bolshevik menace' had, for decades, been harnessed and redirected under the new title of The Cold War, and in the spirit of supporting freedom, Western governments armed the *mujahedeen* insurgents in their Holy War against the Soviets. A young Saudi Arabian named Osama Bin Laden helped establish training camps for fighters across the border, in the mountainous areas of northern Pakistan. He would later become the most notorious terrorist leader in history and be assassinated by US Special Forces after spending years hiding in plain sight in Waziristan.

The League of Nations lasted officially until 1946, but the grand head-quarters building in Geneva – the Palace of Nations – was left empty for the duration of the Second World War. It seemed an appropriate metaphor for the demise of the whole organisation, which had manifestly not achieved its aim of securing world peace. There is no doubt that the League's founders and the majority of its members were well intentioned, but in 1920, the first year if its existence, the League's frailties were brutally exposed. If the desire of the nations who joined the League had truly been to secure peace and protect those who could not protect themselves, there was no better test case than that of Armenia. The League failed, and with the end of Armenia came the beginning of the end of the credibility of the League of Nations, which would ultimately be demolished when the world went to war again. Armenia itself would not become a sovereign nation until after the collapse of the Soviet Union.

Out of remnants of the League, a new supranational organisation was formed, intended to maintain the League's ideals but to do so more effectively. Gertrude's Bell friend, Lord Robert Cecil, gave a speech at the final meeting of the Assembly in April 1946, in which he said, 'The League is dead. Long live the United Nations!' The UN absorbed some of the bodies created by the League, including the International Labour Organisation, which had never managed to make its planned trip to Russia, and also inherited the League's not inconsiderable assets. But the UN has also come under scathing criticism in its lifetime for being ponderous and ineffective, and for standing by and watching in horror while conflict rages. Cooperation between nations has proved no easier in the twenty-first century than in the one before. Modern-day sceptics include the current occupant of the White House, who tweeted on Boxing Day 2016, 'The United Nations has such great potential but right now it is just a club for people to get together, talk and have a good time. So sad!'

Donald Trump's election victory in 2016 shocked foreign governments and signalled an about-turn in the United States' outlook on the world, just as the election of Warren G. Harding did in 1920. Trump was not the first presidential candidate to run on a platform to put 'America first': American isolationism was not a new idea, even in 1920. To claim today that calls for the United States to withdraw from the responsibility of leading the world are regressive is entirely accurate, but it would be wrong to suggest that such a stance is un-American. Woodrow Wilson was the first US president to entangle his nation in the affairs of Europe and he sought not only to ally the US with European nations, but to redefine its entire role on the world stage within the space of a decade. The suspicion with which the League of Nations was regarded by US lawmakers in 1920 was entirely understandable and in keeping with decades of the history of the republic. A return to such ideas, even in a globalised world, should not come as a surprise.

Nearly a century has now passed since Leon Bourgeois addressed the first League of Nations Council meeting in the elegant surrounds of the Quai d'Orsay in Paris. The year that began with such optimism would witness a surge in nationalist sentiment in Europe, unrest and airstrikes in the Middle East, Russian efforts to destabilise Eastern Europe, and the election of an unabashed populist to the White House. It was the discovery of those striking parallels with today that led to the writing of this book.

Acknowledgements

To Lani, my other half, for your never-ceasing encouragement and for enduring being a writer's widow with good grace. And to Mr Pyke, without whose willingness to take on a late starter in his A-level class I would never have studied history.

Dramatis personae

Prince Abdullah

Older brother of Feisal, who was declared ruler of Iraq by the Arab nationalist General Syrian Congress in 1920.

General Allenby

British commander who captured Jerusalem from the Ottoman Turks in the First World War.

Haj Amin al-Husseini

Former officer in the Ottoman army. His inflammatory speech encouraged the *Nebi Musa* riots in Jerusalem in 1920.

Herbert Asquith

Liberal and former wartime prime minister who was Leader of the Opposition in the British Parliament in 1920.

Mustafa Kemal Ataturk

Leader of the Turkish nationalist movement, which took control of eastern Turkey in 1920. Ataturk would go on to be the founder of the modern Turkish state.

Arthur Balfour

Signatory to the famous 'Balfour Declaration' giving British government support to the establishment of a homeland for the Jewish people in Palestine. Formerly Foreign Secretary. In 1920 he attended the League of Nations Council meetings as the British representative.

Gertrude Bell

Talented historian, archaeologist and linguist who was the British Oriental Secretary in Baghdad under A.T. Wilson and Sir Percy Cox.

M. Philippe Bertholot

Head of the French Foreign Service, key negotiator at San Remo, and also instrumental in the agreement of the deal between the British and French over Iraqi oil.

Leon Bourgeois

First Chairman of the League of Nations. Former prime minister of France.

Henry Cabot Lodge

Chairman of Senate Foreign Relations Committee. Republican grandee who was one of those in the 'smoke-filled room' who engineered Warren G. Harding's nomination.

Winston Churchill

Secretary of State for War and Air in Lloyd George's Cabinet. After his fall from grace as a result of the Gallipoli campaign in the First World War, Churchill was still in the process of restoring his battered political reputation.

Michael Collins

IRA leader whose official capacity was finance minister for the breakaway Irish Parliament.

James 'Jimmy' Cox

Governor of Ohio and Democratic candidate in the 1920 presidential election. In favour of League of Nations membership for the United States. On the campaign trail he was consistently outshone by his running mate, Franklin Roosevelt.

Sir Percy Cox

British High Commissioner of Iraq who was tasked with installing an Arab-led government under British tutelage. Gertrude Bell became his Oriental Secretary.

Lord Nathaniel Curzon

Former Viceroy of India. British Foreign Secretary in 1920. A man of great intellect but little grace.

General Anton Denikin

Commander of the anti-Bolshevist White Army in southern Russia. His forces received significant support from Britain until early 1920.

Prince Feisal

Son of Sharif Hussein of Mecca, who had led the Arab army which fought against the Turks with the help of T.E. Lawrence during the First World War.

Mohandas 'Mahatma' Gandhi

British-educated lawyer and former army officer who led a campaign of non-cooperation against British rule in India in 1920. He would go on to lead the Indian independence movement.

General Haldane

Senior British military commander in Mesopotamia. Viewed the establishment of an Arab government as largely a waste of time. Responsible for putting down the 1920 uprising.

Sharif Hussein of Mecca

Arab leader and King of the Hedjaz, the father of Feisal and Abdullah. He had originally agreed a secret wartime deal with the British to create an Arab independent area in modern-day Syria and Palestine, which the British reneged on after the war.

Wolfgang Kapp

German civil servant who was the co-conspiracist in the short lived 'Kapp putsch'.

Leonid Krasin

The Soviet People's Commissar for Trade and Industry. Negotiated the Anglo-Russian trade deal.

T.E. Lawrence

'Lawrence of Arabia'. The British officer who engineered the Arab military campaign against the British during the First World War. Proponent of Arab independence who, along with Gertrude Bell, helped define the borders of the state of Iraq.

General Walther von Lüttwitz

Decorated First World War general who jointly led the attempted coup in Germany in 1920 and ordered the *Freikorps* to march into Berlin.

David Lloyd George

British prime minister in 1920. Led the post-war coalition government.

William Gibbs McAdoo

Married to President Woodrow Wilson's daughter. A natural presidential candidate who seemed incapable of deciding whether he wanted to attain high office.

Edwin Montagu

Secretary of State for India in Lloyd George's Cabinet.

Alexander Mitchell Palmer

Runner in the Democratic primaries. A Quaker, firmly in favour of prohibition, who affirmed Wilson's 'high ideals'.

Jozef Pilsudski

Polish military commander who had fought for Austria-Hungary in the First World War. It was his daring plan that led to the 'miracle on the Vistula'.

Lord George Riddell

Friend and golfing partner of British Prime Minister Lloyd George. In his capacity as a newspaper proprietor he attended the reparations conference in Spa in 1920.

Franklin Delano Roosevelt

Democratic vice presidential candidate in 1920. He would later go on to become the 32nd President of the United States and serve four terms. He was deemed too inexperienced to be the first name on the ticket in 1920 at the age of thirty-eight. By the time he became president he would be crippled by polio.

Ronald Storrs

British governor of Jerusalem at the start of 1920. Famous Arabist once described by T.E. Lawrence as 'the most brilliant Englishman in the Near East.'

Leon Trotsky

Communist revolutionary who was head of the Soviet Army during the Russian civil war.

Mikhail Tukhachevsky

Commander of Russian forces in the Russo-Polish war. An ardent Bolshevist and also the son of Russian nobility.

Warren, G. Harding

Republican Senator from Ohio who, against all odds, secured his party's nomination for the 1920 presidential race. He ran on a campaign to put 'America First' and made innovative use of new media to get his message to the electorate.

Adolf Hitler

German army corporal in 1920 who worked his way into a position of leadership in the *Nationalsozialistische Deutsche Arbeiterpartei*, or Nazi Party. Thirteen years later he became German Chancellor.

Sir Arnold T. Wilson

British Civil Commissioner in Baghdad. Replaced by Sir Percy Cox in October 1920.

Woodrow Wilson

Democratic President of the United States. The League of Nations was his brainchild.

General Pyotr Wrangel

Final general of the pro-Tsarist White Army. Took over from Denikin after the withdrawal to Crimea.

Bibliography

This book would not have been possible without the collections of multiple archives, most notably The National Archives at Kew, London, The Gertrude Bell Archive at Newcastle University, the Woodrow Wilson Presidential Library in Staunton, Virginia, and the diligent records kept by the Secretariat of meetings of the League of Nations, now held by the United Nations' Archives in Geneva.

For the sake of brevity, I have only included in this bibliography books and articles used as sources for specific passages of text and quotations. Special mention should however be made of David Pietrusza's *1920, The year of six Presidents* and Ian Rutledge's *Enemy on the Euphrates, the Battle for Iraq 1914–1920*. Within the limited space of this book it has been impossible to follow all the twists and turns and do complete justice to the characters involved in the presidential race which took Warren G. Harding to the White House, or the uprising in Iraq.

Alikuzai, Hamid Wahed, *A concise history of Afghanistan in 25 volumes: Volume 1* (Trafford Publishing, 2013).

Avrich, Paul, *Kronstadt, 1921* (Princeton University Press, 1991).

Bardon, Jonathan, *A History of Ireland in 250 Episodes* (Gill & Macmillan Ltd, 2008).

Bendiner, Elmer, *A time for angels: the tragic history of the League of Nations* (Weidenfeld and Nicholson, 1975).

Bennett, Richard, *The Black and Tans* (Pen & Sword Military, 2010).

Best, Brian, *Reporting from the front, war reporters during the Great War* (Pen & Sword, 2014).

Bew, Paul, *Ireland: The Politics of Enmity 1789–2006* (Oxford University Press, 2007).

Brady, C.M., 'Indianapolis at the time of the Great Migration, 1900 – 1920', *Black History News and Notes* (Indiana Historical Society, 1996).

Boller, F. Paul, *Presidential Anecdotes* (Oxford University Press, 1996).

Borgonovo, John and Doherty, Gabriel, 'Smoking gun: British government policy and RIC reprisals, summer 1920', *History of Ireland*, Issue 2 (March/April 2009).

Callaghan, Michael, D., 'The British Colonial Office and the League of Nations Mandate for German East Africa, 1916–1920', *Albion Quarterly*, Vol. 25, No. 3 (autumn 1993).

Churchwell, Sarah, *Behold America: A History of America First and the American Dream* (Bloomsbury Publishing, 2018).

Constello Francis, 'Lloyd George and Ireland, 1919–1921: An Uncertain Policy', *The Canadian Journal of Irish Studies*, Vol. 14, No. 1 (July 1988).

Cooper, John Milton, *Breaking the Heart of the World: Woodrow Wilson and the Fight for the League of Nations*, (Cambridge University Press, 2001).

Cronin, Sean, *The Story of Kevin Barry*, (The National Publications Committee, 1965).

Dalrymple, William, *Return of a King, the Battle for Afghanistan* (Bloomsbury Publishing, 2014).

Davies, Normal, 'Lloyd George and Poland, 1919–20', *Journal of Contemporary History*, Vol. 6, No. 3 (1971).

Davis, Wade, *Into the Silence: The Great War, Mallory and the conquest of Everest* (Vintage Books, 2012).

DeBellaigue, Christopher, *The Islamic Enlightenment* (Penguin Random House, 2017).

Dobson, Christopher & Miller, John, *The day we almost bombed Moscow: the Allied war in Russia 1918–1920* (Hodder & Stoughton, 1986).

Drexler, Anton, *My Political Awakening, From the journal of a socialist worker* (CreateSpace Independent Publishing Platform, 2016).

Dugdale, Blanche E.C. *Arthur James Balfour, First Earl of Balfour, K.G., O.M., F.R.S., G.P.*, (G.P. Putnam's Sons, 1937).

Elcock, H.J., 'Britain and the Russo-Polish Frontier, 1919–1921', *The Historical Journal*, Vol. 12, No. 1 (1969).

Ellinwood, Dewitt C., *Between Two Worlds: A Rajput Officer in the Indian Army, 1905–21* (University Press of America, 2005).

Evans, Richard J., *The Third Reich in History and Memory*, (Oxford University Press, 2015).

Eugene H., *Wilhelm II: Emperor and Exile, 1900–1941 Volume 2: Emperor and Exile, 1900–1941 v. 2* (University of North Carolina Press, 1996).

Ferguson, Niall, *Empire: How Britain made the modern world* (Penguin, 2004).

Ferrier, R.W., *The History of the British Petroleum Company, Volume 1 The Developing Years, 1901–1932* (Cambridge University Press, 1982).

Flynt, Larry and Eisenbach, David, *One Nation Under Sex: How the Private Lives of Presidents, First Ladies and Their Lovers Changed the Course of American History* (St. Martin's Press, 2011).

Fromkin, David, *A Peace to End All Peace: Creating the Modern Middle East, 1914–1922* (Henry Holy and Company, Inc., 1989).

Gandhi, Mahatma, *Freedom's Battle: Being a Comprehensive Collection of Writings and Speeches on the Present Situation* (The Floating Press, 2014).

Gartman, Eric, *Return to Zion, the History of modern Israel* (University of Nebraska Press, 2015).

Gilbert, Martin, *World in Torment: Winston Churchill 1917–1922* (Minerva, 1975).

Robert A. Pastor, Stanley Hoffmann, *A Century's Journey: How the Great Powers Shape the World* (Basic Books, 1999).

Gillman Peter and Gillman, Leni, *Wildest Dream: The Biography of George Mallory* (The Mountaineers Books, 2001).

Gokay, Bulent, *Soviet Eastern Policy and Turkey, 1920–1991: Soviet Foreign Policy, Turkey and Communism* (Routledge, 2006).

Hovannisian, Richard G., *The Republic of Armenia, Volume IV Between Crescent and Sickle: Partition and Sovietization* (University of California Press, 1996).

Hennessay, Prof. Thomas, *Dividing Ireland, World War One and Partition* (Routledge, 1998).

Hittle, J.B.E., *Michael Collins and the Anglo-Irish War: Britain's Counterinsurgency Failure*, (Potomac Books, Inc., 2011).

Hughes, Bettany, *Istanbul: A tale of three cities* (Weidenfeld & Nicholson, 2017).

Huneidi, Sahar, *A Broken Trust: Sir Herbert Samuel, Zionism and the Palestinians* (I.B. Tauris, 2001).

Jackisch, Barry, A., *The Pan-German League and Radical Nationalist Politics in Interwar Germany, 1918–29* (Routledge, 2016).

Jacobson, John, *When the Soviet Union Entered World Politics* (University of California Press, 1994).

Johnson, G., *The Berlin Embassy of Lord D'Abernon, 1920–1926* (Palgrave Macmillan, 2002).

Kershaw, Ian, *Hitler* (Penguin, 2009).

Kibriya, Mazhar, *Gandhi and Indian Freedom Struggle* (APH Publishing, 1999).

Kopisto, Lauri, *The British Intervention in South Russia 1918–1920* (Historical Studies from the University of Helsinki XXIV, 2011).

Lawrence, Thomas Edward, *Seven Pillars of Wisdom* (Wordsworth Editions Ltd., 1997).

Leake, Elizabeth, *The Defiant Border: The Afghan-Pakistan Borderlands in the Era of Decolonization, 1936–65* (Cambridge University Press, 2016).

Lynch, Robert, 'The People's Protectors? The Irish Republican Army and the "Belfast Pogrom," 1920–1922', *Journal of British Studies*, Vol. 47, No. 2 (April 2008).

Mack, John E., *A Prince of our disorder: the life of T.E. Lawrence* (Harvard University Press, 1998).

MacLaren, Roy, *Empire and Ireland: The Transatlantic Career of the Canadian Imperialist Hamar Greenwood, 1870–1948* (McGill-Queen's Press, 2015).

McCarthy, Helen, *British people and the League of Nations* (Manchester University Press, 2011).

McWhirter, Cameron, *Red Summer: the summer of 1919 and the awakening of black America* (Henry Holdy and Company, 2011).

Moreman T., *The army in India and the development of frontier warfare, 1848–1947* (Palgrave Macmillan, 1998).

Mulligan, William, *The Creation of the Modern German Army: General Walther Reinhardt and the Weimar Republic, 1914–1930* (Berghahn Books, 2005).

Michaeli, Ethan, *The Defender: how the legendary black newspaper changed America*, (Houghton Mifflin Harcourt Publishing Ltd., 2016).

Morgan, Kenneth, *Lloyd George family letters 1885–1936* (University of Wales Press, 1973).

Morello, John, A., *Selling the President 1920: Albert D. Laskar, Advertising and the Election of Warren G. Harding* (Greenwood Publishing Group, 2001).

Okrent, Daniel, *The Last Call: The Rise and Fall of Prohibition* (Scribner, 2010).

Orde, Anne, *British policy and European reconstruction after the First World War* (Cambridge University Press, 1990).

Paxman, Jeremy, *Empire* (Penguin, 2012).

Pietrusza, David, *1920, The year of six Presidents*, (Basic Books, 2008).

Pipes, Daniel, *Greater Syria: the history of an ambition* (Oxford University Press, 1990).

Popplewell, Sir Oliver, *The Prime Minister and His Mistress* (Lulu Publishing Services, 2014).

Powaski, Ronald E., *American Presidential Statecraft: from Isolationism to Internationalism* (Palgrave Macmillan, 2017).

Ramraz-Ra'ukh, Gilah, *The Arab in Israeli Literature* (I.B. Tauris, 1989).

Reid, Brian Holden, *Military power: Land Warfare in Theory and Practice* (Frank Cass & Co. Ltd., 1997).

Reynolds, John, *Divided loyalties: the Royal Irish Constabulary in County Tipperary, 1919–1922* (University of Limerick, 2013).

Riddell, Lord, *Lord Riddell's Intimate Diary of the Peace Conference and After, 1918–1923* (Victor Gollancz Ltd, 1933).

Robenalt, James, D., *Linking Rings: William W. Durbin and the Magic and Mystery of America* (Kent State University Press, 2004).

Rutledge, Ian, *Enemy on the Euphrates, the Battle for Iraq 1914–1920* (Saqi Books, 2014).

Segev, Tom, *One Palestine Complete* (Little, Brown and Company, 2001).

Stackelberg, Roderick and Winkle, Sally A., *The Nazi Germany source book: an anthology of texts* (Routledge, 2002).

Stevenson, David, *The First World War and International Politics* (Oxford University Press, 1988).

Storrs, Ronald, Sir, *The Memoirs of Sir Ronald Storrs* (G.P. Putnam's Sons, 1937).

Tanenbaum, Jan Karl, 'France and the Arab Middle East, 1914–1920', *Transactions of the American Philosophical Society*, Vol. 68, No. 7 (1978).

Tanner, Marcus, *Ireland's Holy Wars: the struggle for a nation's soul, 1500–2000* (Yale University Press, 2001).

Taylor, A.J.P., *Lloyd George, a diary by Frances Stevenson* (Hutchinson and Co, 1971).

The Chicago Commission on Race Relations, *The Negro in Chicago: a study of race relations and a race riot* (University of Chicago Press, 1922).

Thomas, Martin, *The French Empire between the wars: Imperialism, Politics and Society* (Manchester University Press, 2007).

Townshend, *The British Campaign in Ireland, 1919–1921: the development of political and military policies* (Oxford University Press, 1975).

Ward, Alan J., 'Lloyd George and the 1918 Irish Conscription Crisis', *The Historical Journal* (Vol. 17, No. 1, Cambridge University Press, March 1974).

Weekes, Colonel E.H., *History of the 5th Royal Gurkha Rifles: 1858 to 1928* (Naval & Military Press Ltd, 2011).

White, Gerry and O'Shea, Brendan, *The Burning of Cork* (Mercier Press Ltd, 2006).

Wilde, Major-General Sir A.T., *Regimental History of the 4th Battalion 13th Frontier Force Rifles (Wild's)* (Naval & Military Press Ltd., 2012).

World Peace Foundation, *The First Assembly of the League of Nations* (Double Number, 1921).

Wrangel, Petr, *The Memoirs of General Wrangel: The Last Commander-In-Chief of the Russian National Army* (Duffield & Company, 1930).

Wylly, Col. H.C., *History of the 5th Battalion 13th Frontier Force Rifles: 1849–1926* (The Naval & Military Press Ltd, 2011).

Zamoyski, Adam, *Warsaw 1920: Lenin's failed conquest of Europe* (Harper Collins, 2008).

Notes

Chapter 1: 'The birth of the new world'

1. 'First Council of League in Session', *The Sacramento Union*, Saturday, 17 January 1920, https://cdnc.ucr.edu/cgi-bin/cdnc?a=d&d=SU1920 0117.2.24, accessed 16 February 2018.
2. McCarthy, Helen, *British people and the League of Nations* (Manchester University Press, 2011, p.81–82).
3. Bendiner, Elmer, *A time for angels: the tragic history of the League of Nations* (Weidenfeld and Nicholson, 1975, p.164).
4. Ibid, p.160.
5. Boller, F.Paul, *Presidential Anecdotes* (Oxford University Press, 1996, p.220).
6. Ed. AJP Taylor, *Lloyd George, a diary by Frances Stevenson* (Hutchinson and Co, 1971. P.196–197).
7. Churchill, Winston, S., 'Situation in Russia', 15 October 1919, CAB 24/90.
8. Dobson, Christopher & Miller, John, *The day we almost bombed Moscow: the Allied war in Russia 1918–1920* (Hodder and Stoughton, 1986, p.270).
9. Kopisto, Lauri, *The British Intervention in South Russia 1918–1920*, Historical Studies from the University of Helsinki XXIV, 2011, p.162.
10. Riddell, Lord, *Lord Riddell's Intimate Diary of the Peace Conference and After, 1918–1923* (Victor Gollancz Ltd, 1933, p.162–163).

Chapter 2: Troubles at home

1. Ferguson, Niall, *Empire: How Britain made the modern world* (Penguin, 2004, p.303).
2. Ibid, p315.
3. Stevenson, David, *The First World War and International Politics* (Oxford University Press, 1988, p.106).
4. Wormell, Jeremy, *The Management of the National Debt of the United Kingdom, 1900–1932* (Routledge, 1999, Appendix III, p.733).

5. Orde, Anne, *British policy and European reconstruction after the First World War* (Cambridge University Press, 1990, p.63).
6. Reynolds, John, *Divided loyalties: the Royal Irish Constabulary in County Tipperary, 1919–1922* (University of Limerick, 2013, p.76).
7. Ward, Alan J., 'Lloyd George and the 1918 Irish Conscription Crisis', *The Historical Journal*, Vol. 17, No. 1 (Cambridge University Press, March 1974, p. 109).
8. Sinn Fein Standing Committee, *Sinn Fein Manifesto*, 1918 election.
9. Connacht Tribune, 31 January 1920, quoted in Reynolds, John, *Divided loyalties: the Royal Irish Constabulary in County Tipperary, 1919–1922* (University of Limerick, 2013, p.76).
10. Cabinet memorandum, 4 February 1920, 'Report on a Visit to Ireland, January 1920', CAB 24/97/73.
11. Tanner, Marcus, *Ireland's Holy Wars: the struggle for a nation's soul, 1500–2000* (Yale University Press, 2001. p.288).

Chapter 3: The world's best hope

1. Newspaper Clipping, 'Public Diagnosis Vexes President', 11 February 1920, Cary T. Grayson Papers, Woodrow Wilson Presidential Library.
2. Wilson, Woodrow to Gilbert M. Hitchcock, 26 January 1920, Cary T. Grayson Papers, Woodrow Wilson Presidential Library, Staunton Virginia.
3. Lodge, Henry Cabot, 12 August 1919, quoted in: Powaski, Ronald E., *American Presidential Statecraft: from Isolationism to Internationalism* (Palgrave Macmillan, 2017, p.104).
4. Michaeli, Ethan, *The Defender: how the legendary black newspaper changed America*, (Houghton Mifflin Harcourt Publishing Ltd., 2016, p.67).
5. McWhirter, Cameron, *Red Summer: the summer of 1919 and the awakening of black America*, (Henry Holdy and Company, 2011).
6. The Chicago Commission on Race Relations, *The Negro in Chicago: a study of race relations and a race riot* (University of Chicago Press, 1922, p.3).
7. Brady, C.M., 'Indianapolis at the time of the Great Migration, 1900–1920', *Black History News and Notes* (Indiana Historical Society, 1996).
8. Chicago Commission on Race Relations, p.640.

Chapter 4: Troubles abroad

1. Wylly, Col. H. C., *History of the 5th Battalion 13th Frontier Force Rifles: 1849–1926* (The Naval & Military Press Ltd, 2011, p.90).
2. Dalrymple, William, *Return of a King, the Battle for Afghanistan* (Bloomsbury Publishing, 2014, p.388).
3. The Pioneer Mail, 10 December 1920, *Pioneer Mail and Indian Weekly News*, Vol. 47, p.7.
4. Weekes, Colonel E.H., *History of the 5th Royal Ghurkha Rifles: 1858 to 1928* (Naval & Military Press Ltd, 2011, p.427).
5. Reid, Brian Holden, *Military power: Land Warfare in Theory and Practice* (Frank Cass & Co. Ltd., 1997, p.114).
6. Popplewell, Sir Oliver, *The Prime Minister and His Mistress* (Lulu Publishing Services, 2014, p.65).
7. Viceroy, Army Department to Secretary of State for India, 'Afghanistan. Telegram No. 147', 19 January 1920, CAB 24/96/83.
8. Ibid.
9. Viceroy, Army Department to Secretary of State for India, 'India. Telegram No 151', 28 January 1920, CAB 24/97/36.
10. Montagu, Edwin S. memorandum to Cabinet, 'Situation in the Near East', 13 January 1920, CAB 24/96/55.
11. Ibid.
12. Viceroy, Army Department to Secretary of State for India, 'Afghanistan. Telegram No. 513', 14 January 1920, CAB 25/96/60.
13. Secretary of State for India, 'Afghanistan. Telegram No. P.309 from Secretary of State to Viceroy, Foreign Department', 15 January 1920, CAB 24/96/61.

Chapter 5: Hopeless tangles

1. Bell, Gertrude to Sir Hugh Bell, 18 May 1917, Gertrude Bell Archive, Newcastle University.
2. P. Harding to Director of Military Operations, War Office, 'Note by Major Gabriel on the Arab question', 22 November 1915, FO 371/2486.
3. Charlwood, David, 'The Impact of the Dardanelles Campaign on British Policy Towards the Arabs: How Gallipoli Shaped the Hussein-McMahon Correspondence', *British Journal of Middle Eastern Studies* (Taylor and Francis, 2014).

4. Bell, Gertrude to Dame Florence Bell, 1 February 1920, Gertrude Bell Archive, Newcastle University.
5. Rutledge, Ian, *Enemy on the Euphrates, the Battle for Iraq 1914–1920* (Saqi Books, 2014, p.162).
6. Ferrier, R.W., *The History of the British Petroleum Company, Volume 1 The Developing Years, 1901–1932* (Cambridge University Press, 1982).
7. Ibid, p.357.
8. Best, Brian, *Reporting from the front, war reporters during the Great War* (Pen & Sword, 2014, p.153).
9. Rutledge, p.166.

Chapter 6: A new faith

1. Kopisto, Lauri, 'The British Intervention in South Russia 1918–1920', *Historical Studies from the University of Helsinki XXIV*, 2011, p.166.
2. Dobson, p.273.
3. Ibid.
4. Kopisto, p.162.
5. Holman, Major-General to Churchill, 'The position in South-West Russia', 16 February 1920, CAB 24/98/96.
6. Drexler, Anton, *My Political Awakening, From the journal of a socialist worker* (CreateSpace Independent Publishing Platform, 2016, p.25).
7. Eugene H., *Wilhelm II: Emperor and Exile, 1900–1941 Volume 2: Emperor and Exile, 1900–1941 v. 2* (University of North Carolina Press, 1996, p.294).
8. Lloyd George, on behalf of Supreme Council of the Allied Powers, to Govt. of Holland, 14 February 1920, CAB/24/98/39.
9. Karnerbeek, Minister for Foreign Affairs, to President of the Supreme Council, 'Extradition of the Ex-Emperor', 2 March 1920, CAB 24/100/9.
10. Kershaw, Ian, *Hitler* (Penguin, 2009, p.87).

Chapter 7: 'Native interests'

1. Hughes, Bettany, *Istanbul: A tale of three cities* (Weidenfeld & Nicholson, 2017, p.546).
2. DeBellaigue, Christopher, *The Islamic Enlightenment* (Penguin, Random House, 2017, p.105).

3. Supreme Council of the Allied Powers, 'Allied Policy in Russia', 24 February 1920, CAB 24/99/17.

4. Conclusions of Conference of Ministers held at 10 Downing Street, Monday 9 February 1920, CAB 23/27/35.

5. Ed. Morgan, Kenneth, *Lloyd George family letters 1885–1936* (University of Wales Press, 1973, p.191).

6. Supreme Council Allied Powers, 'Treaty of Peace with Turkey', 17 February 1920, CAB 24/98/65.

7. For a short history of the Turkish efforts to eradicate the Armenians see Charlwood, David, *Armenian Genocide: the great crime of World War 1* (Pen & Sword, 2019).

8. Hankey, Maurice P., 'Synopsis of the Treaty of Peace with Turkey', 21 February 1920, CAB 24/99/6.

9. Ibid.

10. Rutledge, p.163.

Chapter 8: The man who would be king

1. Bell, Gertrude to Dame Florence Bell, 7 March 1920, Gertrude Bell Archive, Newcastle University.

2. Lawrence, Thomas Edward, *Seven Pillars of Wisdom* (Wordsworth Editions Ltd., 1997, p.76).

3. Mack, John E., *A Prince of our disorder: the life of T.E. Lawrence* (Harvard University Press, 1998, p.173).

4. Bell, Gertrude to Sir Hugh Bell, 7 March 1919, Gertrude Bell Archive, Newcastle University.

5. Fromkin, David, *A Peace to End All Peace: Creating the Modern Middle East, 1914–1922* (Henry Holy and Company, Inc., 1989, p.343).

6. Tanenbaum, Jan Karl, 'France and the Arab Middle East, 1914–1920', *Transactions of the American Philosophical Society*, Vol. 68, No. 7 (1978), p.33.

7. Ibid, p.34.

8. Ibid, p.36.

9. Thomas, Martin, *The French Empire between the wars: Imperialism, Politics and Society* (Manchester University Press, 2007, p.43).

10. Pipes, Daniel, *Greater Syria: the history of an ambition* (Oxford University Press, 1990, p.27).

11. Ibid, p28.
12. Bell, Gertrude to Dame Florence Bell, 14 March 1920, Gertrude Bell Archive, Newcastle University.

Chapter 9: The restoration of order

1. Avalon Project, Yale Law School, 'Treaty of Versailles, Part V, 28 June 1919', Lilian Goldman Law Library (http://avalon.law.yale.edu/imt/partv.asp) accessed 2 July 2017.
2. Jackisch, Barry, A., *The Pan-German League and Radical Nationalist Politics in Interwar Germany, 1918–29* (Routledge, 2016, p.35).
3. Ed. Stackelberg, Roderick and Winkle, Sally A., *The Nazi Germany source book: an anthology of texts* (Routledge, 2002, pp.67–68).
4. Directorate of National Intelligence (Home Office), 'A Monthly Review of Revolutionary Movements in Foreign Countries', Report No. 17., March 1920, CAB 24/100/88.
5. Mulligan, William, *The Creation of the Modern German Army: General Walther Reinhardt and the Weimar Republic, 1914–1930* (Berghahn Books, 2005. p.163).
6. Evans, Richard J., *The Third Reich in History and Memory* (Oxford University Press, 2015, p.49–50).
7. Mulligan, p.166.
8. Kershaw, p.94.

Chapter 10: Nothing but force

1. Lloyd George, David to League of Nations Council, 24 February 1920, *League of Nations Official Journal*, March 1920, Annex 1., p.64.
2. Proces-Verbal of the Third Session of the Council of the League of Nations, 19 May 1920, p.62.
3. Balfour, Arthur J. to Cabinet, 'Memorandum by Mr. Balfour on Suggestions made to the 95. Council of the League of Nations in Reference to the Peace with Turkey, 15 March 1920, CAB 24/100/98.
4. Bendiner, p.162.
5. Proces-Verbal of the Fifth Session of the Council of the League of Nations, 19 May 1920, p.139.
6. Balfour, 'Memorandum by Mr. Balfour on Suggestions made to the Council of the League of Nations in Reference to the Peace with Turkey'.

Chapter 11: The Frankenstein monster

1. Cooper, John Milton, *Breaking the Heart of the World: Woodrow Wilson and the Fight for the League of Nations* (Cambridge University Press, 2001, p.321).
2. Ibid.
3. Secretary of State for Colonies to the Governors General of the Commonwealth of Australia, New-Zealand and the Union of South Africa, 'United States Reservations re League of Nations Covenant', 13 March 1920, CAB 24/100/71.
4. Ibid.
5. Cooper, p.3382.
6. Ibid, p.342.
7. Grayson, Cary T., Diary entry, 20 March 1920, Cary T. Grayson Papers, Woodrow Wilson Presidential Library, Staunton Virginia, Grayson.
8. Ronald Lindsay telegram 20 March, quoted in Foreign Countries Report No. 13, 24 March, CAB 24/154/13.
9. Pietrusza, David, *1920, The year of six Presidents* (Basic Books, 2008, p.40, p.84).
10. Ibid, p.84.
11. Cooper, p372.
12. Grayson, Cary T., Diary entry, 25–26 March 1920, Cary T. Grayson Papers, Woodrow Wilson Presidential Library, Staunton Virginia.

Chapter 12: Occupation

1. Viceroy to Secretary of State for India, 'Telegram No 3168 from Viceroy, Army Department, to Secretary of State for India', 8 March 1920, CAB 24/100/35.
2. Moreman T., *The army in India and the development of frontier warfare, 1848–1947* (Palgrave Macmillan, 1998, pp.176–177).
3. Viceroy to Secretary of State for India, 'Telegram No 325 S from Viceroy, Foreign & Political Dept, to S/S for India', 20 March 1920, CAB 24/101/46.
4. General Climo to Viceroy, quoted in Viceroy to Secretary of State for India, 'Telegram No 2931 from Viceroy, Army Department, to Secretary of State for India', 4 March 1920, CAB 24/99/100.

5. Capt. Singh diary, quoted in Ellinwood, Dewitt C., *Between Two Worlds: A Rajput Officer in the Indian Army, 1905–21* (University Press of America, 2005, p.507).
6. Viceroy to Secretary of State for India, 'Telegram No 332 S from Viceroy, Foreign & Political Dept, to Secretary of State for India – Occupation of Waziristan', 23 March, CAB 24/101/88.

Chapter 13: The unhappy country

1. Long, Walter H., 'Irish Self-Government. Some Notes and Observations on a Recent Visit to Ireland by Mr. P J Hannon', 1 March 1920, CAB 24/100/25.
2. Directorate of National Intelligence (Home Office), 'Report on Revolutionary Organisations in the United Kingdom. No. 43'., 26 February 1920, CAB 24/99/48.
3. Directorate of National Intelligence (Home Office), 'Report on Revolutionary Organisations in the United Kingdom. No. 44'., 4 March 1920, CAB 24/99/91.
4. Long, Walter H., 'Irish Self-Government. Some Notes and Observations'.
5. Hennessay, Prof. Thomas, *Dividing Ireland, World War One and Partition* (Routledge, 1998, p.162).
6. Dillon, 'Continuance of Martial Law', HC Deb 11 May 1916 vol 82 cc935-70, http://hansard.millbanksystems.com/commons/1916/may/11/continuance-of-martial-law, accessed 15 August 2017.
7. Asquith, Herbert, 'Statement to Parliament', Prime Minister's Statement, HC Deb 10 July 1916 vol 84 cc57-64, http://hansard.millbanksystems.com/commons/1916/jul/10/prime-ministers-statement, accessed 15 August 2017.
8. Chief Secretary for Ireland, Mr Macpherson, Government of Ireland Bill, HC Deb 29 March 1920 vol 127 cc925-1036, http://hansard.millbanksystems.com/commons/1920/mar/29/government-of-ireland-bill-1, accessed 15 August 2017.
9. Mr John Clynes, M.P. for Manchester Platting, Ibid.

Chapter 14: Withdrawal

1. Walter H. Long, 'Situation in South Russia. Report of a visit by Lieut. Commander G. C. Muirhead Gould', 9 March 1920, CAB 24/100/50.

2. Ibid.
3. Kopisto, p.165.
4. Francis, Charles, Memoirs, digitised by Francis, Roger, http://bejo toandus.typepad.com/charles_and_rose/2013/02/a-russian-interlude. html, accessed 17 August 2017.
5. Lancing College War memorial, Lieutenant Colonel William Henry Bingham, OBE, http://www.hambo.org/lancing/view_man.php?id=353, accessed 17 August 2017
6. Dobson, p.273.
7. Conclusions of a meeting of the Cabinet held at 10 Downing Street, 31 March 1920, CAB 23–20

Chapter 15: The Holy City

1. Samuel, Herbert, 'Interim Report on the administration of Palestine, during the period 1st July, 1920–30 June, 1921', 30 July 1921, UNISPAL documents collections, https://unispal.un.org/DPA/DPR/unispal.nsf /0/349B02280A930813052565E90048ED1C, accessed 20 August 2017.
2. Ramraz-Ra'ukh, Gilah, *The Arab in Israeli Literature* (I.B. Tauris, 1989, p.15).
3. Segev, Tom, *One Palestine Complete* (Little, Brown and Company, 2001, p.140).

Chapter 16: Choosing a candidate

1. *Florence Morning News*, Sunday 13 November 1932, p.4.
2. Pietrusza, p.193.
3. Ibid, p.197.
4. Okrent, Daniel, *The Last Call: The Rise and Fall of Prohibition* (Scribner, 2010, p.8
5. Pietrusza, p.159).
6. Alban B. Butler to Cary T. Grayson, 26 Apr. 1920, Cary T. Grayson Papers, Woodrow Wilson Presidential Library, Staunton Virginia.
7. Grayson, Cary T., Diary entry, 3 March 1920, Cary T. Grayson Papers, Woodrow Wilson Presidential Library, Staunton Virginia, Grayson .
8. A. Mitchell Palmer, 'Extract of a Speech Given at Savannah, Georgia, on 10 April 1920', Cary T. Grayson Papers, Woodrow Wilson Presidential Library, Staunton Virginia.

Chapter 17: Nebi Musa

1. Gartman, Eric, *Return to Zion, the History of modern Israel* (University of Nebraska Press, 2015, p.41).
2. Storrs, Ronald, Sir, *The Memoirs of Sir Ronald Storrs* (G.P.Putnam's Sons, 1937, p.320), published in the United Kingdom under the title 'Orientations'.
3. Ibid, p.348.
4. Segev, p.137.
5. Ibid, p.138.

Chapter 18: Territories, not colonies

1. Callaghan, Michael, D., 'The British Colonial Office and the League of Nations Mandate for German East Africa, 1916–1920', *Albion Quarterly*, Vol. 25, No. 3 (autumn 1993), p. 459, p.456.
2. Ibid, p.456.
3. Report by Inspector General, Kings African Rifles, 31 March 1920, 'Despatches. Tanganyika, Kenya', CO 534/40.
4. Montagu, Edwin, 'Memorandum on the draft Peace Treaty with Turkey', 9 April 1920, CAB 24/103/46.
5. Dispatch from British Representative in Washington, 26 March 1920, quoted in 'Turkish Peace Treaty. Correspondence between President Wilson and the Supreme Council', 26 April, CAB 24/104/91.

Chapter 19: Old enemies

1. Conclusions of the meeting at Cabinet held at 10 Downing Street on 8 April 1920, CAB 23/21/1
2. Morgan, p.191.
3. French govt. to Lord Derby, 9 April 1920, quoted in 'Consideration of the reply to the French Note on the occupation of Frankfurt and other German towns', 10 April 1920, CAB 23/35/15.
4. Foreign Office to Lord Derby, to be passed to Millerand, quoted in Ibid.
5. General Staff, War Office, 'Violations of the Peace Treaty by Germany', 7 April 1920, CAB 24/103/30.

6. Churchill, Winston S., 'Memorandum on Destruction of German War Material', 22 April 1920, CAB 24/104/33.

7. Roddie, Lieutenant Colonel Stewart, quoted in Churchill, Winston S.. 'The Present Situation in Germany, Memorandum to Cabinet 14 April 1920', CAB 24/104/62.

8. Supreme Allied Council to German govt, 'German request to maintain an Army of 200,000. Allied Declaration in answer to German Note', 26 April 1920, CAB 24/104/85.

9. Morgan, p.191.

10. Riddell, p.196.

11. Lord Curzon, 'Memorandum on Foreign Policy and Inter-Allied Debts', 17 April 1920, CAB 24/103/93.

Chapter 20: San Remo

1. Foreign Office, 'Foreign Countries Report No. 15', 21 April 1920, CAB 24/154/15.

2. Kelleway, F. to Cabinet, 'Mesopotamian Oilfields', 22 April 1920, CAB 24/104/19.

3. 'Memorandum of Agreement between M.Phillipe Bertherlot, Directeur des Affairs politiques et commerciales au Ministiere des Affairs Etrangeres, and Professor Sir John Cadman, KCMG, Director in charge of His Majesty's Petroleum Department', CAB 24/108/26, 21 June 1920,

4. Segev, p.144.

5. Hankey, M.P.. 'Treaty of Peace with Turkey. Armenia', 25 April 1920, CAB 24/104/71.

6. Secretary of the Supreme Council to President Wilson, 'Armenia. Despatch to President Wilson. Approved by the Supreme Council at San Remo', 26 April 1920, CAB 24/104/88.

Chapter 21: A nation reborn

1. Zamoyski, Adam, *Warsaw 1920: Lenin's failed conquest of Europe* (Harper Collins, 2008, p.18).

2. Ibid, p.2.

3. Riddell, p.191.

4. Zamoyski, pp.45–46.

Chapter 22: 'Indian measures'

1. Constello Francis. 'Lloyd George and Ireland, 1919–1921: An Uncertain Policy', *The Canadian Journal of Irish Studies*, Vol. 14, No. 1 (July 1988), p.9.
2. Home Office, 'Report on Revolutionary Organisations in the United Kingdom. No. 54.', 13 May 1920, CAB 24/105/81.
3. Riddell, Lord, p.184.
4. Alfred Mond, 'Mural Decoration of the Foreign Office', 6 May 1920, CAB 24/105/42.
5. Churchill, Winston, S., 'Formation of a Special Force for Service in Ireland', 19 May 1920, CAB 24/106/18.
6. Ministerial conference 32, 'The State of Ireland – Requirements of the Irish Government', 11 May 1920, CAB 23/37/32.
7. Ministerial Conference 35, 31 May 1920, CAB 23/37/35.

Chapter 23: Taking the initiative

1. McAdoo, William G. to Woodrow Wilson, 14 May 1920, Woodrow Wilson Presidential Library, Cary T. Grayson papers.

Chapter 24: The cost of peace on the frontiers

1. Montagu, Edwin S to Viceroy, 'India. Telegram No 1714 from S/S for India to Viceroy', Foreign Department, 11 May 1920, CAB 24/106/4.
2. Viceroy to Montagu, 'India. Telegram No 6229 from Viceroy Army Department to S/S for India', 18 May 1920, CAB 24/106/24.
3. Viceroy to Montagu,' India, India. Telegram No 6593 from Viceroy Army Department to S/S for India', 26 May 1920, CAB 24/106/52.
4. Alikuzai, Hamid Wahed, *A concise history of Afghanistan in 25 volumes: Volume 1* (Trafford Publishing 2013, pp.29–33).
5. Wilde, Major-General Sir A.T., *Regimental History of the 4th Battalion 13th Frontier Force Rifles (Wilde's)* (Naval & Military Press Ltd., 2012, p.201)
6. Moreman, p.120.
7. Ibid.

8. Viceroy to Secretary of State for India, 'Withdrawal of Troops from East Persia. Telegram No 6066 from Viceroy, Army Department to S/S for India', 13 May 1920, CAB 24/105/9.
9. Churchill, Winston S., to Sec. of State for India, 'Incidence of the cost of troops in South and East Persia', 29 May 1920, CAB 24/106/65.
10. Churchill, Winston, S., 'Future Methods of Control in Mesopotamia', 12 June, CAB 24/107/36.

Chapter 25: The call to revolution

1. Montagu, Edwin, 'Mesopotamia & Middle East. Question of future control', 1 June 1920, CAB 24/107/2.
2. Bell, Gertrude to Sir Hugh Bell, 1 June 1920, Gertrude Bell Archive, Newcastle University.
3. Secretary of State for India, 'Note on the Causes of the present Unrest on the Euphrates, by Major H.H.F.M. Tyler, C.I.E., Political Officer at Hillah', 3 August 1920, CAB 24/110/54.
4. Lord Curzon, 'Future Administration of the Middle East', 8 June 1920, CAB 24/107/34.
5. Churchill, Winston, S., 'Future Methods of Control in Mesopotamia', 12 June, CAB 24/107/36.
6. The Prime Minister, HC Deb 23 June 1920 vol 130 cc2223–85, http://hansard.millbanksystems.com/commons/1920/jun/23/mesopotamia-1, accessed 17 November 2017.
7. Churchill, Winston, S., 'The Situation in Mesopotamia should it be decided to evacuate North-West Persia and withdraw on all Fronts within the area covered by existing Railheads', 12 June 1920, CAB 24/107/70.
8. Montagu, Edwin, 'Mesopotamia, Political and Military Situation', 15 June 1920, CAB 24/107/76.

Chapter 26: 'Secret murder'

1. Borgonovo, John and Doherty, Gabriel, 'Smoking gun: British government policy and RIC reprisals, summer 1920', *History of Ireland*, Issue 2 (Mar/April 2009), Revolutionary Period 1912–23, Volume 17, http://www.historyireland.com/20th-century-contemporary-history/

smoking-gun-british-government-policy-and-ric-reprisals-summer-1920/, accessed 29 September 2017.

2. Riddell, p.223.
3. Bennett, Richard, *The Black and Tans* (Pen & Sword Military, 2010 p.57).
4. Long, Walter H., 'Government of Ireland Bill', 10 June 1920, CAB 24/107/38.
5. Ulster Ex-Service Men's Association - Ireland. 'Copy of telegram received by H.M. the King from the Ulster Ex-Service Men's Association, Belfast', 17 June 1920, CAB 24/108/6.

Chapter 27: The candidate

1. Grayson, Cary T., to Francis X. Dercum, 7 June 1920, Cary T. Grayson Papers, Woodrow Wilson Presidential Library, Staunton, Virginia.
2. *New York Times*, 'Text of the Republican Platform, Except League Plank; Dispute Over That, and Threat of a Bolt by Borah; Wood Men See Gains; New Yorkers Balk at Butler Pledge', 10 November 1920, https://partners.nytimes.com/library/politics/camp/200610convention-gop-ra.html, accessed 21 November 2017.
3. Pietrusza, p.179, pp.210–211, p.225.
4. Leonard Wood, Address at the Harvard Union, 13 April 1920, The Harvard Crimson, http://www.thecrimson.com/article/1920/4/17/address-given-by-general-leonard-wood/, accessed 21 November 2017.
5. Pietrusza, p.210
6. Ibid, p.225.

Chapter 28: Looking East

1. Riddell, p.204.
2. Jacobson, John, *When the Soviet Union Entered World Politics* (University of California Press, 1994, p.63).
3. Cabinet conclusions, 21 May 1920, CAB 23/21/13.

Chapter 29: A principled man

1. McAdoo, William, G., Press Release, 19 June 1920, Cary T. Grayson Papers, Woodrow Wilson Presidential Library, Staunton, Virginia.

2. Pietrusza, p.246.
3. Ibid, p.251.
4. Grayson, Cary T., Diary entry, 1 July-8 Sept. 1920, Cary T. Grayson Papers, Woodrow Wilson Presidential Library, Staunton, Virginia.
5. Wilson, Woodrow to Homer S. Cummings, 2 July 1920, Cary T. Grayson Papers, Woodrow Wilson Presidential Library, Staunton, Virginia, Homer Stillé Cummings.
6. McAdoo, William, G., Press Release, 19 June 1920.
7. *Palm Beach Post*, West Palm Beach, Florida, 3 July 1920,
8. Pietrusza, p.245, p.248.
9. Ibid, p.248.
10. Cox, James, 'Statement by Governor James M. Cox for the Newspapers After a Conference with President Woodrow Wilson', 18 July 1920, Cary T. Grayson Papers, Woodrow Wilson Presidential Library, Staunton, Virginia.

Chapter 30: The enemy in the room

1. Riddell p.216.
2. Ibid, p214.
3. German Delegation at Spa, 'Execution of Treaty of Peace with Germany. Suggestions as to Payment of Reparation', 11 July 1920, CAB 24/109/10.
4. Riddell, p.216.
5. German Delegation at Spa, 'Food Situation in Germany', July 1920, CAB 24/109/29.
6. Rolin Jacquemyns, 'Protocol of the Conference at Spa on July 9, 1920', 9 July 1920, CAB 24/109/46.

Chapter 31: Revolt

1. Rutledge, p.279.
2. Ibid.
3. Montagu, Edward, S. to Secretary of State for War, 14 July 1920, CAB 24/109/49.
4. Civil Commissioner in Baghdad to India Office, 30 July 1920, quoted Montagu, Edwin S., 'The Causes of the unrest in Mesopotamia', 4 August 1920, CAB 24/110/49.

5. Churchill, Winston, S. to General Officer Commanding Middle East, 14 July 1920, CAB 24/109/24.
6. General Officer Commanding [Middle East] to War Office, 15 July 1920, CAB 24/109/49.
7. Churchill, Winston, S, 'Situation in Mesopotamia', 17 July 1920, CAB 24/109/49.

Chapter 32: Peacemaker

1. Riddell, p.219.
2. Zamoyski, p.53.
3. Elcock, H.J., 'Britain and the Russo-Polish Frontier, 1919–1921', *The Historical Journal*, Vol. 12, No. 1 (1969), pp.137–154 (Cambridge University Press).
4. Zamoyski, p.59.
5. Riddell, p.221.
6. Davies, Normal, 'Lloyd George and Poland, 1919–20', *Journal of Contemporary History*, Vol. 6, No. 3 (1971), pp.132–154 (Sage Publications, Ltd).
7. Riddell, p.223.
8. Davies, 'Lloyd George and Poland'.
9. Riddell, p.227.

Chapter 33: The Imperial Government

1. Anderson, Sir John, 'Irish Situation', 25 July 1920, CAB 24/109/92.
2. Long, Walter, H., 'Irish Situation Committee', 22 July 1922, CAB 24/109/75.
3. Balfour, Arthur, J., 'Ireland. The future of the Home Rule Bill', 24 July 1920, CAB 24/109/86.
4. Cassel, F., 'Martial Law in Ireland. Copy of letter from the Judge Advocate General to the Chief Secretary for Ireland', 19 July 1920, CAB 24/109/65.
5. Secretary of State for Ireland, 'The Situation in Ireland. Notes of a Conference with the Officers of the Irish Government', 23 July 1920, CAB 24/109/96.
6. *Tuam Herald*, A Tale of Terror - Part of Tuam in Ruins - Fearful Destruction of Property - The Police get out of Hand - Details of the Destruction - The Town Hall Wrecked', Saturday 24 July 1920

7. Tanner, pp.288–289.
8. Bardon, Jonathan, *A History of Ireland in 250 Episodes* (Gill & Macmillan Ltd, 2008).
9. Lynch, Robert, 'The People's Protectors? The Irish Republican Army and the "Belfast Pogrom", 1920–1922', *Journal of British Studies*, Vol. 47, No. 2 (Apr., 2008), pp.375–391.
10. *The Sun* newspaper, Christchurch New Zealand, 'Enraged Constables Sack Tuam', 22 July 1920
11. Riddell, p.225.

Chapter 34: The family of nations

1. *League of Nations Official Journal*, Proces Verbal, Eighth Session of League of Nations, September 1920.
2. Secretary of State for India, 'Note on the Causes of the present Unrest on the Euphrates, by 259. Major H.H.F.M. Tyler, C.I.E., Political Officer at Hillah', 3 August 1920, CAB 24/110/54
3. Foreign and Commonwealth Office, The Treaty of Peace with Turkey.
4. Morgan, pp.191–192.

Chapter 35: Armies and treasure

1. Bell, Gertrude to Sir Hugh Bell, 2 August 1920, Gertrude Bell Archives, Newcastle University.
2. Bell, Gertrude to Sir Hugh Bell, 26 July 1920, Gertrude Bell Archive, Newcastle University.
3. Bell, Gertrude to Sir Hugh Bell, 7 August 1920, Gertrude Bell Archives, Newcastle University.
4. Rutledge, p.259.
5. Bell, Gertrude to Sir Hugh Bell, 23 August 1920, Gertrude Bell Archive, Newcastle University.
6. Haldane to War Office, 22 August 1920, quoted Churchill, Winston, S., Situation in Mesopotamia, 2 September 1920, CAB 24/111/29.
7. Bell, Gertrude to Sir Hugh Bell, 23 August 1920, Gertrude Bell Archives, Newcastle University.
8. Churchill, Winston S., 'Situation in Mesopotamia', 20 August 1920, CAB 24/110/91.

9. Civil Commissioner Baghdad to Secretary of State for India, 27 August 1920, quoted in Secretary of State for India, 'Situation in Mesopotamia', 27 August 1920, CAB 24/111/17.
10. Gilbert, Martin, *World in Torment: Winston Churchill 1917–1922* (Minerva, 1975, pp.495–496).

Chapter 36: Miracle on the Vistula

1. Zamoyski, p.67.
2. Ibid, p.71.
3. Ibid, p.88.
4. Ibid, p.71.
5. Ibid, pp.99–100.
6. Riddell, p.232.
7. Elcock, H.J., 'Britain and the Russo-Polish Frontier, 1919–1921', *The Historical Journal*, Vol. 12, No. 1 (1969), pp.137–154 (Cambridge University Press).
8. Robert A. Pastor, Stanley Hoffmann, *A Century's Journey: How the Great Powers Shape the World* (Basic Books, 1999, p.175).

Chapter 37: Non-cooperation

1. Kibriya, Mazhar, *Gandhi and Indian Freedom Struggle* (APH Publishing, 1999).
2. Gandhi, Mahatma, *Freedom's Battle: Being a Comprehensive Collection of Writings and Speeches on the Present Situation* (The Floating Press, 2014).
3. Ferguson, p.305–306.
4. Montagu, Edwin, 'The King's Proclamation to India', 6 January 1920, CAB 24/96/17.
5. Paxman, Jeremy, *Empire* (Penguin 2012, p.235).
6. Viceroy to Secretary of State for India, 'India. Telegram from Viceroy Home Department to S/S for India', 27 August 1920, CAB 24/111/19.

Chapter 38: Tranquillity at home

1. Pietrusza, p.320.

2. Morello, John, A., *Selling the President 1920: Albert D. Laskar, Advertising and the Election of Warren G. Harding* (Greenwood Publishing Group 2001, p.55).
3. Flynt, Larry and Eisenbach, David, *One Nation Under Sex: How the Private Lives of Presidents, First Ladies and Their Lovers Changed the Course of American History* (St. Martin's Press, 2011, p.95)
4. Pietrusza, p.322.
5. Ibid, p.335.
6. Ibid, p.342.

Chapter 39: Dark ages of chaos

1. India Office, quoted in Montagu, Edwin S., 'The Causes of the Outbreak in Mesopotamia', August 1920, CAB 24/110/90.
2. Rutledge, p.353.
3. Cabinet conclusions, 16 September 1920, CAB 23/22/13.
4. Churchill, Winston S., 'Air Staff Memorandum on the Air Force as an Alleged Cause of the Loss of Popularity of the Mesopotamia Civil Administration', 27 August 1920, CAB 24/111/23.
5. Churchill, Winston S. to Sir Hugh Trenchard, 29 August 1920, Quoted, Martin Gilbert, *Winston S. Churchill, Companion Volume 4, Part 2*, 1977.
6. Bell, Gertrude to Dame Florence Bell, 5 September 1920, Gertrude Bell Archive, Newcastle University.
7. Civil Commissioner Baghdad to Sec. of State for India, 'Mesopotamia. Evacuation of Arbil and Koi', 2 September 1920, CAB 24/111/35.
8. Bell, Gertrude to Sir Hugh Bell, 12 September 1920, Gertrude Bell Archives, Newcastle University.
9. Rutledge, p.377.
10. Churchill, Winston, S., 'Situation in Mesopotamia', 2 September 1920, CAB 24/111/29.
11. Haldane to Churchill, quoted Sec. of State for War, 'Military Policy in Mesopotamia. Copy of Telegram from General Commanding-in-Chief the Forces in Mesopotamia to Secretary of State for War.', 30 August 1920, CAB 24/111/15.
12. Bell, Gertrude to Sir Hugh Bell, 19 September 1920, Gertrude Bell Archives, Newcastle University.

13. Churchill, Winston, S., 'Recent Events in Mesopotamia', 30 September 1920, CAB 24/112/12.

Chapter 40: Balbriggan

1. Morgan, p.193.
2. Bennett, p. 94.
3. O'Donoghue, Andrew, *Memoirs – Raids and ambushes*, Clare County Library, http://www.clarelibrary.ie/eolas/coclare/history/war_of_independence/rineen_ambush.htm accessed 22/12/2017.
4. Bennett, p.97.
5. Ibid, pp. 95–96.
6. Extract from 'a letter from an officer in Ireland', dated 28 September 1920, Papers of Andrew Bonar Law, House of Lords Record Office, 102/6/9.
7. MacLaren, Roy, *Empire and Ireland: The Transatlantic Career of the Canadian Imperialist Hamar Greenwood, 1870–1948* (McGill-Queen's Press, 2015).
8. Bew, Paul, *Ireland: The Politics of Enmity 1789–2006* (Oxford University Press, 2007, p.404).
9. Bennett, p. 94.
10. Ibid, p.99.

Chapter 41: The invasion of Armenia

1. Hovannisian, Richard G., T*he Republic of Armenia, Volume IV Between Crescent and Sickle: Partition and Sovietization*, University of California Press, 1996, p.202
2. Ibid, p.194.
3. Ibid, p.201.
4. Ibid, p.208.
5. Ibid, p.212.
6. Ibid, p.209.
7. Ibid, p.213.
8. Ibid, p.219.
9. Ibid, p.254.

10. Council of the League of Nations to Supreme Allied Council, copied to British Cabinet, 'Memorandum: League of Nations. Armenia', 2 November 1920, CAB 24/114/48.

Chapter 42: The final furlong

1. Pietrusza, p.324.
2. Lloyd George, David to Cary T. Grayson, 11 Oct. 1920, Cary T. Grayson Papers, Woodrow Wilson Presidential Library, Staunton, Virginia.
3. Pietrusza, pp.398–399.
4. Morello, p.58.
5. Ibid, p.56.
6. Robenalt, James, D., *Linking Rings: William W. Durbin and the Magic and Mystery of America* (Kent State University Press, 2004, p.163).
7. *San Francisco Chronicle*, California, 11 October 1920.
8. Pietrusza, p.367.
9. Ibid, p.350.

Chapter 43: The coming messiah

1. Bell, Gertrude to Sir Hugh Bell, 17 October 1920, Gertrude Bell Archives, Newcastle University.
2. Rutledge, p.391.
3. High Commissioner, Baghdad to India Office, 26 October 1920, quoted in Secretary of State for India, 'Political situation in Mesopotamia. Telegrams from High Commissioner Baghdad, Mesopotamia and Viceroy', 26 October 1920, CAB 24/114/54.
4. Bell, Gertrude to Sir Hugh Bell and Dame Florence Bell, 10 October 1920, Gertrude Bell Archives, Newcastle University.
5. Bell, Gertrude to Sir High Bell, 17 October 1920, Gertrude Bell Archives, Newcastle University.
6. Bell, Gertrude to Sir Hugh Bell, 24 October 1920, Gertrude Bell Archives, Newcastle University.
7. High Commissioner, Baghdad to India Office, 26 October 1920, quoted in Secretary of State for India, 'Political situation in Mesopotamia.

Telegrams from High Commissioner Baghdad, Mesopotamia and Viceroy, 26 October 1920'.

Chapter 44: 'In Mountjoy jail one Monday morning'

1. Raidió Teilifís Éireann interview, broadcast 29 October 1970, http://www.rte.ie/archives/2015/1021/736454-kevin-barry/, accessed 5 January 2018.
2. Cronin, Sean, *The Story of Kevin Barry*, The National Publications Committee, 1965, p.2.
3. Conclusion, Ministerial Conference 57, 28 October 1920, CAB 23/38/7.
4. Cronin, p.40.
5. Tanner, p.289.
6. Riddell, p.241.

Chapter 45: The end of the White Army

1. Wrangel, Petr, *The Memoirs of General Wrangel: The Last Commander-In-Chief of the Russian National Army* (Duffield & Company, 1930, p.339).
2. Riddell, p. 233.
3. Wrangel, p.323.
4. Avrich, Paul, *Kronstadt, 1921* (Princeton University Press, 1991, p.105).
5. Conclusions, Cabinet meeting 11 November, CAB 23/23/3.
6. Admiralty to C-in-C Mediterranean Fleet, 13 November 1920, quoted Hankey, Maurice, 'Memorandum, General Wrangel's submarines', 13 November 1920, CAB 24/114/97.
7. Lord Curzon to Cabinet, 'Russian trade negotiations', 14 November 1920, CAB 24/114/100.
8. Conclusions, Cabinet meeting 17 November 1920, CAB 23/23/4.
9. Hankey, Maurice, 'Evacuation of Russian Refugees from the Crimea', 22 November, CAB 24/115/26.

Chapter 46: Casting votes

1. Pietrusza, p.402.

2. Grayson, Cary T., 'The President Reacts to Election Returns, Nov. 1920', Cary T. Grayson Papers, Woodrow Wilson Presidential Library, Staunton, Virginia.
3. *Kingsport Times*, Tennessee, 3 November 1920.
4. Cabinet memorandum, 'The Assembly of the League of Nations. Report on the question of the Prime Minister attending the first Session', 3 November 1920, CAB 24/114/76.
5. Dugdale, Blanche E. C. *Arthur James Balfour, First Earl of Balfour, K.G., O.M., F.R.S., G. P.* (G.P. Putnam's Sons, 1937).
6. World Peace Foundation, *The First Assembly of the League of Nations* (Double Number, 1921, p.98).
7. Ibid, p.122.
8. Ibid, p.199.
9. Ibid, p.200.
10. Ibid, p.8.
11. Bendiner, p.163.

Chapter 47: The death of a nation

1. Hovannisian, p.210.
2. Ibid, p.305.
3. Montagu, Edwin, 'Situation in the East', 22 November 1920, CAB 24/115/53.
4. Hovannisian, p.374.
5. Ibid, p.317.
6. Ibid, p.321.
7. Hymans, Paul, 'Armenian Situation. Telegram from President of the Council of the League of Nations', 26 November 1920, CAB 24/115/99.
8. World Peace Foundation, p.191.
9. Hovannisian, p.323.
10. Ibid.
11. Ibid, p.377.
12. Foreign Office, 'Foreign Countries Report No.32', 15 December 1920, CAB 24/154/32.
13. Hovannisian, p.339.
14. Riddell, p.255.

Chapter 48: Democracy and oil

1. Bell, Gertrude to Sir Hugh Bell, 1 November 1920, Gertrude Bell Archives, Newcastle University.
2. Kelleway, Frederick, 'The Anglo-French Petroleum Agreement and Mesopotamia', 15 November 1920, CAB 24/115/10.
3. Bell, Gertrude to Sir Hugh Bell, 7 November 1920, Gertrude Bell Archives, Newcastle University.
4. Rutledge, p.387.
5. Churchill, Winston, S., 'Situation in Mesopotamia', 2 December 1920, CAB 24/116/17.
6. Bell, Gertrude to Sir Hugh Bell, 29 November 1920, Gertrude Bell Archives, Newcastle University.
7. Bell, Gertrude to Sir Hugh Bell, 14 November 1920, Gertrude Bell Archives, Newcastle University.

Chapter 49: Bloody Sunday

1. Cabinet conclusions, 10 November 1920, 'Situation in Ireland', CAB 23/23/2.
2. Montagu, Edwin, S., 'Ireland', 10 November 1920, CAB 24/114/85.
3. Hartline, Martin C. and Kaulbach, M, *The intelligence war between the British and Irish Intelligence Services, Michael Collins and Bloody Sunday*, *CIA Historical Review Program*, 2 July 96, https://www.cia.gov/library/center-for-the-study-of-intelligence/kent-csi/vol13no1/html/v13i1a06p_0001.htm, accessed 21 January 2018.
4. Dorney, John, 'Bloody Sunday', *The Irish Story*, 21 November 1920, http://www.theirishstory.com/2011/11/21/today-in-irish-history-bloody-sunday-november-21-1920/#.WmTHJlRl_IU, accessed 21 January 1920.
5. O'Dowd, Niall, 'Bloody Sunday 1920, Black and Tans kill fourteen', *Irish Central*, 19 August 2016, https://www.irishcentral.com/news/irishvoice/bloody-sunday-1920-black-and-tans-kill-fourteen, accessed 21 Janaury 1920.
6. Hittle, J.B.E., *Michael Collins and the Anglo-Irish War: Britain's Counterinsurgency Failure* (Potomac Books, Inc., 2011).
7. Account of 5th Witness, British Military Inquiry into shootings, held around 8 December 1920, http://www.gaa.ie/centenary/bloody-

sunday-archive/1920-bloody-sunday-eyewitness-reports/ accessed 21 January 2018.

8. Statement by Council for Relatives of Miss Jane Boyle, Ibid.

Chapter 50: Old World, New World

1. Wilson, Woodrow, 'Eighth annual message to Congress', 7 December 1920, *The American Presidency Project*, http://www.presidency.ucsb.edu/ws/index.php?pid=29561 accessed 22 January 2018.
2. Hovannisian, p.302.
3. Chamberlain, Austen, 'Brussels Reparation Conference', 29 November 1920, CAB 24/116/5.
4. Johnson, G., *The Berlin Embassy of Lord D'Abernon, 1920–1926* (Palgrave Macmillan, 2002, p.34).
5. Ibid, p.35.
6. Churchill, Winston S., 'The Disarmament of Germany', 29 December 1920, CAB 24/117/76.

Chapter 51: Friends and enemies

1. Lord Curzon,' The Russian Trade Agreement', 13 December 1920, CAB 24/116/86.
2. Hovannasian, p.308.
3. Cabinet conclusions, 13 December 1920, CAB 23/23/15.
4. Churchill, Winston, S., 'The Situation in the Middle East', 13 December 1920, CAB 24/117/87.
5. Gokay, Bulent, *Soviet Eastern Policy and Turkey, 1920–1991: Soviet Foreign Policy, Turkey and Communism* (Routledge, 2006, pp.21–22).
6. Bell, Gertrude to Sir Hugh Bell, 18 December 1920, Newcastle University Archives.
7. Bell, Gertrude to Sir Hugh Bell, 29 November 1920, Newcastle University Archives.
8. Gokay, p.25.
9. Churchill, Winston, S., 'Payment of Debts by Soviet Russia, 4 December 1920', CAB 24/116/37.
10. Cabinet Conclusions, 22 December 1920, CAB 23/23/20.

Chapter 52: Independent minded

1. Churchill, Winston, S., 'The Palestine Garrison', 18 December 1920, CAB 24/117/24.
2. Segev, p.147.
3. Bell, Gertrude to Sir Hugh Bell, 10 January 1921, Newcastle University Archives.
4. Segev, p.144.
5. Ibid, p.143.
6. Huneidi, Sahar, *A Broken Trust: Sir Herbert Samuel, Zionism and the Palestinians* (I.B. Tauris, 2001, p.47).
7. Viceroy to Montagu, India, 'Telegram from Viceroy Home Department to Secretary of State', 5 December 1920, CAB 24/116/85.
8. Viceroy to Montagu, 2 December 1920, CAB 24/116/57.
9. Viceroy to Montagu, India, 'Telegram from Viceroy Home Department to Secretary of State', 5 December 1920, CAB 24/116/85.
10. Viceroy to Montagu, 12 December 1920, CAB 24/117/33.
11. Viceroy to Montagu, 30 December 1920, CAB 24/118/15.

Chapter 53: A city on fire

1. Dorney, John, 'The Burning of Cork: 11-12 December 1920', *The Irish Story*, http://www.theirishstory.com/2017/12/13/the-burning-of-cork-december-11-12-1920/#_edn1 accessed 29 January 2018.
2. Greenwood, Sir H., 'Failing to Halt', HC, Hansard, 9 December 1920, vol 135, C2447W, http://hansard.millbanksystems.com/written_answers/1920/dec/09/failing-to-halt accessed 29 January 1920.
3. Riddell, p.253.
4. Gillman Peter and Gillman, Leni, *Wildest Dream: The Biography of George Mallory* (The Mountaineers Books, 2001, p.165).
5. Davis, Wade, *Into the Silence: The Great War, Mallory and the conquest of Everest* (Vintage Books, 2012, pp.199–200).
6. White, Gerry and O'Shea, Brendan, *The Burning of Cork* (Mercier Press Ltd, 2006, p.120).
7. Davis, pp.199–200.
8. O'Riordan, Sean, 'Culprit who led burning of Cork finally identified', *Irish Examiner*, 11 December 2010, https://www.irishexaminer.com/

ireland/culprit-who-led-burning-of-cork-finally-identified-139188.
html accessed 30 January 2018.

9. White, p.163.

10. Cholahan, Daniel, quoted in Stairna hÉireann/History of
Ireland,https://stairnaheireann.net/2015/12/12/1920-the-roman-
catholic-bishop-of-cork-daniel-colahan-issued-a-decree-saying-that-
anyone-within-the-diocese-of-cork-who-organises-or-takes-part-in-
ambushes-or-murder-or-attempted/ accessed 30 January 2018.

11. Townshend, *The British Campaign in Ireland, 1919–1921: the development of political and military policies* (Oxford University Press, 1975,
p.140).

12. Cabinet Conclusions, 29 December 1920, CAB 23/23/25.

Chapter 54: Winter in Baghdad

1. Bell, Gertrude, to Sir Hugh Bell, 5 December 1920, University of
Newcastle Archives.

2. Montagu, Edwin S., 'Possibilities of reduction in Mesopotamia.
Telegrams between Sir Percy Cox and Secretary of State for India',
29 December, CAB 24/117/79.

3. General Radcliffe to War Office, quoted in Churchill, Winston S.,
'The Situation in Mesopotamia', 10 December 1920, CAB 24/116/75.

4. Montagu, Edwin., 'Mesopotamia', 24 December 1920, CAB 24/
117/56.

5. Bell, Gertrude to Sir Hugh Bell, 18 December 1920, Gertrude Bell
Archives, Newcastle University.

6. Churchill, Winston, S., 'Mesopotamia', 22 December 1920, CAB
24/117/82.

7. Montagu, Edwin, 'Mesopotamia', 24 December 1920, CAB 24/117/56.

8. Lord Curzon, 'Mesopotamia', 26 December 1920, CAB 24/117/59.

9. Riddell, p.257.

10. Bell, Gertrude to Sir Hugh Bell, 25 December 1920, Newcastle
University Archives.

11. Secretary of State for India, 'Proposed appointment of Feisal as Emir
of Mesopotamia. Withdrawal of troops to Basra Vilayet. Telegrams
circulated by Secretary of State for India', 31 December 1920, CAB
24/118/13.

Chapter 55: Storm clouds

1. Bell, Gertrude to Sir Hugh Bell, 3 January 1921, Gertrude Bell Archives, Newcastle University.
2. Riddell, p.259.
3. Harding, Warren, G., Inaugural Address, 4 March 1921, *The American Presidency Project*, http://www.presidency.ucsb.edu/ws/index.php?pid =25833 accessed 5 February 2018.
4. Riddell, p.288.
5. Dorney, John, Today in Irish History, 'The Truce', 11 July 1921, *The Irish Story*, http://www.theirishstory.com/2011/07/11/today-in-irish-history-%E2%80%93-july-11-1921-%E2%80%93-the-truce-2/#. Wnm9M1Rl_IU accessed 6 February 2018.
6. Bell, Gertrude to Dame Florence Bell, 28 August 1921, Newcastle University Archives.
7. Riddell, p.390.
8. Ibid, p.391.
9. Leake, Elizabeth, *The Defiant Border: The Afghan-Pakistan Borderlands in the Era of Decolonization*, 1936–65, Cambridge University Press, 2016, p.38.
10. Adolf Hitler, *Collection of Speeches 1922–1945*, publisher unknown, 1945, p.43–44, https://archive.org/details/AdolfHitlerCollectionOf Speeches19221945, accessed 9 February 2018.

Index